On the Subject of Religion

NAASR Working Papers

Series Editor: Brad Stoddard, McDaniel College in Westminster, Maryland.

NAASR Working Papers provides a venue for publishing the latest research carried out by scholars who understand religion to be an historical element of human cognition, practice, and organization. Whether monographs or multi-authored collections, the volumes published in this series all reflect timely, cutting edge work that takes seriously both the need for developing bold theories as well as rigorous testing and debate concerning the scope of our tools and the implications of our studies. NAASR Working Papers therefore assess the current state-of-the-art while charting new ways forward in the academic study of religion.

Published

Constructing "Data" in Religious Studies: Examining the Architecture of the Academy
Edited by Leslie Dorrough Smith

Hijacked: A Critical Treatment of the Public Rhetoric of Good and Bad Religion
Edited by Leslie Dorrough Smith, Steffen Führding, and Adrian Hermann

Jesus and Addiction to Origins: Towards an Anthropocentric Study of Religion
Willi Braun
Edited by Russell T. McCutcheon

Key Categories in the Study of Religion: Contexts and Critiques
Edited by Rebekka King

Method Today: Redescribing Approaches to the Study of Religion
Edited by Brad Stoddard

"Religion" in Theory and Practice: Demystifying the Field for Burgeoning Academics
Russell T. McCutcheon

Remembering J. Z. Smith: A Career and its Consequence
Edited by Emily D. Crews and Russell T. McCutcheon

Forthcoming

Discourses of Crisis and the Study of Religion
Edited by Lauren Horn Griffin

Thinking with J. Z. Smith: Mapping Methods in the Study of Religion
Edited by Barbara Krawcowicz

On the Subject of Religion

Charting the Fault Lines of a Field of Study

Edited by
James Dennis LoRusso

SHEFFIELD UK   BRISTOL CT

Published by Equinox Publishing Ltd.

UK: Office 415, The Workstation, 15 Paternoster Row, Sheffield, South Yorkshire S1 2BX

USA: ISD, 70 Enterprise Drive, Bristol, CT 06010

www.equinoxpub.com

First published 2022

© James Dennis LoRusso and contributors 2022

All rights reserved. No part of this publication may be reproduced or transmitted in any form or by any means, electronic or mechanical, including photocopying, recording or any information storage or retrieval system, without prior permission in writing from the publishers.

ISBN-13 978 1 80050 228 4 (hardback)
         978 1 80050 229 1 (paperback)
         978 1 80050 230 7 (ePDF)
         978 1 80050 257 4 (ePub)

British Library Cataloguing-in-Publication Data

A catalogue record for this book is available from the British Library.

Library of Congress Cataloging-in-Publication Data

Names: LoRusso, James Dennis, editor.
Title: On the subject of religion : charting the fault lines of a field of study / edited by James Dennis LoRusso.
Description: Sheffield, South Yorkshire ; Bristol, CT : Equinox Publishing Ltd, 2022. | Series: NAASR working papers | Includes bibliographical references and index. | Summary: "On the Subject of Religion takes as its inspiration the work of the late Jonathan Z. Smith, who challenged scholars to be mindful of the ways in which they imagine religion and religious data. Building on this crucial insight, this book brings together a range of early-career and established scholars of religion to explore how various domains of society-the classroom, academic literature, public debates, and private fundraising-shape, and are shaped, by the contours of the academic study of religion"—Provided by publisher.
Identifiers: LCCN 2022013480 (print) | LCCN 2022013481 (ebook) | ISBN 9781800502284 (hardback) | ISBN 9781800502291 (paperback) | ISBN 9781800502307 (epdf) | ISBN 9781800502574 (epub)
Subjects: LCSH: Religion—Study and teaching. | Smith, Jonathan Z.—Influence.
Classification: LCC BL41 .O55 2022 (print) | LCC BL41 (ebook) | DDC 200.7—dc23/eng20220901
LC record available at https://lccn.loc.gov/2022013480
LC ebook record available at https://lccn.loc.gov/2022013481

Typeset by JS Typesetting Ltd, Porthcawl, Mid Glamorgan

Contents

Introduction: Patchwork or Mosaic? The Fabric of Religious Studies   1
James Dennis LoRusso

Part I: Teaching the Field

1. On the Grammar of Teaching Religious Studies   11
   Leslie Dorrough Smith
   RESPONSES
2. Can't Live with it, Can't Drop it from the Undergraduate Curriculum: World Religions   32
   Rita Lester and Jacob Barrett
3. Practicing Theory   40
   Ian Alexander Cuthbertson
4. The Gaze from Somewhere: Teaching Situated Writing about Religion   51
   Leonie C. Geiger
5. Weaponizing Religious Literacy: "Religioning" as Revitalizing the Field or Reinforcing Neoliberal Values?   61
   Martha Smith Roberts

Part II: The History of the Field

6. The Enduring Presence of Our Pre-Critical Past; or, Same as it Ever Was, Same as it Ever Was   77
   Russell T. McCutcheon
   RESPONSES
7. The Vocation of a Scientist of Religion   94
   D. Jamil Grimes
8. Historicizing Endurance   107
   Andrew Durdin
9. Intercepted Dispatches: A Speculative History of the Future of Religious Studies   121
   Rebekka King

Part III: The Role and Influence of Private Funding in the Field

10. Private Money and the Study of Religions: Problems, Perils, and Possibilities   133
    Gregory D. Alles

	RESPONSES	
11	Drugs, Dog Chow, and Dharma Michael J. Altman	150
12	Between Wittgenstein and Zuckerberg: Selling the Academic Study of Religion in a Buyer's Market John W. McCormack	154
13	Religious Studies: A Pawn in the Culture Wars Natalie Avalos	164

Part IV: International Perspectives on the Field

14	International Perspectives on/in the Field Rosalind I. J. Hackett	175
	RESPONSES	
15	Field of Dreams: What Do NAASR Scholars Really Want? F. LeRon Shults and Wesley J. Wildman	195
16	The Benefit of Comparison Vaia Touna	208
17	"Developing" the Field Yasmina Burezah	217
	Index	225

Introduction

Patchwork or Mosaic? The Fabric of Religious Studies

James Dennis LoRusso

Several months before I was asked to contribute an introduction to this volume, I attended a roundtable discussion at a prestigious university in the northeastern United States exploring a single question: *what does the study of religion have to offer the wider academy?* The event was sponsored by the institution's department of religion with the aim of fostering fruitful dialogue among faculty, graduate students, and researchers from across the humanities and social sciences. As a contingent scholar who, first, was seeking opportunities to build relationships with leaders in the field and, second, remained committed to the critical study of religion, I eagerly jumped at the chance to be part of the conversation.

To my initial disappointment, but not necessarily surprise, the roundtable was attended exclusively by faculty and students affiliated with the religion program. However, some of this hope was restored as the organizer set a promising tone for the discussion when they asserted that the study of religion stands out because it treats "religion" not as a given domain of human experience but as an analytic category through which we examine the world around us. The discussion commenced, and it looked as if the group was about to embark on a robust exchange about the merits of theorizing religion when one of the participants, a recently minted PhD from the department, interjected, confessing that *"I've never really understood how to do theory."* Coming from a colleague whose scholarship I held in the highest esteem, the remark gave me pause, dare I say shocked me. When pressed, they explained that applying theory always seemed like a forced exercise, necessary to somehow gain credibility in the academy. Moreover, for this person, doing theory was a process of trial-and-error, of imposing on the data this-or-that theorist and seeing which one "sticks" or affirms their argument.

Immediately, I indicated my desire to respond and, somewhat flippantly I admit, articulated that doing theory was not like selecting a brand of toothpaste (or something careless to that effect), but rather theory is always already present the moment we ask that first question. As J. Z. Smith states, "it is the perception of incongruity that gives rise to thought" and therefore theorizing emerges from the very process of doing our work (1978: 294). What happened next took me by complete surprise. A senior faculty member rose to the defense of the colleague, stating that they strongly objected to my remarks, suggesting that, as a historian, they found theory overrated that often gets in the way of letting the story speak for itself.

At this point, the tension from the disconcerting silence permeating the room could be cut with a knife. Typically this would be the moment at when I would back down and allow my tenured "betters" to have the last word on the matter, but, for some reason, something compelled me to stand my ground. Filled with anxiety about the words I would soon utter, I steadied myself and spoke, "I agree that historiography may avoid overt theorizing, but we are not historians. We are scholars of religion, and it is our ability to critically engage the category of religion where we make a unique contribution to the wider academy." Boom! I landed my point convincingly, or so I thought, for I was not accustomed to wrestling with the Olympians of academia (and perhaps the gods do not expect to be usurped by mere mortals).

My interlocutor responded carefully and deliberately in a placid, controlled tone that sliced through my fleeting moment of perceived triumph. "You know," they declared, "there *are* some people that claim religious studies to be a unique field of study distinct from other disciplines, but it isn't." They spoke on, reminding me that religious studies is a community of scholars from various disciplines united only in the broadest of shared area or interest: religion. During the remainder to the session, our dispute would manifest again and again, but it became clear to me that we were engaged in a fundamental disagreement about the nature, purpose, and boundaries of our professional identities.

The experience stayed with me for some time in the following weeks and months. Two questions continued to vex me. The first question related to the colleague who initially confessed their confusion over "doing theory." *How could a brilliant junior scholar, nurtured in one of the finest educational environments in the world, not acquire more respect for theory and method in the study of religion?* Secondly, *if we understand religious studies is simply a patchwork of scholars from disparate disciplines, is this something we can properly call a "field of study"?*

To answer both questions, we must consider the structure of this religion program. Like many established programs across the United States, the department of religion that sponsored the roundtable resembles a collection of disparate subfields, each populated with graduate students and faculty who rarely, if ever, transgress these intradepartmental silos. For instance, the doctoral program in American religion expects students to acquire expertise in two ways: by working closely with faculty in the subfield and with scholars located *in other departments* such as anthropology, sociology, or history. All four established qualifying exams for doctoral students focus on some aspect of American religious history and historiography.

To be sure, the program allows doctoral students to engage with scholars at the pinnacle of their respective areas of expertise, and therefore in no way do I intend to impugn the *quality* of education and mentoring received. However, it is significant that programs constructed in this manner provide little substantial engagement with the study of religion *qua* the study of religion. A student may work significantly with anthropologists or historians but likely have little incentive to interact with either students or scholars working in other departmental subfields such as East Asian religions or New Testament. Moreover, despite the stated interdisciplinarity of the program, the fact that qualifying exams target a single methodology—*historiography*—means that students are not expected to complete coursework in or demonstrate broad familiarity with the history, theories, and methods in the study of religion. Ultimately, programs of this kind may very well produce top-notch historians (and the occasional anthropologist) *who study religion* but not who many of us might characterize as scholars *of religion*.

This pattern ripples through the entire academic study of religion, particularly in the United States. For instance, the so-called big tent of the American Academy of Religion brings thousands of scholars together, most of whom will never venture beyond a few program units and affiliate societies that reflect their specific area of expertise. Similarly, we see this design in departments who, in the spirit of interdisciplinarity, eagerly welcome faculty who earned their doctorates in some other field or discipline simply because their object of study is self-evidently religious. The practice of hiring from outside the field is, of course, not generally reciprocated, creating conditions where religion PhDs must compete alongside others from outside disciplines for a diminishing number of permanent faculty positions. However, I digress. My point is that the question remains: *is the academic study of religion a distinct field of study?*

Some suggest that the interdisciplinary quality of religious studies is what constitutes it as a *field of study* rather than a *discipline*, and I largely agree with this sentiment. The study of religion incorporates numerous disciplinary commitments (psychology, anthropology, sociology, philosophy, literature, etc.) and I suspect that the senior scholar who scolded me in the roundtable may have been attempting to convey this view. However, is a field of study simply the sum of its interdisciplinary parts, or something distinct? Surely, one could argue, depending on one's theoretical framework, persuasively for either position. However, I wish to advocate here for the latter. According to Bourdieu, a *field* represents a plane of action in which agents produce, compete, exchange, and jockey for advantage in the acquisition of capital. More importantly, for our purposes, fields are structured internally according to a set of rules or logics (Bourdieu 1984: 168). Bourdieu, of course, is concerned with much broader arenas such as the economic field, or the religious field, but in a cursory sense, we might feasibly attribute these characteristics to a field of study like religious studies. In this sense, therefore, the fact that the study of religion exhibits a distinct logic of its own is what makes it an autonomous field of study from other domains of the academy.

We, as scholars of religion, share a *lingua franca*, engendered through apprenticeships irreplicable in any other space of the wider academy. In other words, the unique combination of interdisciplinary training grounded in a mythology of its own historical genesis equips scholars of religion with the tools to speak not from as interdisciplinarians for whom theory represents a buffet of disparate options. Rather, scholars of religion offer a *transdisciplinary* perspective, enabling them to have meaningful discourse about religion across the boundaries of their respective subfields. A scholars of religions of the Ancient Mediterranean can converse with an expert in Latinx traditions because they each recognize the theoretical platform through which the other articulates their ideas. Yet, when graduate programming privileges the patchwork approach, they fail to provide doctoral students with the opportunity to become fluent in this transdisciplinary field.

All of the contributors to this volume wrestle with these questions, controversies, and fault lines. *What does it mean to be a field of study? How should we narrate our history as field of study? How should one teach the field? What are the material conditions and intellectual disputes through which our collective and individual identities and scholarship get defined?*

The volume is composed of four sections, each featuring a main essay followed by several responses. In Part I ("Teaching the Field"), Leslie Dorrough Smith's main essay grapples with the issue of how scholars committed to non-essentialist approaches to teaching about religion still may inadvertently deploy language that reinforces universalist and essentialized notions of religion. To address this tendency, Smith recounts her efforts to move beyond these limitations by reconfiguring the way we talk about religion in the classroom itself. Rather than referring to religion as an object we might observe and therefore describe, she asks students to consider religion as a *tactic,* as a rhetorical mode employed to mystify and render certain kinds of claims beyond critique. Ultimately, drawing the work of Malory Nye as well as the work of gender and queer theories, Smith suggests educators mute the nominal form, "religion" in favor of the more active "religioning," a term with emphasizes its procedural, dynamic, and contested quality.

In response, Rita Lester and Jacob Barrett discuss their experience with a "pilot" introductory course designed as a "semester-long interrogation of the world religions paradigm." Collaborating with upper-level students to develop the course (itself a crucial ingredient in the holistic critique of reified perspectives on religion), Lester and Barrett utilize the IDEA student self-assessment tool to measure learning outcomes in comparison with more conventional introductory courses offered in previous semesters. Ultimately, the assessment results indicate that students in the pilot course felt better prepared to engage ideas and arguments critically.

Ian Alexander Cuthbertson extends Smith's perspective to critique the way that theory is generally treated in the undergraduate classroom. Whereas theory is frequently treated as a lens through which pre-theoretical data may be explained (i.e., "feminist approaches," "psychology of religion," etc.), Cuthbertson articulates theory in the critical study of religion as a wholly "different *kind* of enterprise" concerned with the discursive foundations of pedagogy itself. In taking J. Z. Smith's maxim seriously, he suggests that theory not only helps us explain various phenomena; it establishes what counts as data in the first place.

Leonie C. Geiger broadens the conversation about breaking out of the entrenched assumptions in how we study religion by asking how we get student to incorporate reflexive practices into their writing. "Situated writing," according to Geiger, "can be seen as a *revelation of one's own tactics* that unveils the sometimes unintentionally hidden strategies" in which our students (and ourselves) remain complicit in our ongoing *invention* of critical religious studies.

Martha Smith Roberts acknowledges the pragmatic challenges facing teachers who are, on one hand, committed to critical approaches to the study of religion and, on the other hand, must navigate the often-competing goals of the contemporary "neoliberal university." The latter, she maintains, place a premium on the values of "tolerance" and "literacy" as worthy pursuits for religious studies, and rather than rejecting these concepts, Roberts prefers to use essentialist notions of religion to "disrupt nominalizing tendencies through investigating the constructed nature of religion in different contexts." Thus, Roberts proposes a progressive model for teaching critical religion that guides students gradually away from notions of religion as an object of study towards an emphasis on "religion as a *strategy*, a classificatory tool that has very real stakes."

Russell McCutcheon assumes the lead essay for Part II ("The History of the Field"), observing that despite the "hard-won gains" by scholars over the last several decades to advance the critical study of religion, the theological and essentialist tendencies nonetheless remain a continuous presence in the field. Justifications for the relevance of religious studies that tout "religious literacy" and "tolerance" by AAR and other voices in the academy peak his concern. First, they treat these goals as self-evidently good, with "little if any critical analysis of the links between these projects and claims that it somehow enhances some untheorized notion of civility." Moreover, these initiatives inherently reinforce the World Religions Paradigm because they often begin from the vantage point that "literacy" is achieved by acquiring sufficient knowledge of the *essential* traits (beliefs, practices, sacred texts, etc.) of a designated range of so-called traditions. For McCutcheon, the more things change, the more they stay the same, as the penchant towards the phenomenological and the normative has not diminished but rather persists as the discourse evolves.

D. Jamil Grimes affirms McCutcheon's concern over the subtle normativity that informs certain modalities of scholarship currently in vogue across the field. In the pursuit of critical study, Grimes reminds readers, they are also "*scientists* of religion" in the broad sense of the need "be independent and objective, to resist the potential impact of passionately held, social, political, and other morally loaded views on a fair reading of the data." To be clear, I do not read his argument as suggesting that objectivity is achievable in some pure, modernist manner. Instead, Grimes understands objectivity and dispassion as aspirational aims and takes issue with scholarship that see in their impossibility a justification for "the field to be a force for certain values" (political, moral, etc.).

Andrew Durdin largely agrees with McCutcheon but argues for a more nuanced and historicized evaluation. However, he challenges McCutcheon's diagnosis that essentialism has persisted but simply found new ways of rearing its head. Instead, Durdin asks readers to consider "how have shifting material and sociological factors at different historical moments generated, hardened, and naturalized certain devices and dispositions, and even given the appearance of being part of a coherent disciplinary tradition ... ?"

In her response essay titled "Intercepted Dispatches," Rebekka King crafts a "history of the future" in which the champions of religious literacy and the "public understanding of religion" have vanquished an all-but-forgotten critical study of religion. This imaginative "speculative, epistolary fiction" explicates, in perhaps hyperbolic fashion, the stakes of adopting uncritically these intiatives for the sake of making the field "relevant" to a wider public.

Part III explores "The Role and Influence of Private Funding in the Field." In his main essay, Gregory D. Alles provides a measured assessment of the role of private funding on knowledge production in the humanities, and in particular the study of religion. Alles, like many of us, remains concerned with the increasingly reliance on private monies in higher education, but he paints the situation as even more pervasive than is typically presumed. His historical account of funding reveals that private funding has always dominated the university, with the exception of a brief period of massive public investment during the mid-twentieth century. Thus, the *privatization* of higher education might be seen not as a decline but rather a restoration of the status quo. Given academia's overwhelming dependence on private philanthropy, Alles unpacks some of the strategies through which power shapes knowledge production. Ultimately, he speculates on what academic life might be like unfettered from the various power structures to which scholars must submit themselves.

In "Drugs, Dog Chow, and Dharma," Michael Altman provides readers with more than a clever title. He anchors an analysis of the way that private capital has informed the emergence, maturation, and continued development of the field in three firms. Moreover, Altman leave us with some provocations for thinking about the ways that fault lines reflect lingering Protestant biases in the academy today.

In contrast to Alles, who characterizes teaching as a means to the end of pursuing research, John McCormack views the classroom as "the primary way scholarship on religion reaches the public." Protecting this platform, perhaps the only forum in which the public may encounter the critical study of religion, should be of singular importance in the face of current pressures to shutter or merge departments, to eliminate or reconfigure majors.

Natalie Avalos draws attention to the reality that impact of private wealth on the study of religion extends to the public domain, that "public funding is shaped by political ideologies that are primarily influenced by private interests." Moreover, because the field has failed to discern and respond to these dynamics, it remains complicit in concealing the deeply entrenched roles of settler colonialism and racialization within the intellectual trajectories of religion research. Avalos challenges "scholars to reconsider the ways that structural violences are not only relevant to the field, but constitutive of it, even incrementally marginalizing its relevance."

Finally, in Part IV ("International Perspectives on the Field"), Rosalind Hackett poses the question: "to what extent can we claim that the non-normative, historical, critical, and contemporary study of religion exists as an international field" in the first place? Drawing on extensive expertise, experience, and engagement globally, Hackett suggests that while a coherent field may not be apparent internationally, a "multifaceted and multilateral" network of scholars, institutions, and professional organizations dedicated to the critical study of religion continues to take shape. Her analysis proves most revealing in the attention she pays to the distinct histories, goals, and challenges that have defined the various regional societies, subfields and journals, and affinity groups that comprise the international community of critical religious studies.

Responding to Hackett's intricate map of the structural integrity of the international field, Shults and Wildman seek to penetrate and identify how the motivational values of North American scholars of religion determine their engagement internationally, particularly the Global South. Data from the *Values in Scholarship on Religion* project (VISOR) reveals some of the ways that NAASR stands out in relation to other scholarly societies such as AAR, ultimately asserting that its members "are uniquely positioned to step up the plate ... and deliver clear and public assessments of the deleterious psychological and political consequences" of religious formations.

Whether there is such a thing as an "international religious studies field" or not, in response to Rosalind Hackett, Vaia Touna's response discusses aspects of the study of religion in Greece and North America, and the benefits of comparing international settings in gaining insight about one's own background. Furthermore, Touna argues, that such a comparative endeavor that stems from being acquainted with other cultures can guard against taken for granted assumptions about that thing we commonly call "religion."

Yasmina Burezah uses her experience in the German development sector as an analogue to Hackett's characterization of the international field of study. Burezah notes that international development work often relies on forms of "distance-making" between "developed" and "undeveloped" in ways that often reinforce entrenched asymmetrical social relations. This mirrors the manner in which the study of religion "necessitates the distance-making of 'the researcher' and 'the religious'," a move that, according to Burezah, leads Hackett to fall short of taking "seriously" the actual content of non-Western scholars of religion.

James Dennis LoRusso is interested in the way that religion interacts with markets, businesses, and workplaces in the production of social inequalities. He is the author of *Spirituality, Corporate Culture, and American Business: The Neoliberal Ethic and the Spirit of Global Capital* (Bloomsbury, 2017) and has published on wide range of subjects, including spirituality in the workplace, corporate chaplaincy and the state of academic labor.

References

Bourdieu, Pierre. 1984. *Distinction: A Social Critique of the Judgement of Taste.* London: Routledge, Kegan & Paul.
Smith, Jonathan Z. 1978. *Map Is Not Territory: Studies in the History of Religions.* Leiden: Brill Publishing.

Part I

Teaching the Field

Chapter 1

On the Grammar of Teaching Religious Studies

Leslie Dorrough Smith

Introduction

Years ago, I had a former colleague who—tongue in cheek—used to tell students that if their parents asked them why they had to take religious studies (or insert any other humanities) courses, they could tell them that there could be a lucrative career going around and winning all of the trivia contests offered at every bar, restaurant, nursing home, and civic center. After the laughter ensued, this was often followed by "No, really, here's what religious studies classes can do for you ..." and the usual list of personal and social competencies (enhanced social ethics, cultural sensitivity, religious literacy, etc.) were rolled out.

Like many jokes, though, that one stung a bit, but perhaps not just for the reasons you might think. For even though the audiences who heard these things were themselves probably somewhat aware that they were receiving a sales pitch for a class or degree that likely wasn't on their radar, what always caused me to cringe the most was that I wasn't sure that my colleagues ever really understood how much they were implicated in their own joke. Indeed, for many university students, religious studies primarily involves the accumulation of intellectual trinkets from exotic places because this is how their professors teach the field, even if such faculty don't intend for it to be received that way.

Although the field itself is now populated by scholars who, perhaps more than ever before, claim a focus on more theoretical and methodological concerns, we should not confuse this interest with the critical application of method and theory, an issue that was the topic of the NAASR 2015 conference.[1] Indeed, there is a widespread, uninterrogated, essentialist impulse still remaining in the research of many who claim theoretical savvy. I've described this as the "accessories" approach, wherein one can treat theory and method in religious studies like an accessory—an academic sidekick, if you will—that can be used or excluded at will with no compromise to one's research (Smith 2017: 179-190). This technique has been used by large swaths of our field to claim theoretical expertise that simultaneously does not disturb a number of forces, among them progressive religious

---

1. That conference resulted in the volume *Theory in a Time of Excess: Beyond Reflection and Explanation in Religious Studies Scholarship* (Hughes 2017).

groups, several of the preconceived notions of our students, nor the agendas of the neoliberal university setting.

It's likely that a good portion of that scholarship is generated by people who are relatively unaware of what remains uninterrogated. But my interest in this essay lies more with thinking about how those of us who are very actively committed to anti-essentialist scholarship still fall back on a series of older conventions that may, even in the best of circumstances, take our teaching to essentialized places we do not wish to go. Though part of this more frequent theorizing about religious studies and our classroom teaching will hopefully have already led us to question the equation of "a good course" with 75 minute-sessions of factoid-vomiting (i.e., the stereotypical undergraduate class), I believe we are only at the beginning of conversations about what critical pedagogies in the religious studies context might look like.

This is not because our field has been uninterested in pedagogy, although as J. Z. Smith argued in the 1980s, the field is so relatively young that it's to be expected that we've come to the pedagogical table later than others (Smith 1991: 185). But at least since my entry into graduate school in the early 2000's, teaching statements, teaching certificates, and other forms of pedagogical focus have simply been par for the course as part of graduate professionalization. Much of this emphasis on our careers as teachers has been valuable and has exposed many of us to technologies, strategies, and vantage points that benefit our students. However, at least some of what are marketed as cutting-edge pedagogical perspectives today have been focused on a set of essentialized conceptualizations about who students are and how they learn ("millennials are such and such a way and need this or that kind of classroom," etc.). Even as we are encouraged to nimbly adapt to a different kind of student in a different kind of situation, we rarely ask what dynamics generate these notions of difference, all of which are often described as inevitable generational or economic shifts.[2] Moreover, many of us were taught pedagogical techniques outside of a religious studies context, either in Scholarship of Teaching and Learning (SoTL) modules or in those designed more broadly for humanities scholars. It is thus not clear that even in a time of pedagogical focus that many of us are on the same page.

In this essay, I want to indulge one of my curiosities about what forms a more robust religious studies pedagogy might take by grappling with the types of rhetoric we use in our classrooms, considering how our linguistic choices influence our students' conceptualization of religious studies as a type of inquiry. More specifically, this essay will explore what is at stake if we start talking about the category of religion more frequently in active, if not verb, form. This is not to say that its most common status as noun or object has no bearing, accuracy, or utility. It is to argue, however, that some of the discursive vocabulary we employ may be suitably critical but still not achieve certain educational goals. For the sake of a brief definition, I'm defining critical skills as cognitive tools that provide the ability to recognize and analyze the multitude of ways in which power creates

---

2. My thanks to Richard Newton, whose insights here have been particularly helpful.

knowledge.[3] Put differently, these tools foster an awareness of how description, classification, interpretation, argumentation, and other forms of reality-making are informed by the power dynamics of a particular social speaker's position. My presumption is that our students (not to mention, often, we, ourselves,) are so steeped in perennialist thought that a grammar disruption may well be a useful tool in helping to generate critical thought.

I'll offer my own insights that come from experimenting with this idea in my undergraduate courses with students who take them primarily for general education credit. Although I teach a variety of courses, our major program is small enough that very few of our classes have prerequisites, and thus most of our students are non-majors who see their religious studies course as one among several harrowing trials they must pass through on the way to a degree. Many of those reading this essay, I suspect, have experiences like mine in the sense that the student we most frequently teach may not have any particular commitment to the concepts of our specific courses apart from their desire for a good grade and our success at making the topics interesting and timely.

I am hardly the originator of this idea to present religion in its verb form; as I'll shortly discuss, several others have wrestled with the significance of this concept. But the reason that I'd like to re-introduce it in this setting, one where we are talking about how we teach the field, is that student misconceptions (if not misapprehensions) about a critical approach to religion is probably the most consistent teaching hurdle that I face day to day. Even as many of us interested in discursive methods and theories have made clear the importance of thinking of religion as a political strategy, a classificatory schema, etc.—all descriptors that appear to be focusing on religion as something people *do*—it is often the case that so long as religion retains its status primarily as a noun then the discussion has already been framed by a certain folk grammar that lends itself quite well to both reification and mystification. I know this is true in my own classroom, for even though I frequently describe religion as a type of tactic, many of my students find importance in the tactic only because of the things it facilitates or creates, when what I wanted them to see was that the object of interest was actually the tactic itself.

This conversation may seem obvious to some, and I submit at the outset that what I am proposing may look like more a tweak than a sea-change, but tweaks often yield some rather tangible results. Moreover, reviving this conversation seems more urgent to me for a couple of reasons that pertain to the conditions under which we work and the popular conventions that frame our scholarship. First, this is a time of extreme financial deprivation and uncertainty for many colleges and universities. Virtually all of us are aware of the closing of departments, programs, indeed, entire institutions, and even those who are at financially healthier schools are being asked to prove themselves in terms of majors,

---

3. I'm tipping my hat here to Foucault's claim that power creates knowledge, and not the other way around. While this concept is everywhere in Foucault's work, see, in particular, Foucault (1995 [1977]: 194; 1990 [1978]: 92ff.).

numbers, and job skills in ways never before. What was already an incredibly precarious job market has become even more so, it seems, and the tiny sliver of those who can secure tenure track jobs will find that they can expect far less from them in many ways than scholars in other times. The economic forces characterizing higher education as of late should confront us with the fact that we likely will, increasingly, have less time with our students. We must thus be impeccable in how we perform our work.

Second, I see this as a time when many of us interested in discursive approaches to religion have achieved at least some degree of consensus around the argument that religion involves strategic acts of classification used by individuals and groups to align their social conditions with their interests. Moreover, I think it's fair to say that many of us have shifted the focus from the strategic acts of certain religious groups to direct that same lens on the scholars who study them. This is evidenced by the fact that our work is quite often about scholarly strategies that fail certain critical tests, a point raised to show how, at times, scholars in our own field are difficult to distinguish from religious insiders. By no means am I arguing that these insights regarding a discursive approach prove that some of us have "figured it all out," but simply that many of us seem to be interested in similar types of arguments, and thus it might be a good time to collectively consider how we teach them.

In short, my proposition is that there may be something immensely helpful to be gained by thinking about what our students hear when we talk about critical approaches to religion, not what we are saying, or even what we *think* we are saying. Again, I can only talk about my own students (the majority of whom are midwestern Americans, usually in their early 20s, about half of whom are first generation college attendees) with any sort of specific expertise. Yet I suspect if we have learned anything from the scholars before us whose insights into forces such as habitus, interpellation, implicit bias, ideology, etc., matter at all, then we should take to heart that both we and the students to whom we speak are nodes in a web of social creation and contestation that directly influences not just what we say and why we say it, but also speaks volumes to our collective capacity to hear, understand, and apply.

What Should Our Classrooms Offer?

Before working through what is at stake in changing the grammar of how we talk about religion, I think it's important to consider broadly what types of things we think students should be learning in our classrooms, as this undoubtedly should form how we approach the study of religion. Bureaucratically speaking, many of the teaching competencies and outcomes that are used in university documents focus both on facts and skills. This seems a reasonable balance at first glance, for in the simplest sense, most of us recognize certain types of data as worth studying while also identifying a set of skills at hand that aid in the analysis of this data. There is also, hopefully, a conversation about why that data was selected over numerous others and what that reveals about our own scholarly and/or disciplinary interests. Put simply, there is nothing to theorize about if we do not first have data (alongside an awareness of how we selected it as such), and rich, diverse examples of it, more specifically.

But if we were to examine these learning outcomes that dot our syllabi and other documents more thoroughly, we would often find that the verb form (what students will do, and here I submit a stereotypical list:[4] "Learn about," "Analyze," "Consider the importance of," "Account for the development of") often plays second fiddle to the words on the other end of that sentence ("the world religions;" "global cultures"; "religious tolerance"; "major ethical systems"). So even when we have constructed lists of outcomes that we think are critically robust, we may find that the nouns outweigh the verbs in the minds of many. Why? I would wager that a rather formulaic way of looking at these outcomes is to assume that the words at the start of the sentences are applicable in most every discipline, and thus, because they are more generic, perhaps seem less important. On the other hand, the words at the end of these sentences are often portrayed as more interesting because this is where specific disciplines or fields are recognized; it's what makes us, us. I don't believe I oversimplify the matter when I say that, for many of us, this separation of analysis from data is part of our job security.

So this arrangement may have very practical benefits, but is it pedagogically helpful? As usual, J. Z. Smith has something to say about that. In Smith's essay, "The Introductory Course: Less is Better," he provides a characteristically unique take on what the introductory course should do, which, I would argue, is advice that we can transfer to virtually any other religious studies course. To Smith, the word "religion" is the least interesting part of the concept of "introductory course in religion" (Smith 1991: 185). Rather, the function of such a course is to (and here I summarize Smith): introduce students to college level work; train them in the skills of interpretation and self-conscious examination; teach them about argumentation, and specifically the role that "definitions, classifications, data, and explanations" play in argument-building; and teach them all this in the context of comparison, and preferably with examples that reach opposing conclusions so as to challenge students in using their burgeoning analytical skills (ibid.: 191).[5] The content of the course, he concludes, really isn't so important, except that you *can* use religion as an exemplar to achieve these ends (ibid.: 188, 192). According to this model, critical thinking skills involve recognizing the structures, forms, functions, and uses of human arguments, biases, and epistemologies.

Smith offers this advice, in part, to tell the reader that there isn't one particular topic that must be addressed in such a course so long as one is skill-building in a way that supports critical thinking. Yet arguments like this have ruffled the feathers of many, for, true to the larger gist of Smith's other arguments about

---

4. These echo Bloom's Taxonomy, which is often used as the central model for how to structure and assess learning.
5. The larger argument of the centrality of argumentation to the introduction course is the theme of the entire essay.

the subject of our field, the pedagogical model he supplies here doesn't posit a uniqueness about religion, which is often what sustains its presence in university catalogs. While many of us might agree that religion is just one social institution like any other, I would contend that there still are reasons why these particular skills might be best mastered in places like the religious studies classroom.

My thinking is that there are often dynamics in the religious studies classroom that are not experienced as frequently in most other disciplines. As Russell McCutcheon notes, one of the interesting things about teaching religion is that it may be one of the only educational settings where students are deemed experts at the start—where their experiences with an entrenched cultural perennialism means that they are likely to have already pre-authorized their anecdotal perceptions of what religion is and how it works (McCutcheon 2018: 68–73).This is why we may want to reconfigure the role of the introductory religious studies course as one where we teach students about the politics of categorization and the dynamics of power more generally, so that they learn "how to be curious about the taken-for-granted," as McCutcheon puts it, and have the intellectual tools at hand to do something with that curiosity, no matter where life may take them (ibid.).

But there are other disciplines that wrestle with this, as well, and the one with which I'm most familiar is the field of gender studies, where I was co-trained alongside religious studies and where I currently co-teach. It is important to take note of other fields with this same set of issues because it gives us additional places to look for how others have pedagogically responded when their main subject must constantly be de-naturalized in a cultural climate that pushes against this impulse. For those of us who teach gender studies and other critical identity categories (race, sexual orientation, etc.), the same problems are abundant, for insomuch as a student has formed even a rudimentary conceptualization of where they fit in our society's matrices of identity, their initial interest in the course is often tied to the reinforcement of their foregone conclusions. (More insights from gender studies momentarily).

Thus if we can agree that a large portion of what we owe our students is training in the laboratory of argument, categorization, and the ability to interrogate the taken-for-granted, then there is often no better place to do that than in a topical setting where students often already presume their own expertise. (As an aside, this is why I suspect many of us have students who struggle in our classes. It's not because we are asking them to use conceptual skills they do not have, but because the material isn't what they thought it would be.) The religious studies classroom is ideal (even if not entirely unique) in offering this opportunity, simply because we have a wealth of naturalized, essentialized claims from which to draw.

If we can agree that these are things we want to teach, does this render those aforementioned learning outcomes completely irrelevant? While I suspect many of us look upon such outcomes and their associated assessment cycles as things that are to be endured rather than celebrated, even those of us most cynical about their utility are probably influenced by them. For even if we do not work at confessional schools, many, if not most of us, are subject to other forces (our departments, research supports, and larger philanthropic institutions) that determine the sort of teaching we will do (i.e., what sorts of pursuits will receive funding), and those trickle down quite directly to affect the shape of syllabi (Newton 2019: 240). I have yet to find a humanities scholar who has not been called to defend themselves in economic terms, and if they cannot do that, in value-laden terms (in that order of preference).[6] Undoubtedly, all of us—competing in tight markets, pushed to justify our worth- have an array of sales pitches we use to validate our existence.

For instance, religious studies courses are often described as important because they reveal to students some mysterious element of "the human experience" and/or they expose (if not promote) a "moral compass" common to the aforementioned humans (Newton 2019: 238). (Obviously, I place all of these in scare quotes to question their critical purchase). To place this thinking in contradistinction with Smith and McCutcheon's earlier arguments, a very large majority of universities market the skills learned in a religious studies class as those that lead naturally to, or are uniquely in the service of, some idea of the "good life" and the "good society" that enables it. The larger narrative undergirding this marketing technique argues that religious studies is, in effect, a field that is "enchant[ed]" (to use Richard Newtons' phrasing) with special qualities that will resolve major social problems and simultaneously promote social unity. Yet insomuch as this approach presumes that our work is "intrinsically significant," Newton continues, "we lose the critical distance to question the actions and institutions fostering its appearance as such. Our students do as well" (ibid.: 236).

This presumption of enchantment often shows up in very benign ways, particularly in words that have lost this overt ethical or evaluative tenor but still retain its spirit. These are often codewords for concepts common to progressive religiosity. More specifically, Rebekka King notes, catchphrases such as "religious literacy, cultural reflexivity, and global engagement" are often the means of talking about otherwise "theological categories [that] have been reshaped in a way that retains their *a priori* mold" (King 2019: 249).[7] While I read King's invocation of the concept of "reshaping" to mean that there are other ways that these concepts could be rendered that gives them a more critical edge, it would be naïve to think that these more analytically robust forms are what most audiences tend to hear. What I believe they tend to hear, to put it bluntly, is that certain instances of religion are intrinsically good and thus don't need analysis beyond knowing certain descriptive facts ("who," "what," "when," "where"). Those deemed not intrinsically good have been "hijacked," and they get the final, often most critical, question ("why").

---

6. I'll mention later Richard Newton's excellent essay on the difference between teaching that religion (and its related cognates) hold some type of value, and the very different proposition that the study of religion is the study of mechanisms of *valuation* (see Newton 2017).
7. One could make the same argument about the AAR's recently released "Religious Literacy Guidelines," which I will shortly discuss. By this I mean that they certainly sound less openly perennialist in certain ways, but insomuch as they presume that there is a certain self-evident truth about various religious groups, they miss how religious discourses are authority moves that groups use for certain ends.

This does not mean that we have no way to construct a rigorous and critical version of religious studies via outcomes such as those mentioned above. It does mean, however, that the ways in which our field has been justified have often been analytically weak and, as such, have often tended to move away from this type of rigor as a means of self-defense. I admit that this may sound a bit oversimplistic, but consider that our largest professional organization, the American Academy of Religion (AAR), has just released guidelines on what should constitute "religious literacy" for two-and four-year colleges. Although that list is ripe for critique if our pedagogical concern is focused on critical thought, for the sake of brevity I will simply mention that two of those items include the ability to "discern accurate and credible knowledge about diverse religious traditions and expressions" and to "distinguish confessional or prescriptive statements made by religions from descriptive or analytical statements" (American Academy of Religion 2019).

To the uninitiated ear these may certainly sound like robust educational goals, but we don't have to dig very far into these statements before we hit the hard (and, I would argue, far more critical) questions, for these are the ones that interrogate power at all levels of human production: Whose versions of a particular instance of religion will be deemed "accurate and credible knowledge"? What forces influence this decision-making process? How, precisely, does one distinguish between the prescriptive and the descriptive, if we know that one feature of power is that it is naturalized to the degree that it becomes relatively invisible? Are we arguing that such a separation is possible, or is this something akin to an ideal type that has heuristic value but perhaps relatively less analytical weight? And are we critically comfortable with granting "religions" such agency that we will refer to them unproblematically as entities that "ma[k]e confessional or prescriptive statements"?

This extremely short list of questions I've just posed merely scratches the surface, and, as one might expect, there is plenty to say about the full list, as well as the forces that have contributed to the development of the concept of religious literacy itself. But for the sake of example here, I will simply note that providing our students with a laboratory wherein they can experiment with and deconstruct notions of argumentation, difference, and analysis will almost certainly increase their *critical* literacy, which, for me, is the central goal of my teaching. In this sense, I believe that the aforementioned learning outcomes and other related bureaucratic documents can be quite important, pedagogically speaking, so long as we examine them from a critical vantage point and also give our students a taste of what it means to see those very statements as part of the power continuum that we all inhabit. Perhaps it goes without saying, however, that the term "critical" may not mean the same thing to everyone deploying it.

On "Religion" as a Verb

Up to this point, I've argued that our classrooms should be focused primarily on building critical thinking skills and that our field provides a particularly good venue in which to test them because of the fact that our data involves a larger number of taken-for-granted claims. I've also noted that several of the dominant ways in which we market our classes may appear to enhance principles important to critical thought but may, in fact, simply reify certain non-critical concepts. So how can we transform these outcomes into something more analytically sound? For many of us, the answer to this has meant focusing on religion as a type of rhetoric that groups use to achieve certain goals. But as I earlier mentioned, I'm not sure that even when we explain this in what we believe are adequate ways that students are always hearing what we think we're teaching.

I began to consider this conundrum in my own teaching several years ago when I started to explicitly use the word "tactic" as my go-to synonym for religion in the introductory classroom, which was a switch for me away from other default terms like "discourse" and "institution." As background, I often start by teaching Lincoln's conceptualization of religion as a type of discourse that stands out from other kinds in its appeal to a transcendent authority (I boil this down to "an authority beyond critique"; Lincoln 2003: 5ff.). I couch this discussion in a larger conversation about the processes of reification and naturalization. With those things in mind, I then challenge students to think of religion as a discursive *tactic* used in the service of certain social goals.

This usually requires some explanation of how the terms we use to describe religion from a critical perspective differ from insider descriptions. I begin by noting that a functionalist perspective is interested in how certain things work, operate, or serve specific goals in a society. Such a perspective is not particularly concerned with whether these things are "good" or "right," since these tend to be insider terms more concerned with which insider speakers should be granted legitimacy over others. Knowing that there are very few objective ways that one could measure such legitimacy claims, I emphasize that, in our class, we'll stick with the more critical realm of functionalism since that approach is less likely to directly engage insider debates that cannot be resolved through academic analysis. This means that we are more interested in asking what the *function* of the terms "good" or "right" are in any particular socio-historical moment rather than presuming that those terms have an eternal and self-evident meaning.

In this light, I equate the term "tactic" with a strategic method of communicating, not unlike other mechanisms of persuasion such as guilt trips, flattery, or logic (and here I list any number of persuasive techniques that may be familiar to them), hopefully presenting them with a correlate that allows them to more easily recognize that the speaker in religious discourses usually has an interest in using that particular method. I am also careful to note that talking about something as a "tactic" does not necessarily imply that the thing in question is bad, ill-intentioned, or even objectively wrong (as an aside, the term "method" might be a useful substitute if "tactic" may prove problematic in tone). We then discuss how appealing to a deity, a self-evident ethical obligation, or an invisible reality are persuasive practices in their own right, ones that could be used for an infinite number of ends.

I have now approached religion from this "tactic" angle for two semesters in a world religions class I teach (our department's bread and butter, as I suspect it is for many reading this chapter), and I have done the same for several years in an Introduction to Religious Studies class that I approach more as a primer on critical elements of the field. No matter the course, though, this conversation happens alongside an introduction to how power dynamics in cultures typically operate. While this tactical approach (again, one that takes place within a conversation about order, reification, and power) has certainly helped students become more functionalist in their mindsets, it is still true that a not insignificant minority thinks of the tactic model as what the "bad religious people" do (that is, they "use" religion for selfish gain). Naturally, the "good religious people" are more readily seen as *not* tactical because, presumably, their motives are pure, or more to the point, aligned with perennialist notions of religion. I don't regard this as a complete pedagogical backfire by any means, for there will always be that minority. But what started to increase my students' understanding of these concepts is when I kept the tactical approach but began to periodically discuss religion in the active, verb tense, as "religioning" or "religionizing" (yes, they're awkward, and not my own terms, as I'll discuss shortly).

Moving into the realm of verbs in the study of religion invites the question: "What's the problem with nouns?" The issue is not so much an inherent problem with nouns as it is a sort of rhetorical tendency that emerges with their use, for without a clear and unequivocal emphasis on the human active, a certain sort of disembodied entity tends to find its way into our work. If our conversation is all about objects, then it's all too easy for scholars and students alike to conceptualize some sort of authentic, core "real" that somehow grounds those objects, leaving us to think that what we should be analyzing is their outer shell (McCutcheon 2012: 238–239). Alternately, students may be able to demonstrate their use of more critical methods in some circumstances but in selective others may differentiate between those things cultures make and other things that "just are," which is one risk associated with the tactical approach just mentioned (Newton 2019: 242).

Several scholars have provided us with models of religion that emphasize an active process and which therefore may be helpful in uncovering what is at stake if we remain in the realm of nouns. Consider Naomi Goldenberg's assertion that religion is the name of a particular type of power play—selectively used just as it is selectively withdrawn—and thus the language of religion as an "it" creates the appearance of an essence rather than acknowledging that it is, instead, an authorizing technique (Goldenberg 2018a: 92). When a social group claims to act for religious reasons, she notes, this "is meant as a gesture toward principles of power, regulation and control. In short, the word and its cognates now imply attitudes and practices of making order whether in regard to public institutions or to intimate feelings, habits, thoughts, actions and 'ways of living'" (Goldenberg 2018b: 129). This model is not unlike one of Richard Newton's pedagogical perspectives, which involves using DeCerteau's notion of "scriptural economies." This term denotes the ways in which cultures produce any number of naturalized discourses (texts and scriptures among them) that then become tools through which humans either grant or deny each other authority and thus determines where they sit in a cultural economy of social value (Newton 2017: 4, 10). The goal of using this method, Newton notes, is that we might teach students to analyze "the ways humans inflate the worth of themselves and others" through "the language game that is religion" (ibid.). Still yet, McCutcheon argues a similar point about activity even more explicitly when he notes that we must "mov[e] from studying settled nouns to dynamic verbs if we are to do something other than what participants are already doing for themselves—i.e., that we move from studying the meaning of the Bible (a ritual activity, really) to studying how meaning is negotiated and managed *by people*, or how the discursive object 'Bible' is created, maintained, and used *by people*" (McCutcheon 2012: 237). The question is how to emphasize the "by people" part without unintentionally creating the outer shell/inner core dichotomy.

While I hope it is clear from this brief selection that scholars are talking about a more active way to describe religion, what I want to consider for a moment are two examples that explicitly take up the issue of moving from the static to the active by proposing a new term through which to describe this process. Malory Nye's now almost 20-year-old essay on the topic of shifting our thinking to conceptualize religion as a verb was inspired, he notes, by Catherine Bell's use of the term "ritualization" in place of "ritual." Bell proposed the former based on her own qualms with the fact that the term "ritual" was used in far too passive, essentialized ways. In particular, Bell was concerned with the popular dichotomization between ritual (understood as "action") and belief (understood as "thought") (Nye 2000: 468).[8] Nye's concern over Bell's choice of the noun form "ritualization" lies with the fact that "...the use of a noun does still suggest something tangible that has its own agency, rather than as a form of expressing the agency of the people who actually do the practice," and thus he's not sure that "ritualization" goes far enough to correct the problem (ibid.: 469).

What Nye is pointing out is quite important, for as earlier mentioned, it's possible for problems to ensue in the classroom when we describe religion primarily, if not often exclusively, as a type of social institution. Although I don't disagree with the sociological meaning behind that vantage point, for students that perspective may unwittingly permit them to create a dichotomy whereby they separate the "human form" (the social institution) from the supposedly "real" or "spiritual" foundation that made the institution possible in the first place. So what should we do, instead? For his part, Nye offers the use of "religioning" to bypass the possibility of slipping into the reification of religion as an essentialized entity:

> Religioning is not a thing, with an essence, to be defined and explained. Religioning is a form of practice, like other cultural practices, that is done and performed by actors with their own agency (rather than being subsumed by their religions), who have their own particular ways and experiences of making their religiosities

---

8. Catherine Bell's attention to the concept of ritualization as a verb can be found in *Ritual Theory, Ritual Practice* (Bell 1992).

manifest. A discourse of religioning also moves away from looking at "religion" in terms of "religions" (Christianity, Islam, Hinduism, etc.), but instead looks at religious influences and religious creativities, and the political dynamics through which certain conceptualisations of religious authenticity are produced and maintained.

(Nye 2000: 468)

While I can agree in general strokes with this characterization of religion as a cultural practice, I have two concerns: first, I would not want to make an argument for actors' agency without also commenting on its limits, for social life is never as free as we imagine. Put differently, "religioning" is often not permitted to happen all the time and in every way in specific social circumstances, a fact that is absolutely critical to its portrayal as a type of activity. Second, I am unclear in what way Nye uses the adjective "religious" when he discusses "religious influences and religious creativities." One unfortunate interpretation of this—unfortunate because it amounts to a circular, essentialized description—might be seen in my students' tendency to keep the sense of activity but deprive it of any critical content, as when they might say that people are "religioning" simply when they "do religious things" (pray, engage in rituals, etc.). If we are going to maintain our critical senses, it is vital to focus the conversation back on the reasons why a figure or group might choose to use the adjective "religious" rather than presume that what's really interesting about the adjective is that it has a stable, self-evident meaning (Smith 1998: 281-282). To do otherwise—to indiscriminately use "religious" without a thoroughgoing explanation of what role it plays in our own categorizations—is itself a form of reification.[9]

This concern is shared by Ian Alexander Cuthbertson, who argues that Nye leaves residues of an underexamined "religion" in this definition that is simply being made manifest in his larger argument. While I can surmise that Nye might have been using that adjective as a heuristic tool to designate "religioning" in action, the problem is that it's hard to tell which option (if any of these) Nye was implying. In response to Nye, Cuthbertson's recommendation is to propose the term "religionization" (note that we're back to a noun), or the process by which what he calls "imagined bodies" are used to reframe the stuff of life into a particular classification system (Cuthbertson 2018: 101). His more comprehensive definition is as follows:

In referring to an imagined distinction, the category "religion" can be used instead to describe intellectual strategies used for separating human existence into discrete spheres along with the specific consequences these strategies entail. Although religion may not exist as a self-evident object in the world, discursive strategies that rely on "religion" and the distinctions this category implies clearly do. These strategies are not objects, however: they are ongoing processes or events.

(Cuthbertson 2018: 99-100)

---

9. This argument is present in many places, but one particularly well-known one is Tim Fitzgerald's critique of Bruce Lincoln (see Fitzgerald 2006: 392-423).

Here I find resonance between my own talk of tactics and Cuthbertson's talk of strategies, as well as some of the recognitions of continual renewal and activity that the power dynamics of almost all cultures demand to maintain the status quo. Cuthbertson pushes the conversation further away from reification by describing religion as a series of what start as intellectual strategies. I am not sure that "religionization" is a term that, when explained in the fullness Cuthbertson provides, will necessarily promise the best pedagogical outcomes because it once again situates the topic at hand within the framework of nouns (recall this was also Nye's concern with Bell's "ritualization"). Yet I still find the intention behind it quite attractive in the sense that it denotes an active process, of something happening across time, of one thing continually becoming something else.

But I would be neglecting what, for me, has undoubtedly been one of the most influential perspectives in allowing me to make this shift if I did not mention the degree to which gender and queer theories have helped me to conceptualize the move from describing what are often considered cultural products to cultural *processes*. And perhaps the twists and turns of my own education should give me (us?) pause on how our students' thinking might operate. When I was a student, I had difficulty conceptualizing religion as a discursive strategy until my exposure to critical theory in the gender studies classroom. At this point, the critical theory backdrop in my own mind was set, so to speak, and I could connect these principles back to my religious studies training. Like many of our students, my own conceptualizations of religion were so firmly rooted in essentialized, noun form that I needed an analog from another area of cultural life to displace that way of thinking.

So what analogous lessons did I learn? Simply put, I learned that power is often described as inevitable and natural when, in fact, it must be endlessly reconstituted to maintain its authority. To choose a widely popular example of this, I imagine that most of us are familiar with Judith Butler's argument that gender is not a static reality, but a type of ongoing cultural performance of certain behaviors, appearances, mannerisms, and attitudes that are socially constructed via appeals to the body (i.e., sex) (Butler 1990: 34). We are not born a particular gender, she notes, nor do we so much "become" one, as if one has arrived somewhere after a long plane ride. Butler contends, rather, that gender's fragility is why we must constantly repeat it in front of others via our clothing, our mannerisms, our communication, etc. Students seem to understand gender as an activity when one explains it as a constant process: "I'm gendering when I get dressed, I'm gendering when I walk to class, I'm gendering when I stand before you and speak, I'm gendering when you and I speak, etc." Because it is an always-shifting, and thus precarious, power relationship, gender's continual rehearsal and display must be demanded to legitimize the subjects formed through it as well as to naturalize its existence as somehow inevitable (ibid.: 45).

Many of us also know that Butler also questions the naturalness of the category of sex (and thus provides a noteworthy example of how one can avoid creating the outer shell/inner core dichotomy). While she does not, of course, deny that different people have different reproductive organs and genitalia, her larger point is that there are any number of other biological markers that could have been chosen if one wanted to organize humans based on body types (Butler 1990: 8–12). This reminds me of Marilyn Frye's argument preceding Butler's, which is that even as we cover our bodies, we are socially pressured to constantly announce what body parts are under our clothing if we are to be accepted by others (again, note the focus on repetition, activity, naturalization). This means that, to the degree that dominant cis-gender norms are followed, our gendered social interactions are an ongoing series of genitally or reproductively focused pronouncements: "I know we're talking about how our families are these days, or the state of the weather, but I'm also telling you more subtly about the parts under my clothing" (Frye 1983: 23–24).

Some might conclude from these rather popular examples that I'm simply calling for a renewed application of postmodern critique when I discuss "religion as verb." While that is not entirely wrong, it misses the larger point. I'm actually arguing for an awareness of the shift from object or states of being to active processes (or, from stative to dynamic verbs, for those who like the references to grammar) that postmodernist thought has so successfully brought to our awareness. Borrowing these techniques from postmodern thought and applying them to religious studies should not imply the terrors that some like Leonardo Ambasciano foresees when he argues that doing so will "leav[e] a wasteland of conceptual ruins" in our wake in so much as Ambasciano equates deconstruction with the utter eradication of what appears to be, to him, the entire field (Ambasciano 2019: 142).[10] In my mind, the only reason one might conclude this is if one was already, first, overly attached to the ontology of static essences, and second, suffering from a failure of imagination by which one could not see how identifying society's working as a series of shifting, adapting processes is itself a type of reconstruction of critical thought (and not its utter eradication; ibid.).

We could spend considerable time wordsmithing the best (or, as the case might be, least worst) verb form of "religion," but I fear that such efforts would simply result in a reification contest of competing terminologies. I am thus not proposing that there is a perfect term for this, as will become quite evident below, nor do I profess to have mastered the technique. What I can say, however, is that my own students' ability to critically consider religion as a certain type of process that leads to certain types of effects has been sharpened substantially the more that I've interjected an active discourse regarding religion into my teaching.

Pedagogical Strategies

In light of these experiences, what I wish to do in the space that follows is to simply offer some suggestions about how we might use terms like "religioning," "religionize," or other variants we might imagine that more decisively place

---

10. Ambasciano's rendering of postmodernism's effect on religious studies is, in my mind, highly caricaturized.

religion in the realm of human creation and activity, one informed by power relations, and in so doing, disrupt the reification process. My emphasis from this point on will be on where I've had pedagogical luck with this practice, as well as what other concepts I've needed to use and/or emphasize to make this idea work in my own classroom.

First, as I mentioned, I pepper in a verb form of religion ("religioning," "religionizing," etc.) in my speech here and there, as well as in my visual presentations. I explain these terms as verbs that designate a much broader series of events, discourses, actors, etc., the function of which is to create an authority claim that appears to be beyond critique (whether situated as the act of a deity, "self-evident" truths, etc.). These terms may sound a bit awkward, but I'm not sure that's entirely bad, since an awkwardness to the term can make it that much more memorable. What I don't want to do is to phrase it as "using religion," because students jump too quickly to the presumption that uses are abuses. "Using religion" is problematic also because it can preserve the idea that there is some idealized version of religion beyond human agendas that represents its pure core.

Second, I go to considerable lengths to discuss religion as a discursive practice so as to offset the overly simplistic "beliefs, rituals, ethics, texts" format, and I include a discussion about human inconsistency alongside that. My goal, in other words, is to be able to describe these "elements" of religion as hardly separate entities, but as different manifestations of a similar, shifting, flexible discursive process that may serve several different social functions at once to institutionalize a particular type of social order. This is in keeping with Lincoln's argument that all of the physical, psychological, institutional, etc. elements of religion are extensions first of its rhetoric (Lincoln 2003: 5ff.).

The tougher (but for students, often more interesting) work that takes place here is that parallel conversation about human inconsistency. If students can recognize that humans are consistently inconsistent, then they can better understand religioning as a technique that may appear in one form over here (say, a religious text), but pop up again in what seems to be a diametrically oppositional form over there (say, the choice by a certain group to ignore what a religious text says, all in the name of their religion). Once students can recognize that as human interests change so their religionizing changes, much of the hardest work is done. This is an incredibly important point, because without noting inconsistency as feature of human social groups, it is often very hard for students to mentally avoid charges of hypocrisy or "inauthentic" religion.

Third, where this principle often begins to "stick" for my students is with examples that focus on moments of change and transition. I tend to emphasize the many times when a group claims something is "cultural, not religious," which invites us to ask a series of questions that we can place in verb form ("This group was religionizing this event, but now they've stopped. Why?"). Other good resources for examples are the aforementioned inconsistencies that emerge in every religious group, ones that students are most likely to want to call illegitimate or hypocritical, alongside other moments of inconsistency or difference that do not fit popular stereotypes.

Regarding the rhetoric that something is cultural, not religious, I always start with the precursor that religion is an element of culture, and thus cannot be separated from it. I liken the dominant religion within a culture to a mirror in the sense that the hegemonic religion will usually reflect the qualities of the culture it inhabits. Once I have established that the "culture vs. religion" dichotomy is inherently flawed, I can draw on examples such as these:

- One that I've included in my own work is the example of Bob Jones University (BJU), which was one of the last evangelical universities to openly ban interracial dating, something that was policy as late as the 1990s and justified as divine will. When, in the early 2000s, the school rescinded their ban, they explained their previous policy by arguing that it was a manifestation of the "segregationist ethos of American culture" that had also afflicted other Christian groups (Smith 2020: 61). God had been dropped from the argument, in other words.

  To my students I might approach it this way: In the 1990s, BJU was religioning when it came to race, but by 2000s that religioning stopped. What, culturally, had changed, and does this give us any insight into this series of stops and starts? And what does this tell us, more to the point, about how religion worked for the group in this instance? Why use it in one moment but stop using it in another? The important thing I emphasize along the way is that this is not a shift in the object at hand (a racist policy), but a change in the way that a group describes it. Religionizing is thus revealed as, among other things, a very specific mode of description, but only one among many.

- Another effective example that disturbs the false dichotomies of religion vs. culture or religion vs. politics is Goldenberg's conceptualization of religion as a category of governance, or a tool "that functions as a key component in the technology of contemporary statecraft" (Goldenberg 2015: 80). Goldenberg has shown how nation-states often selectively surrender authority to certain religious groups as a way to manage those very groups, permitting them to engage in behaviors that would otherwise be considered inappropriate if not illegal in exchange for their more general acquiescence to the formal, dominant governing structure (Goldenberg 2020). Often, Goldenberg notes, these behaviors involve acts of violence or harm against women and children in the name of preserving the sense of a private realm free from unwarranted government interference. In one case from 2013–2014, Goldenberg describes how New York city Mayor Bill DeBlasio's campaign vowed to permit the practice of *metzizah b-peh* (oral suction after circumcision) on newborn boys, even though the act—a traditional practice among certain ultra-Orthodox Jewish groups—had been linked with the spread of herpes, and subsequently brain damage and even death in some infected children. In this case, because the ultra-Orthodox community was highly resistant to regulate this act, and DeBlasio needed the ultra-Orthodox vote to maintain his own power, the practice was allowed to continue under the auspices of religious freedom (ibid.: 10–11).

When considering a case such as this, we can describe both the city government and the ultra-Orthodox community as entities religioning (i.e., deploying religious discourses) for various purposes. Put differently, we might ask how an act that would be considered child abuse in one realm could get "religioned" into a matter of civil liberties. This query might naturally be followed up with another: when groups or individuals are religioning/religonizing, what does this do to their relative status and/or power within the subcultures in which they operate? This is an interesting set of questions to juxtapose with instances of faith-healing in the US wherein parents have been found guilty of neglect and homicide in the deaths of their children after refusing to provide them with medical care.[11] Very simply, there have been times when governments intervene in such acts, and times when they haven't, and the outcome of these cases often depend on the political impact of the group in question. Closely examining the power relationships at play when groups are religionizing certain behaviors will often reveal the reasons behind the inconsistency.

A second grouping of examples that often work well with students involves inviting them to compare two or more actors whose identities are both described using the same traditionally religious adjectives (in the examples I'll provide below, "Christians" or "Hindus") but whose platforms are marked by utter difference or incompatability. The goal in each instance is to identify the religioning that is going on and what cultural factors motivate its use.

- In one of my introductory courses, I have students read two articles, both written by self-described Christians, about gay marriage (both were written on the eve of the 2015 *Obergefell v. Hodges* decision legalizing gay marriage in the US). One of the articles is written by a progressive seminarian who tacitly proclaims his support for gay marriage by liberally citing all of the ways in which the Bible is inconsistent and historically bound (and thus, the argument goes, Christians can and should ignore the few passages that speak about homosexuality). He does quite a lot of religioning. Another article is written by a very conservative Christian Right author who argues forcefully against gay marriage using virtually no religioning at all;

---

11. As an interesting example of discourse surrounding the legality of faith healing in light of notions of religious freedom, see Merriam and Tuttle (2009).

rather, her arguments are grounded mainly in nationalist rhetoric, citing gay marriage as a violation of the Constitution and the Bill of Rights.

I point out to students that both people are religionizing in the sense that they are using some sort of naturalized authority to ground their claims, not to mention their self-proclaimed Christianity. But the fact that they both claim the same label and yet come to different conclusions can be explained as something more than "people have different opinions," which is where I fear the analysis ends in our students' minds if we do not push it further. Why would the self-identified conservative Christian NOT be religionizing in overt ways when that aspect supposedly defines her identity? Conversely, why would the progressive seminarian focus so heavily on the Bible—engaging in very active religionizing—if he's just attempted to undercut the authority of its literal reading?

Here we talk about intended audiences and persuasive power: the conservative activist needs not attempt to persuade other conservatives, for they are likely already on board with her. Rather, her essay is marketed towards those more likely to identify with nationalist or patriotic labels than religious ones, and the reverse is true for her interlocutor: more progressive thinkers already agree with him, so he needs to focus his persuasion by religionizing in ways that conservatives are more likely to hear. Both are religioning, in a sense, but if we can recognize it as a tactic and the essays we read as part of the persuasive process, then we will be able to see that behind their common label ("Christian") are different rhetorical processes that benefit them in light of their intended audiences and different goals.

- A final example I might offer is a question that I ask most of my world religion students after having read primary texts from Gandhi on how he represents Hinduism, alongside a series of news reports on the BJP's own version of Hinduism. There isn't much unusual about this exercise if we compare it to what other world religions classes often discuss; we contrast Gandhi's insistence that Hinduism recognizes the value of all humans and all religions with the BJP's history of discrimination and violence against Muslims and Dalits in the name of this very Hinduism. Almost always, students love Gandhi and are enraged by the BJP, and this impulse to see Gandhi as more "authentically" Hindu is something we address in a larger discussion on how conversations on authenticity are really a type of social contest.

They are usually quite ready, then, to answer an essay question on how advocates of each side are "religioning" when they represent Hinduism in the way they do, and the social factors that naturalize those different vantage points. To put that differently, they are prepared to see "Hinduism" as an umbrella term that can used by a variety of different actors for a variety of ends. But that's not what I ask them. Rather, I ask them how our class was religioning when we wanted to normalize Gandhi's statements as "real" Hinduism. This throws some of them for a loop, but the majority get the point that if religion refers to a process of making order, of granting "authority beyond critique" to one particular group over another, then scholars (and their students!) can engage in the same sort of rhetorical processes as the people they claim to study.

Like most habits, a change in language is hard. As we know, however, it's not hard just because we must break out of a particular type of repetition, but because our language is the mechanism through which our cognitive worlds are both formed and shared. Attempting a reinvention of how we use language thus means a reinterpretation of the intellectual frameworks through which we make sense of the data around us. I present these ideas with the full knowledge that implementing them in certain types of courses may be more challenging than in others, but I hope to open up a discussion on what a more active, process-focused representation of religion might look like, how it might be taught, and what it might mean for our attempts to create more critical classrooms.

Leslie Dorrough Smith is associate professor of religious studies at Avila University (Kansas City, MO), where she is also the director of the Women's and Gender Studies Program. She is the author of *Compromising Positions: Sex Scandals, Politics, and American Christianity* (Oxford University Press, 2019) and *Righteous Rhetoric: Sex, Speech, and the Politics of Concerned Women for America* (Oxford University Press, 2014). Her research interests focus on American evangelicals and politics, critical theory, and the use of method and theory in both religious studies and gender studies.

References

Ambasciano, Leonardo. 2019. *An Unnatural History of Religions: Academia, Post-Truth, and the Quest for Scientific Knowledge*. London: Bloomsbury Academic.
American Academy of Religion. 2019. "AAR Religious Literacy Guidelines." Retrieved www.aarweb.org/aar-religious-literacy-guidelines#academic%20approach (accessed October 3, 2019).
Bell, Catherine. 1992. *Ritual Theory, Ritual Practice*. New York: Oxford.
Butler, Judith. 1990. *Gender Trouble: Feminism and the Subversion of Identity*. New York: Routledge.
Cuthbertson, Ian Alexander. 2018. "Preaching to the Choir? Religious Studies and Religionization." In Brad Stoddard (ed.), *Method Today: Redescribing Approaches to the Study of Religion* (pp. 96–105). Sheffield: Equinox.
Fitzgerald, Tim. 2006. "Bruce Lincoln's 'Theses on Method': Antithesis." *Method & Theory in the Study of Religion* 18(4): 392–423.
Foucault, Michel. 1990 [1978]. *The History of Sexuality, Volume 1: An Introduction*. Trans. Robert Hurley. New York: Vintage.

Foucault, Michel. 1995 [1977]. *Discipline and Punish: The Birth of the Prison*. Trans. Alan Sheridan. New York: Vintage.
Frye, Marilyn. 1983. "Sexism." In Marilyn Frye, *The Politics of Reality: Essays in Feminist Theory*. New York: Crossing Press.
Goldenberg, Naomi R. 2015. "The Category of Religion in the Technology of Governance: An Argument for Understanding Religions as Vestigial States." In Trevor Stack, Naomi R. Goldenberg, and Timothy Fitzgerald (eds), *Religion as a Category of Governance and Sovereignty* (pp. 280–292). Leiden: Brill.
Goldenberg, Naomi R. 2020. "Toward a Critique of Postsecular Rhetoric." In Leslie Dorrough Smith, Steffen Führding, and Adrian Hermann (eds), *Hijacked: A Critical Treatment of the Public Rhetoric of Good and Bad Religion* (pp. 37–47). Sheffield: Equinox.
Goldenberg, Naomi. 2018a. "Forget About Defining 'It': Reflections on Thinking Differently in Religious Studies." In Brad Stoddard (ed.), *Method Today: Redescribing Approaches to the Study of Religion* (pp. 79–95). Sheffield: Equinox.
Goldenberg, Naomi. 2018b. "Response to the Responses." In Brad Stoddard (ed.), *Method Today: Redescribing Approaches to the Study of Religion* (pp. 128–130). Sheffield: Equinox.
Hughes, Aaron W. (ed.). 2017. *Theory in a Time of Excess: Beyond Reflection and Explanation in Religious Studies Scholarship*. Sheffield: Equinox.
King, Rebekka. 2019. "Competencies and Curricula: The Role of Academic Departments in Shaping the Study of Religion." In Leslie Dorrough Smith (ed.), *Constructing "Data" in Religious Studies: Examining the Architecture of the Academy* (pp. 246–255). Sheffield: Equinox.
Lincoln, Bruce. 2003. *Holy Terrors: Thinking About Religion After September 11*. Chicago, IL: University of Chicago Press.
McCutcheon, Russell. 2012. "A Tale of Nouns and Verbs: Rejoinder to Ann Taves." *Journal of the American Academy of Religion* 80(1): 238–239.
McCutcheon, Russell. 2018. *"Religion" in Theory and Practice: Desmystifying the Field for Burgeoning Academics*. Sheffield: Equinox.
Merriam, Jesse, and Robert W. Tuttle. 2009. "Faith Healing and the Law." Retrieved from www.pewforum.org/2009/08/31/faith-healing-and-the-law (accessed October 2, 2019).
Newton, Richard. 2017. "Locating Value in the Study of Religion." *Method and Theory in the Study of Religion* 29(4–5).
Newton, Richard. 2019. "Teaching in the Ideological State of Religious Studies: Notes Towards a Pedagogical Future." In Leslie Dorrough Smith (ed.), *Constructing "Data" in Religious Studies: Examining the Architecture of the Academy* (pp. 235–245). Sheffield: Equinox.
Nye, Malory. 2000. "Religion, Post-Religionism, and Religioning: Religious Studies and Contemporary Cultural Debates." *Method & Theory in the Study of Religion* 12(1–4): 447–476.
Smith, Jonathan Z. 1991. "The Introductory Course: Less is Better." In Mark Juergensmeyer (ed.), *Teaching the Introductory Course in Religious Studies: A Sourcebook* (pp. 185–192). Atlanta, GA: Scholars Press.
Smith, Jonathan Z. 1998. "Religion, Religions, Religious." In Mark C. Taylor (ed.), *Critical Terms for Religious Studies* (pp. 269–284). Chicago, IL: University of Chicago Press.
Smith, Leslie Dorrough. 2017. "Theory is the Best Accessory: Branding and the Power of Scholarly Compartmentalization." In Aaron W. Hughes (ed.), *Theory in a Time of*

Excess: Beyond Reflection and Explanation in Religious Studies Scholarship (pp. 179–189). Sheffield: Equinox.

Smith, Leslie Dorrough. 2020. *Compromising Positions: Sex Scandals, Politics, and American Christianity*. New York: Oxford.

Chapter 2

Can't Live with it, Can't Drop it from the Undergraduate Curriculum: World Religions

Rita Lester and Jacob Barrett

Can the gateway undergraduate course in the study of religion be designed to disturb the "taken-for-granteds," de-exoticizing what Leslie Dorrough Smith (Chapter 1, this volume) calls the "accessories" approach, and challenging a more narrowly focused operational definition of religious literacy even if that gateway course was the rightly critiqued-within-an-inch-of-its-life but institutionally and popularly resilient world religions?[1]

Religious studies courses take as our subject the authorizing techniques by which meaning is created and negotiated by people, a highly motivated process of classification and bricolage used to align social conditions and claims with selective interests. When people invoke religion for the things they do and desire, it frames their arguments in a way that appear stable and self-evident but religionizing (Smith, Chapter 1, this volume), the appeal to an authority beyond critique, is indicative of power, the sleight of hand that distracts from the process, its material effects, and privilege.[2] Religion as a hegemonic discourse, as Joseph Laycock summarizes Foucault, "operates by presenting the interests of the dominant group as the interests of everyone" and this exercising of power is only "tolerable only on the condition that it mask a substantial part of itself," hiding "its own mechanisms" (Laycock 2020: 23). That said, what to do about my university's well-connected gateway course, world religions? Private, liberal arts colleges[3] have long hosted a world religions course as a prerequisite or outgrowth to

---

1. World religions at Nebraska Wesleyan University serves philosophy and religion, international studies, and diversity requirements. In spring 2019 we piloted a redesigned world religions with explicit critique of the world religions paradigm. This course rejects the standard textbook, show-and-tell, and multiple-choice exams replacing them with examinations of clichés about religion and intentionally provocatively juxtaposed case studies based on J. Z. Smith's advice for teaching, assessed through written arguments about interpretations and power. The pedagogical goal: critical and self-interrogation of cultural bias and the influence of colonialism. Curricular goals: introduce theorizing in the gateway, critically engage what students expect a world religions course to do, and ensure that scores for IDEA evaluation prompts indicated as essential are maintained or improved.
2. At 2019 NAASR, Naomi Goldenberg, from the audience, suggested the "political study of religion" instead of "the scientific study of religion."
3. Like Nebraska Wesleyan University (www.nebrwesleyan.edu).

Christian missions that took an ecumenical turn. As Leslie Dorrough Smith notes, we are never as free in creating as we imagine,[4] that is, the course/s in which we examine religionizing exists in the space negotiated between curriculum, student expectations, and funding trends.[5] But, as Kathyrn Lofton encourages scholars in another regard: "It was made by us ... we have the tools to take it apart and to try again."[6]

Tactics for Teaching Religionizing as a Tactic

Whether in distributive or integrative curriculum, world religions survives as a well-connected course. Although I have used Prothero's and Pew religious literacy[7] quizzes as first session activities, I do so in a move that Steven Ramey calls "critical embrace" (Ramey 2016: 48–60); that is, not as a promise that students will get better at trivia but to make apparent the disconnect between devotion and knowledge, to expose the work of definitions and classifications (like "scripture"), and to initiate a semester-long interrogation of the world religions paradigm. Instead of eliminating world religions from the course catalog[8] we piloted a world religions that overtly attempts to challenge assumptions implicit in the world religions paradigm, replacing memorization of emic or normative claims, big glossy textbook, encyclopedic approaches to religious literacy,[9] and implicit theological/interfaith goals, with examinations of widely held clichés about religion (Stoddard and Martin 2017) buttressed by intended-to-be-provocatively juxtaposed case studies, with a schedule scaffolded and designed according to Jonathan Z Smith's rules from "Approaching the College Classroom,"[10] which are:

1. Students should gain some sense of mastery. Among other things, this means read less rather than more. In principle, the students should have time to read each assignment twice.

2. Always begin with the question of definition and return to it.

---

4. Saba Mahmood (2011) questions the Kantian ethical self valorized in US feminist scholarship on religion, and Elizabeth Bucar (2011) argues for dianomic agency.
5. The pervasive reality of the impact of private and public funding trends on religious studies are more broadly and historically examined in Gregory Alles presentation at the 2019 NAASR (published as Chapter 10 of this volume).
6. Currently acting dean of humanities at Yale and author of *Consuming Religion* (Lofton 2017).
7. Unlike cultural literacy arguments which initially ignored discursive power, religious studies should argue that religious literacy is *not* limited to normative factoids, emic narratives, or selective encyclopedic entries.
8. I sympathize more with a department or program that would eliminate the world religions course, less if assigns to contingent faculty or renames it without changing content *à la* Huston Smith's *The World's Religions* (Smith 2009), first published as *The Religions of Man* in 1958.
9. Although the entries at the end of his 2007 *Religious Illiteracy* is an example of this approach, Prothero's newest world religions textbook is the best of this albeit problematic WRP industry if you need to have a more traditional textbook, and its reasonably priced.
10. Jonathan Z. Smith's rules from "Approaching the College Classroom" (Smith 2012).

3   Make arguments explicit. Both those found in the readings and those made in class.

4   Nothing must stand alone. Comparison opens space for criticism.

5   A student only knows something well if she can apply it to something else.

6   Students have learned something when they can be reflective about their initial understanding.

Admittedly easier to manage in smaller courses because it is assessed through discussion and written arguments about interpretations and analyses of power, the proposed learning outcome in gateway course in religious studies is a critical interrogation of cultural bias with a focus on the influence of the European Enlightenment, Christian theism, and colonialism. As Jolyon Baraka Thomas writes in his book on the construction of religion and religious freedom in Japan, "the academic study of religion," not just world religions, reflects "imperial encounters with cultural difference, sublimated Protestant supercessionism, anti-communist Cold War politics, and tenacious crypto-theological attempts to posit a transhistorical universal human religiosity" (Thomas 2019: 245). In this way, a world religions course that doesn't support the WRP, even attempts to dismantle it, is both a useful introduction to the study of religion and an effective integrative curriculum service course for students who may never take another religion class.

We Go to Class with the Students We Have

Because there is a gap between professorial plans and student takeaways,[11] I redesign and pilot courses collaboratively with upper-level students whose senior project research intersects with course inquiry.[12] Although successful completion of the course is a prerequisite, what such students bring is not content mastery but a clearer understanding of how students manage assignments, respond to activities, and engage delivery platforms. A readily accessible but limited tool for consistently collecting students' self-ratings of learning is IDEA[13] which indicates that students continue to report high self-ratings for "gaining a basic understanding" and "developing knowledge ... of diverse perspectives." As initially and tentatively measured, the "learning to analyze and critically evaluate ideas" self-rating is noticeably higher in the pilot course that explicitly critiques the WRP.

---

11. One of Leslie Dorrough Smith's concerns is how even professors committed to anti-essentialist scholarship teach unintended lessons of essentialism.
12. Peter Felton's model at Elon University on Students as Learner and Teachers (see www.centerforengagedlearning.org/about-us/staff/peter-felten).
13. See www.ideaedu.org/services/student-ratings-of-instruction. Although using and citing this, the research on bias in student evaluations should give our institutions pause in overvaluing student evaluations in tenure and promotion considerations.

Table 2.1 Comparison of course evaluation surveys on selected questions.

IDEA Prompt	Fall 2017	Spring 2017	Pilot Spring 2018
1. Gaining a basic understanding of the subject (e.g., factual knowledge, methods, principles, generalizations, theories)	87%	88%	88%
2. Developing knowledge and understanding of diverse perspectives, global awareness, or other cultures	N/A	N/A	88% (72% ranked 5 on a 1–5 scale)
3. Learning to analyze and critically evaluate ideas, arguments, and points of view	63%	73%	84%

It appears that critiquing the WRP didn't hurt the learning goals, even improved one of them: learning to analyze and critically evaluate ideas, arguments and points of view. In the future, the gap I may need to turn my attention to is between student expectations and my expectations regarding "values and spiritual development." According to Barbara Walvoord's research on introduction to religion courses at over 500 private and public universities in the US and UK, this gap is widespread. Students rate "values and spiritual development" much higher than faculty:

- 51–54% students at sectarian/ religiously affiliated school choose "values and spiritual development" as essential.
- 70–73% of students at non-sectarian/non-religiously affiliated schools choose "values and spiritual development" as essential.
- While 1/3 Faculty in religiously affiliated schools did NOT choose "values and spiritual development" as an essential goal.

(Walvoord 2008: 133)

If I decide to rate "values and spiritual development" as more important that I have thus far in order to, say, investigate "spiritual but not religious" (SBNR), two of Walvoord's recommendations may prove helpful: focus on the impact of claims, and focus on behavior not belief (ibid.: 95). Future revisions will include religioning as an exoticizing, fragmenting, commodifying self-help practice (yoga: Altglas 2014; Oprah: Lofton 2011), and the secularization two-step,[14] the division between religion and non-religion (Thomas 2019), "good belief" and "bad belief" (Coviello 2019: 29), "religion" and "superstition" (Josephson-Storm 2017), what a modern state welcomes and what isn't tolerated (Asad 2003).

---

14. Peter Coviello in *Make Yourselves Gods* says he got this phrase from Nancy Bentley (Coviello 2019: 27).

Interfaith and Religious Studies

The funding initiative of the America Association of Colleges & Universities in conjunction with The Interfaith Youth Core(AAC&U/IFYC) directly impacts my course content and the university curriculum because its mission is for students, faculty and staff to have what it calls interfaith skills.[15] As can be seen in the six programs it highlights, the AAC&U/IFYC initiative accepts non-religious studies faculty teaching "interfaith skills" and "religious diversity" and two of the six programs highlighted explicitly house interfaith programs in non-religious studies departments.[16] At a time of, as Leslie Dorrough Smith notes, financial struggles and uncertainty, how can Religious Studies faculty critically embrace universities' interfaith interests and funding opportunities, eye wide open regarding the ways in which interfaith "masks ... a kind of privilege in which the powerful decide who will be tolerated and on what terms" (Laycock 2020: 23)? Make the history and assumptions of interfaith the subject of courses and build a new program housed in religious studies[17] designed to offer historical, contextual and theoretical examinations of how religious diversity has been conceived of, why, and to whose benefit, consistent with the learning goals of the department and university.

As with learning goals that historically examine, denaturalize, de-essentialize sex/gender, we cannot assume wide-spread or permanent critical gain in de-centering Christian theism in Religious Studies.[18] Our agency to teach religion as a tactic in the gateway course or to tactically engage interfaith trends

---

15. See www.aacu.org/summerinstitutes/ifyc/2019/goals.
16. Six programs highlighted by AAC&U/IFYC three-year project funded by the Teagle Foundation, two of which are housed in Interdisciplinary Studies and Economics and Business (see www.ifyc.org/sites/default/files/resources/CurricularPrograms%20-%20Rebecca%20 Bates.pdf).
17. Religious diversity minor goals: analyze the categories of religion, religious diversity, and interreligious studies including the histories, theoretical models, and scholarship that inform them, recognize and explain the ways in which religious traditions and interreligious encounters are embedded within cultural, political and economic systems, produce nuanced and critically self-aware reflections on ways that religious traditions and religious communities have and continue to interact and critique existing models for understanding and facilitating multi-religious encounters in curricular and co-curricular settings and offer constructive suggestions for improvement in equity.
18. Like Smith, my initial training in denaturalizing a subject was in feminist studies Anti-sexism (invoking what Ibram X. Kendi says about anti-racism in *How to Be an Antiracist*) is not as far along as some of us might imagine or want. Russell McCutcheon's "The Enduring Presence of Our Pre-Critical Past; or, Same as it Ever Was, Same as it Ever Was" (Chapter 6, this volume) advises that teachers have long entrenched habits to undo with each new generation of students. Also, thanks to F. LeRon Shults for putting a sharp point on this at the 2019 NAASR/AAR: gender studies critiques sexism, African-American studies critiques racism, religious studies critiques theism.

and outside funding in the curriculum shapes the field we teach and the field on which we play.[19]

Rita Lester is professor of religion at Nebraska Wesleyan University. Her interests include undergraduate education in religious studies, from first-year introductory to senior capstone project courses.

Jacob Barrett is an MA student in the religion in culture MA program at the University of Alabama. His research explores questions about religion and governance, law, and the state through contemporary examples from American politics.

Appendix

There are six programs in interfaith and interreligious studies highlighted by the AAC&U Interfaith Youth Core three-year project funded by the Teagle Foundation (www.ifyc.org/sites/default/files/resources/CurricularPrograms%20-%20Rebecca%20Bates.pdf), plus Elon University held in high esteem by AAC&U as a model of high impact, experiential and engaged learning. The following programs include majors, minors and certificate programs at both public and private undergraduate institutions and are included here to situate NWU in the larger, national spectrum of populations, offerings, and rigor. I include here only to show that although NWU's new minor fits on this spectrum, it is also acceptable to AACU IFYC if the "interfaith" goals are constructed and delivered in professional programs, business or other fields.

California State University (CSU) Chico—Certificate in Interreligious and Intercultural Relations

California State University Chico is a public institution located in Chico, California, with an undergraduate population of over 15,000 students. CSU Chico has created an interdisciplinary certificate in interreligious and intercultural relations. The certificate includes five academic courses, a senior internship in religious diversity, and one course regarding religious diversity in a professional or disciplinary context.

Saint Mary's College of California—Interfaith Leadership Minor

Saint Mary's College of California is a private institution affiliated with the Roman Catholic Church in Moraga, California, and serves 2,800 undergraduate students. The college launched an interdisciplinary interfaith leadership minor in the fall of 2015, which is housed within the School of Economics and Business Administration. The minor consists of 6 courses, which includes four courses regarding the intersection of interfaith cooperation and anthropology, business, ethics, communication, and psychology, two interdisciplinary electives, and a quarter-credit interfaith leadership praxis course.

---

19. This field of play metaphor is Bucar's, in the conclusion of *Creative Conformity* of the interplay between male clerics and the women she classifies as creative conformers for the feminist tactics in production of ethical knowledge (Bucar 2011: 160).

Elizabethtown College—Interfaith Leadership Studies Major

Elizabethtown College is a private institution affiliated with the Church of the Brethren in Elizabethtown, Pennsylvania, and serves 1,900 undergraduate students. Elizabethtown launched the country's first major in the fall of 2015, which includes 6 required courses centered around interfaith leadership, two courses in religious literacy, three courses related to religious diversity and civil society, and two courses in professional skills and experiential learning.

Oklahoma City University (OCU)—Interfaith Studies Minor

Oklahoma City University is a private institution affiliated with the United Methodist Church in Oklahoma City, Oklahoma, and serves about 2,300 undergraduate students. OCU has created an interfaith studies minor which launched in the fall of 2015. Replacing their pre-existing world religions minor, the interfaith studies minor is housed in the Wimberly School of Religion and consists of six courses: two religion courses, three electives (at least one of which must be taken outside of the School of Religion), and an internship in an interfaith setting.

University of Toledo—Interreligious Studies Concentration within the Religious Studies Major

The University of Toledo is a public research university located in Toledo, Ohio, and serves over 18,000 undergraduate students. Toledo has developed an interreligious studies concentration, which is housed within the religious studies major. The concentration consists of 12 credit hours, selected from courses in multiple disciplines including religious studies, philosophy, peace and justice, film, and history. This concentration provides a more extended study of interreligious dynamics by way of case studies, theory, community service, and internships.

Elon University—Interreligious Studies Minor

Elon is a private liberal arts university in North Carolina held in high esteem by AAC&U for its engaged learning. Located in central North Carolina, it serves about 6,000 undergraduate students and has developed an interreligious studies minor, housed in religious studies. The program consists of six courses (1–4 credits each), selected from courses in religious studies and Spanish, with internship and research possibilities. Housed in religious studies, other electives are accepted from other departments on a case-by-case basis for approval by religion chair.

References

Altglas, Veronique. 2014. *From Yoga to Kabbalah: Religious Exoticism and the Logics of Bricolage.* Oxford: Oxford University Press.

Asad, Talal. 2003. *Formation of the Secular: Christianity, Islam Modernity.* Stanford, CA: Stanford University Press.

Bucar, Elizabeth. 2011. *Creative Conformity: The Feminist Politics of US Catholic and Iranian Shi'i Women.* Washington, DC: Georgetown University Press.

Coviello, Peter. 2019. *Make Yourselves Gods: Mormons and the Unfinished Business of American Secularism*. Chicago, IL: University of Chicago Press.
Josephson-Storm, Jason. 2017. *The Myth of Disenchantment, Magic, Modernity, and the Birth of the Human Sciences*. Chicago, IL: University of Chicago Press.
Laycock, Joseph P. 2020. *Speak of the Devil: Hope the Satanic Temple is Changing the Way We Talk About Religion*. Oxford: Oxford University Press.
Lofton, Kathyrn. 2011. *Oprah: The Gospel of an Icon*. Berkeley, CA: University of California Press.
Lofton, Kathyrn. 2017. *Consuming Religion*. Chicago, IL: University of Chicago Press.
Mahmood, Saba. 2011. *Politics of Piety: The Islamic Revival and the Feminist Subject*. Princeton, NJ: Princeton University Press.
Ramey, Steven. 2016. "The Critical Embrace: Teaching the World Religions Paradigm as Data." In Christopher Cotter and David Roberson (eds), *After World Religions: Reconstructing Religious Studies* (pp. 48–60). Abingdon: Routledge.Smith, Huston. 2009. *The World's Religions*. New York: HarperOne.
Smith, Jonathan Z. 2012. "Approaching the College Classroom." In Christopher Lehrich (ed.), *On Teaching Religion: Essays by Jonathan Z. Smith*. Oxford: Oxford University Press.
Stoddard, Brad and Craig Martin (eds). *Stereotyping Religion: Critiquing Cliches*. London: Bloomsbury Academic.
Thomas, Jolyon Baraka. 2019. *Faking Liberties: Religious Freedom in American-Occupied Japan*. Chicago, IL: University of Chicago Press.
Walvoord, Barbara. 2008. *Teaching and Learning in College Introductory Religion Courses*. Oxford: Blackwell Publishing.

Chapter 3

Practicing Theory

Ian Alexander Cuthbertson

Introduction

In "On the Grammar of Teaching Religious Studies" (Chapter 1, this volume), Leslie Dorrough Smith outlines some of the issues that those of us who work and teach within the critical religion framework face in our classrooms. In this response, I focus on two questions posed by Smith: what do our students expect from our courses? And what should our classrooms offer our students? Like Smith, my own priorities as an educator are shaped by an interest in examining how and why labels like "religion" are claimed and defended along with the specific practical and political consequences these claims and defenses entail. Her suggestion that we consider how our "linguistic choices influence our students' understanding of religious studies as a type of inquiry" (Smith, Chapter 1, this volume) is apt, as are the specific pedagogical strategies she describes.

But I am also interested in the ways the field of religious studies itself, the typical progression of religious studies degrees, and the ways theory is presented (or ignored) in religious studies classrooms risks presenting "religion" as a coherent and stable object of study and thereby reifying an imaginary distinction between religion and not-religion. In other words, I am interested how our field and classrooms engage in religionization,[1] or the "event or process of imagining religion to be both separate and unique" (Cuthbertson 2018: 100). I explore these issues in the first part of this response and argue that our students' expectations are shaped by implicit metatheoretical stances that impede the critical skills that many of us attempt to foster in our classrooms.

Finally, I am interested in addressing some of the problems that both students and teachers face when our students do not have "any particular commitment to the concepts of our specific courses apart from their desire for a good grade"

---

1. While I am pleased that Smith has found the term "religionization" to be helpful in achieving the linguistic disruptions she describes, I did not intend the term to be a "verb form" of religion (Smith, Chapter 1, this volume). Rather, I intended the term to describe "ongoing discursive processes involved in constructing religion as a separate sphere of human activity, one modeled on inherited ... distinctions between religion and the secular." Religionization describes processes according to which complex and ambiguous events (praying) are described and conceived as apparent manifestations of a stable and separate object (religion).

(Smith, Chapter 1, this volume). My own experiences teaching large first-year undergraduate religious studies courses and, more recently, teaching mandatory general education humanities courses have led me to consider how those of us who mostly teach general education requirements can strive to foster student engagement. In the second part of this response, I describe my own experiences with the Universal Design for Learning (UDL) framework, specifically its focus on significant and self-relevant learning, and explain why these approaches are helpful given the fact that many of our students view our courses as merely "one among several harrowing trials they must pass through on their way to a degree" (Smith, Chapter 1, this volume).

The Field

The field of religious studies has been amply criticized in recent decades. These critiques, which can be grouped under the framework of critical religion, have claimed religious studies scholarship mistakenly frames its ostensible object of study as unique or *sui generis* (McCutcheon 1997) ignores or else replicates problematic assumptions concerning the nature of religion and the universality of that category (Balagangadhara 2005; see also Fitzgerald 2000); or merely replicates larger theological and ecumenical projects (McCutcheon 1997). My own thinking, writing, and teaching have been influenced by these critiques in important ways.

The central problem is that religious studies reifies a particular and problematic conception of the world in which "religion" exists as a self-evident object or separate sphere of human activity. As I have argued elsewhere, nothing is self-evidently "religious," instead certain texts, institutions, practices, and objects are designated as "religious" for specific purposes (Cuthbertson 2018: 105). My concern here is not about language or precision or definitions or categories. All categories are fluid. My concern is that the widespread notion that phenomena can be *unproblematically* categorized as religious or secular has practical and political consequences. As Naomi Goldenberg notes, "religion" is particularly significant term because it is "accorded special status in laws and foundational national documents such as constitutions" (Goldenberg 2018).

This view that religion can neatly be separated from other spheres of life or that certain texts, institutions, etc., are straightforwardly "religious," is not only prevalent in legal and governmental discourse; it is implicit in the very notion of a discrete field of religious studies. From the vantage point of the AAR's annual program, the field of religious studies not only involves studying various religions and religious denominations but also involves examining religion through the lenses of various disciplines (anthropology, sociology, psychology, philosophy, cognitive science); exploring how religion is expressed in specific geographical areas (Africa, Japan, China, Europe, North America); investigating apparently distinct religious phenomena (ritual, myth, literature, ethics, yoga); and interrogating the connections between religion and a host of other phenomena (sport, affect, cities, ecology, economy, food, migration, politics, popular culture, public schools, sexuality, science fiction, sound, secularity, animals; American Academy of Religion 2020). Unless religion is seen as a coherent and bounded object which unites these disparate approaches, the field of religious studies dissolves into an incomprehensible mess of unrelated topics.

Religionization is also prevalent in religious studies curricula—for unless "religion" constitutes an actual object of study, why bother taking courses or pursuing a degree in religious studies? The courses we teach religionize. As is the case with the AAR's program units, courses with the conjunction "and" in their titles such a religion and popular culture, religion and the environment, or religion and gender reify, naturalize, and solidify both "religion" and whatever noun appears to the right of the conjunction. Given undergraduates' desire to accumulate "intellectual trinkets" (Smith, Chapter 1, this volume) and departments' desire to increase enrollment, I can accept that these formulations are perhaps practically or economically unavoidable. I recall, for instance, colleagues at a departmental meeting debating whether a course titled "religion and sex" would attract more undergraduates than one titled "religion and gender."

Theory

Smith is right when she notes that students who struggle in courses informed by the critical religion approach do so—not because they lack the required conceptual skills to think differently about "religion"—but because "the material isn't what they thought it would be" (Smith, Chapter 1, this volume). But our students' conceptualizations of religious studies as a type of inquiry are shaped not only by received "anecdotal perceptions of what religion is and how it works" (Smith, Chapter 1, this volume) but also by the structure of religious studies programs and the embedded expectations concerning the distinction between data and theory that these imply.

I encountered this disconnect between the learning outcomes that *I* wanted to foster and those my *students* expected when teaching a course entitled religion and popular culture at Queen's University. Whereas I wanted to de-naturalize both categories and designed tutorial activities in which students would engage with instances of religionization, students complained they weren't learning enough about religion. As one student put it, "I didn't sign up for a theory course." But this notion that there are *courses* and then there are *theory courses* is itself a problem. The very structure of religious studies programs implies a metatheoretical stance in which data (religions, religious texts etc.) precede theory and in which theory can therefore be seen as an optional accessory or tool for engaging with pre-existing objects of study.

Students and scholars alike have differing views on the meaning and uses of the term "theory." According to Tenzan Eaghll, "the field of religious studies is characterized by a sort of theoretical anarchism" (Eaghll 2019: 36). But this anarchism results not only from competing theoretical claims and definitional strategies, it also results from confusion concerning what "theory" means in the first place. In his article "The Meaning of Theory," Gabriel Abend notes that although theory is one of the most important words in the scholarly lexicon, confusion about the meaning of "theory" routinely creates conceptual muddles and miscommunication (Abend 2008: 173). Abend helpfully identifies seven distinct senses of the word, each with its own presumed nature and use.

Theory$_1$ refers to a general proposition that establishes a relationship between two or more variables (Abend 2008: 177). Durkheim's view that religion provides social cohesion, for instance, is an example of theory$_1$. This use of theory assumes the relationship described is generally applicable and of interest to non-specialists. When Juhn Y. Ahn describes the complex negotiation between the aspiration to tackle "theoretical" problems with which any scholar can identify and the desire to focus on the specifics of our particular research in his article "Do We Need Theory in Religious Studies?", he is actually asking a question about the necessity of theory$_1$ (Ahn 2010: 25).

Theory$_2$ refers instead to an explanation of a particular social phenomenon. Approaches that claim religious beliefs are a product of normal human cognition, for instance, are examples of theory$_2$ (Abend 2008: 178). When Patrick Hart argues that all theory is really explanatory and thus an instance of "myth making" in his article "Theory, Method, and Madness in Religious Studies," he is actually reducing all varieties of theory to theory$_2$ (Hart 2016: 21).

Theory$_3$ is concerned instead with meaning and interpretation. Theory$_3$ provides an explanation, but this explanation is not necessarily causal. Instead, theory$_3$ offers an original interpretation or reading of some phenomenon or text (Abend 2008: 178). When David Loy (1997) argues that the market should be interpreted as religion, for instance, he is engaging in theory$_3$.

In the first three senses of the word "theory" in Abend's lexography, theory is interested in "saying something about empirical phenomena in the social world" (Abend 2008: 178). In the context of religious studies, theory in these senses either describes relationships between religion and other phenomena, explains how or why religion (or religious beliefs etc.) are caused, or else provides novel interpretations of religious texts or other phenomena with reference to religion. Theorizing in this sense assumes the prior existence of religion as a pre-existing empirical object.

Snowblowers

I first encountered a version of this metatheoretical view as a graduate student in the mid-2000s when one of my professors explained that theory is like a snowblower. Her point was that theory was all well and good when applied to particular data (religions, religious texts, religious institutions) but that theory on its own was like a snowblower without any snow: useless.

This theory-as-snowblower metaphor is also implicit in the course progression of many undergraduate religious studies programs. In Canada, for instance, those religious studies programs that require majors to complete theory courses typically require these in the third or fourth year. This structure seems to imply that theory is only useful later on in an undergraduate's career when they have accumulated sufficient empirical snow in their introduction to such-and-such a religion course to require a theoretical snowblower.

Other metaphors have been used to describe the purpose and place of theory in religious studies. Smith, for instance, describes the widespread view that theory is a mere sidekick or optional accessory—something that adds a bit of glamour or gravitas—but which a scholar or student can usually do without. Again, this view is implicit in departmental structures.

In the Canadian context with which I am most familiar, while many undergraduate religious studies programs offer theory courses, these are rarely mandatory for religious studies majors. Upon surveying twenty major Canadian universities that offer religious studies degrees, I discovered that only six of these have required theory courses.[2] The remaining fourteen or seventy percent either do not offer theory courses at all or else these are optional. The University of Toronto, for instance, provides religion majors with two options in their final year: a theory course entitled "Constructing Religion" or else a capstone seminar that emphasizes the integration of the study of religion with contemporary public life (University of Toronto 2020).

The problem is not that a majority of Canadian religious studies majors might very well complete their undergraduate degrees without ever taking a theory course. The problem is students are being presented, in the very structure of their degrees, with an *implicit* metatheoretical stance that sees theory as an optional accessory and religion as an already-existing empirical "thing." Is it any wonder my student was so frustrated by my theory-driven religion and popular culture course that he felt the need to remind me that he had not, in fact, signed up for a theory course?

But the theoretical movement that critical religion recommends, in which scholars and students shift their focus from religion as a discrete object to "religion" as a rhetorical strategy, tactic, or language game, is a different *kind* of theoretical enterprise. Here, the focus is not on empirical data but rather on the nature of language and classification; what Abend refers to as theory$_7$ in his lexography (Abend 2008: 181).

In preparing this response, I was surprised to learn the theory-as-snowblower metaphor has already been described and criticized. Russell McCutcheon (2015) encountered this metaphor in the late 1980s as a doctoral student of Will Oxtoby at the University of Toronto. McCutcheon criticizes this view as one in which

---

2. I analyzed the program progressions of the 15 largest Canadian research universities along with other major universities offering religious studies programs in each province including (in alphabetical order): Concordia University, Dalhousie University, McGill University, McMaster University, Memorial University, Queen's University, University of Alberta, University of British Columbia, University of Calgary, University of Manitoba, Université de Montréal, University of Ottawa, University of Prince Edward Island, Université de Québec à Montréal, University of Saskatchewan, University of Toronto, University of Victoria, University of Western Ontario, Waterloo University, and York University.

theory "signifies a collection of tools to help us manage all of the many splendid presentations competing for our attention, merely organizing them and placing them in some sort of chronological or causal order" (McCutcheon 2015: 6). Some varieties of theory do, in fact, perform this organizational task. But the kind of theoretical engagement that critical religion recommends does not. From the perspective of critical religion, theory$_7$ does not move empirical snow around, it *creates* the snow. As McCutcheon puts it, theory is "more like a snow-making machine at a ski resort: for without the device there is nothing to move around and no hills to be groomed" (ibid.: 7).

McCutcheon's metaphorical reversal is helpful in that it demonstrates the primacy of theory$_7$. In this view, *theories*, and not self-evidently interesting religious data, are the driving force of our intellectual labor (McCutcheon 2004: 165). Theory$_7$ does not create the empirical world around us, but it does create bounded objects of study. In other words, theory$_7$ directs out attention and allows us to carve interesting things out of otherwise undifferentiated stuff. Theory$_7$ also involves explicit or implicit normative views. We delimit objects of study (snow) precisely because we already have scholarly or practical goals (ensuring there is plenty of snow on the ski slopes but none in the ski resort bathrooms, for instance).

It is impossible to build a curriculum without theory$_7$. Yet is often tempting to pretend this is not the case. Expectations from both our students and departments concerning objectivity, for instance, can push teachers to conceal their political or pedagogical goals. We are expected to present the sheer *facts* of Hinduism in our introduction to Hinduism courses. Even in those courses that are explicitly labeled "theory courses," the expectation is that we will present the *facts* of these theories and perhaps the fact that they have been criticized in various ways. We may seek to obscure our political and pedagogical agendas but these are precisely what allow us to determine which apparent facts (texts, concepts, examples) we include in our syllabi and which we leave out (Smith, Chapter 1, this volume). Theory$_7$ is what we use to shape our courses. Without a theoretical system in place, "there is nothing to sort through and nothing to arrange, and thus no delimited field in which to dig, for we have no way to mark anything as significant and worth talking about, worth finding, or worth piecing together" (McCutcheon 2015: 7). All of our courses are in their choice of materials and progression theory$_7$ courses—even if we often hide this from our students.

While our students and departments may expect us to conceal or ignore the theoretical$_7$ commitments (sometimes called biases) that always and inevitably structure our courses, this is neither necessary nor helpful. Jonathan Z. Smith (2007) has described this kind of obfuscation as "introductory lying," which often results in the mystification of both our object of study and our students. One way to avoid this mystification involves being explicit about our goals and theoretical leanings. If we are interested in having our students view "religion" as a strategy or tactic then we ought to make this point explicitly at the outset and repeat it throughout the semester, as Smith suggests. I have found that focusing on theory from *day one* in my own courses is another way to disturb the notion that religion already exists unproblematically "out there" in the world.

Because I want my students to understand that theory$_7$ always comes first, delimits our objects of study, and entails normative views, I designed my undergraduate religious studies courses with this argument in mind. In the first class I asked my students to write down their own definition of religion. We then spent the first few weeks learning about "key theories" and considering what kinds of "things in the world" each theory picks out and which it ignores. I asked my students not only to consider whether hockey or Netflix or consumerism are religions but also which theories support that view. I also asked them to consider the normative views each theory implies. In other words, if we argue that sports or consumerism are religion what are we really saying about either sports, consumerism, or religion? Eventually, we returned to the definitions they wrote down in the first class. I asked them to consider the kind of objects their definition picked out along with the normative views it contained.

Putting theory in the foreground often frustrated my students and this approach probably entails its own mystifications. But by the end of the semester most students seem to have grasped my argument. On the last day, I asked them to revisit their original definitions and to write a new one. Many students ended up arguing that "religion" is "in the eye of the beholder" and that what we end up calling "religion" reflects particular goals and values. I agree with Smith that we ought to reconfigure the role of the introductory religious studies course as one where we "teach students about the politics of categorization and the dynamics of power" (Smith, Chapter 1, this volume). Focusing explicitly on theory$_7$ from the very beginning is one helpful way to achieve this goal.

Significant Learning

I no longer teach in a religious studies department. The students I meet each semester at Dawson College are *required* to take the humanities courses I teach. Most of them have very little interest either in taking a humanities course or in learning about religion. Because my college offers both pre-university and vocational programs, many of my students are in fact training to become nurses, laboratory technicians, or graphic designers. Given this lack of interest, why focus on religion?

The short answer is that, despite the fact I have spent the last fifteen years thinking about "religion," there is no good reason to do. Which isn't to say that I haven't offered courses that are, ostensibly, "about religion." I have come to realize, however, that whatever the topic, my courses are really about asking appropriate questions, thinking critically, and developing meaningful self-relevant creative answers. Inspired by the Universal Design for Learning (UDL) framework, I have restructured my courses to emphasize transferable self-relevant student abilities rather than facts, knowledge, or worse, factoid-vomiting (Smith, Chapter 1, this volume).

The UDL framework focuses on expert learning. From the UDL perspective, the goal of education does not only or even primarily involve the transmission of knowledge from teachers to students but rather the development of key student abilities. UDL considers how to structure learning environments to reduce barriers to learning in a variety of ways (Meyer et al. 2014). In part, this involves designing courses to be as accessible as possible to all students, whether or not they happen to be in disabling situations. But UDL also focuses on student motivation and purpose. Recognizing that cognition and emotion are linked (Jaggar 1989; Cavanagh 2016), UDL focuses on the affective dimensions of learning (Meyer et al. 2014: 54). Before students can recognize which concepts are significant or develop the kinds of arguments we expect in college-level classes, they must first be engaged and motivated.

This intersects with what L. Dee Fink (2013) calls "significant learning experiences." For Fink, significant learning arises most often when content-centered approaches to teaching are replaced with learning-centered approaches that focus instead on processes (ibid.: 27). In this model, courses should not be "about" a particular topic (religion, say) but rather should be about analyzing, thinking, synthesizing, and creating—privileging verbs over nouns (ibid.: 4–5). Importantly, this implies a shift from learning to *doing*. As Fink puts it, "whatever it is that you want students to learn how to do, that is what they need to be doing during the course" (ibid.: 105).

If our goal is to train our students in the laboratory of critical thought then the course topic is unimportant. As instructors, we likely feel as though the particular topics we teach are "interesting and timely" (Smith, Chapter 1, this volume). We feel this way because we opted to be trained in our particular field. We feel this way because we are already interested in our subject material. But our students might see things differently. From the perspective of UDL, the solution to a lack of student interest is not to *explain* why our course topics are interesting or to somehow *create* student interest but rather to provide students with multiple options for engagement and expression (Meyer et al. 2014: 91). From the UDL perspective, this involves optimizing student choice and autonomy; optimizing relevance, value, and authenticity; and heightening the salience of goals and objectives (ibid.: 111).

Optimizing choice and autonomy can be as simple as providing several options for texts to be analyzed or topics to be explored. In my own courses, I go somewhat further in that the final projects for my courses are student-directed. I ask my students to pick their own topic or focus and to explain why their chosen topic will permit them to demonstrate a mastery of course competencies (the *doing* component). This approach requires considerable scaffolding and continued feedback, but in my experience often produces meaningful learning outcomes. While some students select topics that fit neatly within the framework of the course, others opt instead to explore something tangential or unrelated to the topic of the course itself. Allowing students to design their own evaluations gives them the freedom to pick topics in which they are already interested. As a result, students are typically more motivated, interested, and hard-working, which results in superior work.

Providing multiple options for course topics or including student-directed projects can also heighten the relevance and perceived value of both our courses and of student work. Students in the nursing or graphic design programs at Dawson are right to wonder why their humanities courses are relevant to their personal and career goals. One way to address these concerns is to emphasize "transcendent" learning goals (Cavanagh 2016: 154–155). We might argue that students who are uninterested in religion or the humanities ought to take these courses because they provide intrinsically valuable knowledge (e.g., "religious literacy") or else generally transferable skills (e.g., critical thinking). Another way to address these concerns involves encouraging students to *create* self-relevance in our courses. In this approach, students are asked to reflect on their personal and professional learning goals and are encouraged to connect these to the specific course competencies. I use this approach in the student-directed projects I assign. In their project proposals, I ask students to explain not only why their chosen project will demonstrate mastery of course competencies but also why the project is relevant to their own specific personal or professional goals.

Student-directed projects also limit construct-irrelevance or the extent to which evaluation scores are influenced by factors not related to the construct (the concept or competency) being evaluated. If I am evaluating my students' ability to analyze an argument then requiring them to do this in a written essay introduces construct-irrelevant factors. Students could equally demonstrate their analytical skills orally either in person or in an audio or video recording. Likewise, Unless I am evaluating my students' ability to answer questions within a particular time frame on a particular day (which might be useful in some fields but does not reflect what scholars in the humanities or religious studies typically do), traditional examinations introduce a host of unhelpful construct-irrelevant factors. If we are interested in having our students apply the skills they have developed, then multiple-choice exams and essay questions are unlikely to be adequate measures of these abilities (Gravel et al. 2015).

The format of the student-directed projects I assign is open. Students are encouraged to express their mastery of course competencies in whatever format best suits their interests and abilities. Because most of my students are already familiar with traditional essay formats, many opt to write essays. Others argue instead that their thinking is best expressed by other means. While having an open project format decreases construct-irrelevant barriers for students who are in disabling situations, it also encourages all students to connect the medium of expression to other relevant personal or professional goals.

Student-directed projects are not only more interesting and enjoyable to grade than hundreds of nearly identical essays, they are also more interesting, enjoyable, and challenging for students. Student-directed projects require not only critical thinking but also purposeful *creative* thinking. While the degree of creativity varies with the project topic and medium students propose, student-directed projects ask students to creatively imagine how the kinds of work we do in class can be applied to relevant examples outside the course itself. Those students who propose non-essay media for their projects are able to harness their creative abilities. Ideally, our students should develop not only critical abilities but also the ability to apply their thinking and learning to new contexts. Critical thinking is immensely valuable but if it only requires our students to "take in information, question its assumptions, and break it into segments" then, something important is missing (Finn 2015: 78). I want my students to be able to apply critical insights—to *do* something with them, in other words. Giving students the freedom to apply their learning to contexts that matter to them provides space for the creative application of the critical abilities we foster. It makes the kind of work we do in class and the arguments we analyze relevant and important. It answers the question, perhaps, of why our students should be taking our courses in the first place.

Ian Alexander Cuthbertson is a professor at Dawson College, Montréal. Ian is broadly interested in exploring how the category "religion" is deployed to legitimize certain beliefs, practices, and institutions while delegitimizing others.

References

Abend, Gabriel. 2008. "The Meaning of Theory." *Sociological Theory* 26(2): 173–199.
Ahn, Juhn Y. 2010. "Do We Need Theory in Religious Studies?" *Bulletin for the Study of Religion* (39)1: 24–27.
American Academy of Religion. "Program Units." Retrieved from www.aarweb.org/annual-meeting/program-units (accessed May 2, 2020).
Balagangadhara, S. N. 2005. *"The Heathen in his Blindness ...": Asia, the West, and the Dynamic of Religion*. Daryaganj, New Delhi: Ajay Kumar Jain for Manohar Publishers and Distributors.
Cavanagh, Sarah Rose. 2016. *The Spark of Learning: Energizing the College Classroom with the Science of Emotion*. Morgantown, VA: West Virginia University Press.
Cuthbertson, Ian Alexander. 2018. "Preaching to the Choir? Religious Studies and Religionization." In Brad Stoddard (ed.), *Method Today: Redescribing Approaches to the Study of Religion* (pp. 96–105). Sheffield: Equinox.
Eaghll, Tenzan. 2019. "Religion, Theory, Critique, and Epistemological Anarchy: A Review Essay." *Bulletin for the Study of Religion* 48(1–2): 35–39.
Fink, L. Dee. 2013. *Creating Significant Learning Experiences: An Integrated Approach to Designing College Courses*. San Francisco, CA: John Wiley & Sons.
Finn, Patrick. 2015. *Critical Condition: Replacing Critical Thinking with Creativity*. Waterloo, Canada: Wilfred Laurier University Press.
Fitzgerald, Timothy. 2000. *The Ideology of Religious Studies*. Oxford: Oxford University Press.
Goldenberg, Naomi. 2018. "Response to the Responses." In Brad Stoddard (ed.), *Method Today: Redescribing Approaches to the Study of Religion* (pp. 128–130). Sheffield: Equinox.
Gravel, Jenna W., et al. 2015. "Universal Design for Learning in Postsecondary Education: Reflections on Principles and Their Application." In Sheryl E. Burgstahler (ed.), *Universal Design in Higher Education: From Principles to Practice* (pp. 81–100). Cambridge, MA: Harvard Education Press, 93.

Hart, Patrick. 2016. "Theory, Method, and Madness in Religious Studies." *Method and Theory in the Study of Religion* 2: 21.

Jaggar, Alison M. 1989. "Love and Knowledge: Emotion in Feminist Epistemology." *Inquiry* 32(2): 151-176.

Loy, David. 1997. "The Religion of the Market." *Journal of the American Academy of Religion* 65(2): 259-290.

McCutcheon, Russell T. 1997. *Manufacturing Religion: The Discourse on Sui Generis Religion and the Politics of Nostalgia*. New York: Oxford University Press.

McCutcheon, Russell T. 2004. "Dispatches from the Religion Wars." In Timothy Light and Brian C. Wilson (eds), *Religion as a Human Capacity: A Festschrift in Honor of E. Thomas Lawson* (pp. 161–189). Leiden: Brill.

McCutcheon, Russell T. 2015. *A Modest Proposal on Method: Essaying the Study of Religion*. Leiden: Brill.

Meyer, Anne, et al. 2014. *Universal Design for Learning: Theory and Practice*. Wakefield: CAST Professional Publishing.

Smith, Jonathan Z. 2007. "Afterword: The Necessary Lie: Duplicity in the Disciplines." In Russell T. McCutcheon (ed.), *Studying Religion: An Introduction* (pp. 74–80). London: Equinox.

University of Toronto. "Religion Specialist." Retrieved from https://fas.calendar.utoronto.ca/religion-specialist-arts-program-asspe015 (accessed May 2, 2020).

Chapter 4

The Gaze from Somewhere
Teaching Situated Writing about Religion

Leonie C. Geiger

> No textual staging is ever innocent (including this one).
> (Richardson et al. 2005: 96)

During my undergraduate studies, I was teaching a tutorial for first year students in the study of religion at a University in Germany.[1] In this tutorial, students ought to become familiar with the basics of the study of religion. One student approached me afterwards with research ideas for a paper: He wanted to write about disabled veiled Turkish Muslims in a big German city. I inquired where his interest in this topic came from and eventually asked him what role a reflection on his male, white German, Christian background—which he did not hesitate to mention again and again during class—could play during this inquiry. He was confused by my question. "What does it mean to reflect on my background? *How do I do that in my paper?*"

Since then, this question has been stuck in my mind, while giving seminars inside and outside academia, but especially while writing papers—*how do I actually do that?* As a starting point one could draw on feminist scholars like Maria Matsuda, Kathy Davis, Leslie McCall, Donna Haraway, Ruth Frankenberg, or Judith Butler who have written about situating oneself and the methodological, and especially analytical, implications of this:

> The assumption is that your social location will inevitably shape the ways you look at the world, the kinds of questions you ask (as well as the questions you haven't thought of asking), the kinds of people and events that evoke sympathy and understanding (as well as those that make you feel uncomfortable or evoke avoidance).
>
> (Davis 2014: 23)

Yet, the student's legitimate question was *how* to create this sort of self-reflectivity in his paper. What kind of practical implications does this act have on the concrete products of academic writing? Therefore, this response will focus on the

---

1. I want to thank Prof. Dr. Adrian Hermann and the team of the *Department for Religion Studies* at the *Forum Internationale Wissenschaft* (FIW) in Bonn, Germany, for their elaborated feedback on this response.

urgent need to talk about *the meaning of "writing reflectively" in our field* and its practical application: the teaching of reflective writing about religion, something I will call "situated writing." Holding a German BA and Dutch MA, I will build this response to Dr. Smith's "On the Grammar of Teaching Religious Studies" (Chapter 1, this volume) my status as a PhD *student*, who has just freshly finished the Master degree, holding the transitional position of educating others while still being educated.

"On the Grammar of Teaching Religious Studies"

At first glance, my call for a more applied teaching of reflective writing in the study of religion and Smith's examination of the grammar of teaching religious studies seem to address two different "most pressing issue(s) in need of consideration when addressing scholarship on religion."[2] However, this surface appearance is deceptive as the methods that Smith advocates for can provide the necessary preconditions in the classroom for the kind of self-reflective writing that I am interested in. "On the Grammar of Teaching Religious Studies" offers a strong vision of what a more active, process-oriented presentation of issues can look like in the study of religion classroom with a focus on a critical reflection of how the rhetoric of "religion" is used. Her concern is how an appropriate critical examination of religion in the classroom can be achieved; one that builds on a consistently anti-essentialist scholarship, and which thereby aims at grammar disruption to foster critical thinking, skills, and literacy. Smith understands "critical skills as tools that provide the ability to recognize and analyze the multitude of ways in which power creates knowledge" (Smith, Chapter 1, this volume).

Smith's chapter examines the effects of how using religion in a more active form in the classroom based on her teaching experiences can serve to prevent and deconstruct essentialist understandings of religion. She is particularly concerned with the active processuality of religion, the inconsistency of human interests as they are expressed in religion, and the avoidance of dichotomies of such as inside versus outside, good versus bad or normal versus abnormal. Given that these tendencies tend to cluster in students' definitions of religion, Smith proposes to shift the focus from the product to the process. Therefore, the focus in her didactic considerations lies on the category religion as a verb. Cornerstone for this is a functionalist approach that examines statements of legitimacy in terms of their function in certain socio-historical moments. In this context, her chapter introduces the concept of "tactic" as a "strategic method of communicating, not unlike other mechanisms of persuasion" (Smith, Chapter 1, this volume). This is followed by the important remark that the term "tactic" does not necessarily have to be negatively connotated; a point I will take up again later. Smith combines this "tactical approach" with the periodical use of the verb form of religion,

---

2. From the call for papers for the NAASR 2019 Annual Meeting (see https://naasr.com/2019/01/16/naasr-2019-annual-meeting-cfp/).

"religionizing" and "religioning," to shift the focus to analyzing religion as an activity in the classroom. Eventually, Smith offers three concrete pedagogical strategies that translate her considerations into practical ones. After the introduction of religion as a verb, as mentioned above, she focuses on the discursive embeddedness of religion and on human inconsistencies, for which she offers, in the final step, examples of transition and moments when changes and, above all, the principle of inconsistency are revealed.

How are these issues linked to my own concerns? Smith's chapter proposes a critical pedagogy in which her teaching aims at *unlearning* "religion." Her pedagogical strategies are meant to—abstractly speaking—create (non-permanent) *disorder* in her students' attitudes to religion. She addresses the necessity to closely accompany as a teacher this process from the normative harmony of colloquial definitions of religion to critical disorder, to more questions, from the product to the process, from the static to the dynamic. Her proposed strategies transport in an inventive manner what Suzanne Owen characterized as "'religion' literacy," a "knowledge and understanding of how 'religion' is constructed (by scholars, media, popular culture, etc.), the interests being served (issues of power, etc.) and the implications of this construction" (Owen 2020: 215).

The Tactics of Using "Tactic" as "Religion"

As she writes, one interest of Smith's essay lies "with thinking about how those of us who are very actively committed to anti-essentialist scholarship still fall back on a series of older conventions that may, even in the best of circumstances, take our teaching to essentialized places we do not wish to go" (Smith, Chapter 1, this volume). Before I engage with the urgent need to talk about (teaching) situated writing about religion, I want to offer some remarks on one part of Smith's pedagogical strategies: her use of "tactic" instead of "religion," what I call the tactics of using "tactic" as "religion." I certainly do not aim at a "reification contest of competing terminologies" (ibid.) and yes, it is "time to collectively consider how we teach" (ibid.) critical thinking (and writing!) in the study of religion. Indeed, especially reading about the use of "tactic" as religion, I was amazed how this grammar disruption builds up critical thinking (and writing). Every now and then I began using "tactic" instead of religion, as well as version of "religionizing" and "religioning" in German and was impressed with the kinds of thinking processes this speaking it out loud facilitated. It was like saying something implied but never expressed explicitly. However, while re-reading the chapter, one sentence irritated me: "I don't regard this [students who still understand tactic as 'bad religion'] as a complete pedagogical backfire by any means, for there will always be that minority" (ibid.). I want to briefly follow up on this remaining minority and try to better understand the reasons for its existence. Considering the fact that the term tactic is negatively connoted, it is not surprising that there is a minority of students for which "bad religion" is associated with "tactic" whereas "good religion" or good religious people are the not selfish and egoistic ones, the ones not following a tactic. In the *Collins Dictionary* three synonyms for "tactic" are: "1. Ploy, 2. Gambit and 3. Stratagem" (Dictionary.com 2022). Smith addresses this issue, but I still wonder whether the term "tactic" in the singular rather homogenizes instead of leaving space for all the negotiations and other communication processes that characterize the *inconsistent* phenomena scholars of religion look at? A tactic is a "plan, procedure, or expedient for promoting a desired end or result" (ibid.) and therefore implies a very active and well-planned form of operation. Most importantly, as it is commonly used in military contexts tactic implies having to hide—in order to be successful—one's "real" and "actual" purpose, making tactic something that is potentially essentialist. I am curious therefore, after the elaborations on nouns and their essentialist character, why Smith chose in her teaching next to her use of the verbs "religioning" and "religionizing" the noun "tactic" in the singular. Wouldn't it be much more appealing to avail oneself of the plural "tactics" or of the neologisms "tacting" or "tactings"?

Furthermore, the crux with tactics is that the opponent must *not know* neither what the concrete tactics look like nor that a tactic is followed at all. Yet, we as researcher using the word "tactic" instead of religion assume—provocatively put—the position of the auctorial narrator, to use a metaphor from literature, the one that discovered the true intentions behind the tactic, the one that knows everything and is omniscient. However, it is crucial as a *student* being introduced to the study of religion to understand that this position is not attainable. Indeed, it is deeply problematic—"Only the god trick is forbidden" (Haraway 1988: 589). This argument, however, can also be turned around: Thinking about "tactics," in the plural, as different, partially inconsistent forms of communication may also enable students to better grasp the one thing that is crucial for critical thinking and writing: We as researchers pursue tactics too. What seems important to me, however, is the plural—"tactics"—for as Smith puts it "humans are consistently inconsistent" (Chapter 1, this volume), and so are their tactics. Consequently, there is no neutral, objective researcher, who brings "the truth" down on paper from above, disembodied, God-like. This is furthermore crucial in order to avoid giving students the false impression that they have been fooled their whole life and just now discovered *the* truth about religion. Research is also situated, pursues strategies and tactics, and has criteria for assessing research as "good" or "bad." Especially the latter are hardly stable, considering the history of the philosophy of science and various schools and paradigms. This insight serves as the premise for my understanding of self-reflectivity: Research, including academic writing, is a process with effects that are not static and sometimes even inconsistent—which I describe with the term "situated writing." Such a self-reflective critique is necessary, since the study of religion as an academic field has a legacy that contributed decisively to the construction of eurocentric and racist imaginations as well as (neo-)colonial misrepresentations.

Why Do I Think that Teaching Self-reflective Writing is the Biggest Issue?

Why is reflective writing about religion such an unexplored matter in the discourse about teaching, especially considering the fact that to learn how to carefully construct arguments marks the very beginning of every academic career? If we critically engage with teaching the study of religion, and critically address and try to deconstruct essentialisms, we also need to question its hegemonic main product: the text as a written form of knowledge production: "Styles of writing are neither fixed nor neutral but rather reflect the historically shifting domination of particular schools or paradigms. Social scientific writing, like all other forms of writing, is a sociohistorical construction and, therefore, is mutable" (Richardson et al. 2005: 960).

So, is reflective writing—situated writing—about religion an unexplored matter because of the inherently personal and elusive character of this act? Or is it just not perceived as *relevant* enough? Maybe because it is attributed to feminist methods and methodology? Or because of our (special?) research matter religion? Indeed, is there actually a difference in (self-reflective) academic writing about religion and for instance gender—assuming of course that both are somehow separable? Smith shows that what is special about teaching the study of religion are the students' presumptions about religion. They enter the classroom having their own definitions of what marks a good, an abnormal, or a bad religion. When students write their first papers, they should at best be trained in critical thinking in order to question the above-mentioned essential or biased presumptions about religion. These critical thinking skills taught in the classroom are not limited to writing papers, but also have implications on what and especially how we do research. Indeed, I am curious to hear if the quality of the papers Smith's students submitted did increase with the students' new critical thinking skills and Smith's linguistic choices in class.

Let us return to the question about the special character of reflective writing about religion. It is possible to argue that the relation of research and objects of research is indeed more complex when it comes to religion considering, that the tactings on both sides somehow lay claim to truth—religious and scientific. Yet, even if one argues that there is *nothing special* about writing about religion, what about the existing discourse about religion, especially the discourse about religion as a sui generis phenomenon? Doesn't this discourse, in turn, have effects? Thus, the question is what kind of effect this discourse has on teaching and writing self-reflectively about religion? Furthermore, assuming the scholar of religion stands in a critical distance towards its subject-matter, something often called "methodological agnosticism," it is crucial to think about engaging reflectively, about situating oneself, and to then transport this into the written outcome of the research: the suspension of religious truth claims creates, after all, an inherent power relation between the discipline and its subject matter. Indeed, even if one argues that the job of the scholar of religion is to be a critic, one that follows the "ambitious project of deconstruction" (Goldenberg 2015: 310) of religion as just "not a stand-alone, stable, unchanging and universal given of human life, but rather is a protean and paradoxical term disguising dense and multilayered histories that are as enthralling as they are difficult to unravel" (ibid.: 309) this still does not suspend scholars from questions of how their empirical others are constructed.

So why does teaching reflective writing about religion seem so unimportant? Another possible answer might be that writing is perceived not as embedded in the act of *doing* research but as the mere documentation of research, which resulted in the unfavorable overlooking of the issue I am addressing. The premise of my response is that writing about the results of research is *not* external to the process of doing research; it is understood as a "method of inquiry."[3] In line with Smith, I define language not as a passive medium, but as active and reality creating.

A turning point in my engagement with such self-reflectivity was a two-month field work in Bolivia. I conducted 50 long face-to-face interviews with Bolivian women for a study on clinical and cultural psychology aiming at better understanding the impact of traumatization on women's empowerment. I had to ask questions that were at times very uncomfortable and triggered negative emotional reactions in my interviewees. Even though, I was trained for this scenario, the study's idea of objective and therefore *innocent* data gathering left me with very mixed feelings. It took me a while to process this experience. To be interviewing, as a German scholar, young Bolivian women about traumatic incidents in their past made me become somehow *differently* aware of the necessity of self-reflectivity, of situating oneself, and of decolonial discourses in academia: the research in Bolivia was surely not innocent and I even though I tried as best as I could, I was *not* a neutral body unbiasedly reading out loud a Spanish questionnaire.

Indeed, during the whole course of my studies, the need to reflect on my perspectivity was repeatedly underscored, discussing the "the conquering gaze from nowhere" (Haraway 1988: 581) which is "the gaze that mythically inscribes all the marked bodies, that makes the unmarked category claim the power to see and not be seen, to represent while escaping representation" (ibid.). Yet, sitting in front of my computer after this field trip to Bolivia, trying to write my master's thesis, I realized this was hardly practically taught and my tutorial student's confusion came to my mind again. I was often confronted with the doctrine of just being aware of your own intersections and to reflect on these during my research. A doctrine that does not take into account the *practical* epistemological implications of this reflective act for academic writing. Consequently, it does not tell you *what it means for the academic text to reflect on our own intersections.* How to learn a critical engagement with my own identity as a scholar if I do not know *how* to draw conclusions from my own reflections? Still processing my

---

3. Laurel Richardson (2000) used this terminology to stress that writing should be seen as integrated into the process of knowledge production—therefore as an as method of inquiry and proposes *Creative Analytic Practices* (CAP) that challenge the traditional academic writing styles.

research experience in Bolivia, I became very insecure about writing my thesis, in which I examined the triangle of religion, gender, and development in the field of German Christian development cooperation. The concrete research topic of my thesis was very different from the research in Bolivia. My data mainly consisted of interviews with German employees from various organizations. It was their perspective that interested me. Yet, the same questions and uncertainties arose. What presumptions do I have and how do they influence the way I understand, and thus *interpret* and code my material and eventually write it down? I was "desiring to be in command of language but also having to admit that language, discourse, genre and style act as tricksters that are not to be controlled 'just like that'" (Lykke et al. 2014: 3)—I had to balance between a critical distance and emic terms, had to struggle with the feeling of betraying my interlocutors from Christian development organizations for being very critical about the idea of development. Kim Knibbe, who also engaged with this feeling observed: "The many small acts of betrayal that come with doing fieldwork and writing about it, are not often a subject for discussion in the handbooks for qualitative research" (Knibbe 2011: 155). Thus, I became very aware of the inseparable entanglement of what and how something is studied and wondered, once again—What does this mean for writing my thesis? Therefore, in what follows, I want to offer some suggestions on how to practice and how to teach applied self-reflective, situated writing about religion.

What Can the Teaching of Applied Self-reflective Writing about Religion Look Like?

I want to come back to my first-year student's plan to do research as a white, Christian, German abled man on disabled, veiled Turkish Muslims. This research is already challenging considering the inherent asymmetrical power distribution. Yet, the aim of self-reflectivity cannot be to force the student to essentialize his own identity and turn these identity markers into naturalized labels such as white, Christian, German, or abled. Situating oneself is not a process of ticking identity boxes combined with also checking what Judith Butler called the entry "embarrassed 'etc.' at the end of the list" (Butler 1990: 182), a practice that would only be reproducing the issues that are supposed to be solved by this act of self-reflectivity.

Before I give some suggestions based on my own experience, I would like to point out the intersection between my proposal and Smith's critical pedagogy. Smith's pedagogical strategies, which promote a critical understanding of religion as well as of science and its role in society, are the prerequisites and the foundation for my ideas. Without a theoretical understanding of why this kind of situated writing is necessary or at least desirable, this kind of written knowledge production is not feasible—or is, conversely, just understood by the students as another *do* in the jungle of *do's* and *don'ts* of academic writing. Indeed, crucial for my explorations in the field of situated writing about religion was the fact that

I was not only lucky to be trained in critical thinking but also that my teachers would stimulate me to not just assimilate academic knowledge and methods but especially to also question them.

Drawing on Smith's concept of tactics, situated writing can be seen as a *revelation of one's own tactics* that unveils the sometimes unintentionally hidden strategies. Therefore, the *first* result of self-reflectivity is *disorder* and thus even more open questions. This however is not to be understood negatively or in a deconstructive manner. Indeed, Smith's approach creates this disorder as well. The task of the teacher is to accompany this process from normative harmony to critical disorder and to welcome this disorder and the questions it raises. Therefore, reflective writing means to think and to write *with disorder*. This raises the question of my concrete understanding of order and disorder: Order always presupposes a principle of sorting. Disorder is, in simple terms, consequently solely the absence of a sorting principle, and accordingly disorder is characterized above all by an interruption of meaningful connections. Two principles of order that students learn right at the beginning of their scientific education are methods and theories, yet shouldn't they also learn principles of disorder?

Secondly, the tension between the act of solely situating oneself and its practical implications for writing arises precisely because writing is an attempt at making stable, at fixing a point in the ongoing process of self-reflectivity. The scholar clearly faces a tension, not to say a contradiction in that the production of a text creates a stable point in the fluent process of knowledge generation. This allows to better understand that—despite the already mentioned essentialist character of the act of writing—simply ticking the boxes of identity marker[s] is not helpful, since it makes invisible the necessary entanglement of writing self-reflectively with the research object. If the text is a static product, and not a dynamic process, it is important to understand that situated writing is about making decisions within disorder. Importantly, a teacher can only provide tools for situated writing and for decision-making, but cannot take these decisions out of students' hands. Creativity is often understood as a tool that restores order (Richardson 2000; Lykke 2010) and when I was a student being creative was an advice many teachers gave to me. However, it is important to keep in mind that for students to be using creativity in academic writing (in addition to all the do's and don'ts) can be hard work and therefore demands a high level of supervision for the students not to fall back on simple non-critical concepts.

Thirdly, after creating disorder and taking decisions in this disorder there is one last important step in self-reflective writing—no matter what the disorder and the following decisions look like: providing *intersubjective traceability* (i.e., the possibility of retracing the steps and methods followed in the research) and *intersubjective transparency* (i.e., justifying the research interest and the choice of method). This may sound trivial and surely constitutes one of the main principles of academic writing. But it is highly relevant and, in my experience, not as easy as it seems. Providing intersubjective traceability and transparency allows one's text to appear as a product, yet *embedded in processes*. This furthermore means that there is no right and wrong in situated writing, but just a better and worse way of argumentation. Indeed, as we all operate alongside different intersections there cannot be one general solution to these questions. Still, my concept of situated writing does not advocate for atomizing individualism. There is not the one simple answer, but infinite possibilities within disorder created by the processes of self-reflectivity. Consequently, teaching self-reflective writing requires breaking with another norm: the all-knowing teacher or adviser. At the same time, it demands a higher level of supervision in teaching.

To conclude, in this response, I primarily attempted to address the urgent need to talk about the meaning of "writing reflectively" in our field and its practical applicability, the teaching of situated writing about religion. In practicing situated writing, the main point is not to fall back too quickly on old familiar principles that restore order, but to recognize and be stimulated by disorder. In the way that my student was confused about my remark on the role of self-reflectivity, I was confused as well by the richness of the disorder this created. Moreover, I was confused while writing my master's thesis and admittedly still am when situating myself and trying to draw conclusions from that. Yet this, as I hope to have shown, is part of the process.

Leonie C. Geiger is a PhD candidate at Forum Internationale Wissenschaft (FIW)—Department for Religion Studies, University of Bonn (Germany). Her research interests include postcolonial studies, gender and critical race theory, intersectionality, secularity, everyday life and religion, theory of religion, and German development cooperation.

References

Butler, J. 1990. *Gender Trouble: Feminism and the Subversion of Identity*. New York: Routledge.
Davis, K. 2014. "Intersectionality as Critical Methodology." In N. Lykke et al (eds), *Writing Academic Texts Differently: Intersectional Feminist Methodologies and the Playful Art of Writing* (pp. 17-29). New York: Routledge.
Dictionary.com. 2022. "Tactic." Retrieved from www.dictionary.com/browse/tactic?s=t (accessed May 2, 2022).
Goldenberg, N. R. 2015. "Afterword." In T. Stack, N. R. Goldenberg, and T. Fitzgerald (eds), *Religion as a Category of Governance and Sovereignty* (pp. 309-311). Leiden: Brill.
Haraway, D. 1988. "Situated Knowledges: The Science Question in Feminism and the Privilege of Partial Perspective." *Feminist Studies* 14(3): 575-599.
Knibbe, K. E. 2011. "Secrets, Gossip and Betrayal: Doing Fieldwork on the Role of Religion in Moral Orientation in a Dutch Catholic Province." *Fieldwork in Religion* 6(2): 151-167.
Lykke, N. 2010. *Feminist Studies. A Guide to Intersectional Theory, Methodology and Writing*. New York: Routledge.
Lykke, N., et al. 2014. "Editorial Introduction." In N. Lykke (eds), *Writing Academic Texts Differently: Intersectional Feminist Methodologies and the Playful Art of Writing* (pp. 1-13). New York: Routledge.
Richardson, L. 2000. "Writing as a Method of Inquiry. In Norman K. Denzin and Yvonna S. Lincoln (eds.) *Handbook of Qualitative Research*, 2nd edition (pp. 23-48). London: Sage.

Richardson, L., and St. Pierre, E. A. 2005. "Writing: A Method of Inquiry." In N. K. Denzin and Y. S. Lincoln (eds), *The Sage Handbook of Qualitative Research*, 3rd edition (pp. 959–978). London: Sage Publications.

Owen, S. 2020. "Benign Religion as Normal Religion." In L. Dorrough Smith, S. Führding, and A. Hermann (eds), Hijacked. A Critical Treatment of the Public Rhetoric of Good and Bad Religion (pp. 212–217). Sheffield: Equinox Publishing.

Chapter 5

Weaponizing Religious Literacy
"Religioning" as Revitalizing the Field or Reinforcing Neoliberal Values?

Martha Smith Roberts

Leslie Dorrough Smith's chapter on the grammar of teaching religious studies raises important questions about the difficulty of teaching religion without falling into essentialist categories. I go into the classroom with the best of anti-essentialist intentions; however, I also know that many of my class activities have the potential to reify religion and can easily go awry if I am not paying careful attention to my own language and my students' assumptions. Many of us do, as Smith notes, utilize method and theory in our research and writing, but we might fall back on easy designations, intentionally or not, when we teach in the religious studies classroom. In this chapter, I want to share some of the assignments and classroom activities I have used to demystify and de-essentialize the category of religion and to discuss the possible pitfalls, and actual failures, of these strategies. I will also interrogate my own use of the language of *religious literacy* and *tolerance* in light of Smith's remarks about shifting our grammar. Much like religion, I see these terms less as nouns and more as verbs—as processes, actions, or negotiations of power. I agree with Smith that recognizing and utilizing this grammatical nuance can be helpful as we try to communicate the importance of the category of religion, and the value of the field of religious studies itself, to those outside of the field—this includes our students, but also our institutions and administrations. As Smith notes, "a grammar disruption may well be a useful tool in helping to generate critical thought," and I am hopeful that this sort of disruption can make change possible in the multiple sites and spaces of the classroom, institution, and public discourse (Smith, Chapter 1, this volume).

Grammar and Value

Before we dive into pedagogical examples of this disruption, I first want to talk about what is at stake in Smith's work in a larger sense. Smith's discussion of grammar is connected to the issue of *value*. Smith argues that careful attention to our own discursive constructions of religion and the field of religious studies is required in order to understand the ways in which value is created and maintained in relation to broader power negotiations in our academic institutions. What pedagogical value does religious studies have that other humanities do not? If the study of religion, as Smith argues, is something that even non-majors will benefit from, how can we communicate this value without relying on the uniqueness of religion as the reason for our courses' (and departments') importance? Can we show value and maintain our anti-essentialist bona fides? I wonder if we can think about concepts, like religious literacy and tolerance, as ways of framing the kind of knowledge we find so valuable while also reflecting the knowledge that our universities and institutions recognize as having value. Or, as a colleague of mine put it recently, can we "do what is expected and maintain our own integrity while we're at it"? In other words, can we meet the university's expectations and institutional requirements and use their language, but still do critical work? This is what I see Smith doing here as well, teaching religion in ways that show value to a variety of invested parties (including institutions and students), while also maintaining critical and theoretical integrity.

In my "Introduction to American Religions" class, I try to do this work by teaching students about religious literacy. I frame the course in terms of learning about religious tolerance and cultivating civil public discourse on religion. I tell my students that they will leave the class with deeper historical knowledge of American religious culture and feel more comfortable and confident talking to people about religion in public conversations. I also communicate the value of learning about historical acts of intolerance against religious groups in a time when anti-religious violence is on the rise. These are practical learning outcomes that align with larger university goals of diversity, tolerance, and a liberal arts education meant to produce "autonomous thinkers, discerning moral agents and active citizens of a democratic society."[1] My classes attempt to accomplish those things in a way that also cultivates an anti-essentialist and theoretically sophisticated view of American religions. I teach about tolerance and religious literacy as processes, not as products in and of themselves. However, I would wager that many university administrations do not necessarily make this distinction.

In fact, the value of religious studies departments is in many ways predicated on the fact that the university sees the *content* of religion as self-evidently important. My learning outcomes are open to this utilitarian and administrative interpretation because the term religion, in its nominal form, communicates the idea that I am teaching about a stable, essentially consistent content, and not a process of human meaning-making that it is unstable, contingent, and contextual. In this reading, knowing about religions that exist in the world is in and of itself the valuable skill that students will gain from a religion course and take with them into the job market; the value of religion lies in its uniqueness. To the contrary, I am very much in agreement with Smith that the value of our courses and departments is not found in the uniqueness of religion, but rather in the particular dynamics that emerge from the study of religion as a space where the

---

1. This phrase comes from the mission statement of my SLAC (Denison 2020).

taken-for-granted is present and ready to be challenged (Smith, Chapter 1, this volume). As Smith notes, "The religious studies classroom is ideal (even if not entirely unique) in offering this opportunity, simply because we have a wealth of naturalized, essentialized claims from which to draw" (ibid.) This gives us a space in which lessons of classification, argumentation, critical thinking, and negotiations of power are consistently present. The value of the religious studies class, it seems, is simultaneously to be found in both the noun and verb forms. And while *religion* does much of the institutional work, *religioning* provides the space for the development of critical skills for our students.

This slippage between grammatical forms is a fraught with the tensions in value that Smith is unpacking in her work. The cultural norms and negotiations of power that load religion's nominal form with value are the same ones that we try to expose in our classrooms. Can we rely on one as a means to the other? As much as I resist commodifying religion as a unique object of study that is self-evidently valuable knowledge for the student to learn and take into the world, I cannot help but agree that students who study religion (as a verb/practice/process) *will* be better critical thinkers, communicators, and observers of their world, all of which may make them more desirable job applicants as well. Smith's definition of "critical skills as cognitive tools that provide the ability to recognize and analyze the multitude of ways in which power creates knowledge" is a helpful notion, in that it recognizes that the tools we cultivate are teaching not simply "description, classification, interpretation, argumentation, and other forms of reality-making" but also how these processes "are informed by the power dynamics of a particular social speaker's position" (Smith, Chapter 1, this volume). This gives me hope that the employable subjects that emerge from my classes are also very aware of the systems of power they are engaging with. Again, however, to use language that supports both interpretations is itself a necessary and dangerous game of hermeneutic gymnastics that can easily work against my larger aims.

In other words, I realize that my uses of religion, religious literacy, and tolerance are truly a nod to the "agendas of the neoliberal university setting" insomuch as I rely on these terms' many possible interpretations to meet the needs of my multiple audiences (Smith, Chapter 1, this volume). On my best days I think of this as a subversive strategy or decolonizing project, on others I truly hope I am not fooling myself. Or as Smith cautions, I hope I am not "very committed to anti-essentialist scholarship" but still falling "back on a series of older conventions that may, even in the best of circumstances, take our teaching to essentialized places we do not wish to go" (ibid.). There exists a compromise in this alignment with power, and the cognitive dissonance that this produces is quite real. I acknowledge it, and I hope that the discussion in these chapters can engage with the issues of value that Smith raises in her paper. Can we utilize these multiple notions of value simultaneously without losing our integrity?

Religious Literacy and Tolerance in Religious Studies

The concepts of religious literacy and tolerance have served as fruitful sites where I have been attempting to negotiate this balance of value in the classroom. Many scholars discuss religious literacy as a hierarchy of learning that moves from facts to familiarity to assessment. This encompasses many notions of religious literacy, some focusing on gaining factual knowledge, others on the uses of that knowledge to encounter and engage with outsider traditions, and still others on the ability to assess, apply, and reflect upon that knowledge (Jacobsen and 2012; Ennis 2017; Prothero 2007). The intricacies of this broad definition, however, are often oversimplified into a content-based understanding of the knowledge necessary to make one religiously literate.

Religious literacy quizzes can perpetuate this view of literacy as simply memorization and regurgitation. In *Religious Literacy: What Every American Needs to Know—And Doesn't,* Stephen Prothero argues that Americans' ignorance of religion has fueled contemporary acts of violence and discrimination from Waco to Islamophobia. And while his book makes a nuanced argument for multiple types of religious literacy, if passing the quiz at the end of the book is the goal of religious literacy, then we have oversimplified the concept into a simple matter of content knowledge. I would argue instead that content knowledge is just the beginning of the process of religious literacy. In the pedagogical examples below, I will discuss the ways that content quizzes like Prothero's can provide all kinds of opportunities for critical thinking and anti-essentialist discussion in the classroom. Starting with descriptive knowledge can be a useful mode of navigating the multiple meanings of the value of religious literacy in the classroom. It offers students a way of thinking about what they know about religion, how they talk about religion, and how that compares and contrasts to the ways in which scholars, practitioners, politicians, and others do this same kind of descriptive work.

Much like Prothero's religious literacy quiz, scholars like Diane Moore, Diana Eck, and others, have also discussed the centrality of content knowledge in teaching religious literacy (Moore 2007; Eck 2002).[2] Many of these discussions build on content to show the possibilities of religious literacy in terms of skills and competencies. The AAR Religious Literacy Guidelines, published in October of 2019, contain suggested outcomes for students that begin with content-centered goals, such as "discern accurate and credible knowledge about diverse religious traditions and expressions" and "recognize the internal diversity within religious traditions." The outcomes move from content to context, expecting that students will also learn to "explain how religions have shaped—and are shaped by—the experiences and histories of individuals, communities, nations, and regions" and to "interpret how religious expressions make use of cultural symbols and artistic representations of their times and contexts," and finally, to "distinguish confessional or prescriptive statements about religion from descriptive or analytical

---

2. See also Chapter 6 of this volume by Russell T. McCutcheon, where he does an in-depth look at religious literacy, and connects this discussion to the political project of the nation state as well.

statements" (American Academy of Religion 2019). The AAR guidelines reinforce the notion that the study of religion is descriptive and analytical, content and skills based. The use of the terms religion and religious here tend to reinforce a more stable object of study than one might be comfortable with in terms of anti-essentialist pedagogy. However, this set of guidelines reminds us that the stable object of religion remains the centerpiece for illustrating the value of the study of religion in higher education: the necessity of religious literacy and learning about religion.

These notions of religious literacy are often the basis for our own learning outcomes, and can be translated into skills-based, or competency-based, religious studies programs. Jenna Gray-Hildenbrand and Rebekka King use the competencies of description, analysis, and critique as the framework for Middle Tennessee State University's religious studies major (Gray-Hildenbrand and King 2019). Eugene Gallagher and Joanne Maguire recently published a student-centered text on religious studies skills that focuses on close reading, critical thinking, and comparison (Gallagher and Maguire 2019). These sorts of constructions of religious studies utilize the broader understanding of religious literacy to offer the possibility of aligning our own conceptions of the value of religion and religious studies with those of other stakeholders (universities, departments, students, parents). I revisited Malory Nye's article on "Religion, Post-Religionism and Religioning" that Smith referenced in her chapter and was reminded that he ends that piece with three possible developments in the field: (1) dissolving religious studies, (2) recreating religious studies as "religion and culture," or (3) "rethinking the vocabulary and discourse of the discipline ... that is to think of and discuss religion as something which is done, as practice, as religioning" (Nye 2000: 473). The pedagogical studies that I find most compelling are those that seem to take up this third possibility, often using language of competency or skill to communicate it to others. At the classroom level, the examples that Smith provides in her paper offer ways to envision how religioning can accomplish this.

Because I have not yet tried to use verb forms, like religioning, in the classroom, my examples center on ways to disrupt nominalizing tendencies through investigating the constructed nature of religion in different contexts. In fact, I often lean into the nominal form of religion at first as a way to establish the strong hold the dominant structure has on our thinking, and *then* try to shift to discussing religion as a *strategy*, a classificatory tool that has very real stakes. While this is not a grammatical shift in my language, it is a thorough shift in grammar in other ways. Thus, I can appreciate the move that Smith makes to from religion to religioning. The very messiness of the word, the strangeness of the verb form, draws attention to the shift in thinking we are asking students to make. This awkward formulation might reflect the religioning process itself: the constructed, piecemeal, agreed upon usage that never quite fits, but still serves a useful purpose for the group identity and communication.

Religioning may also offer students a much more dynamic and empowering understanding of the role of religious strategies at work in their world and their lives. Many of my students may start the class by claiming identities that are disconnected from religion: "I don't have a religion" or "I am not religious." But religioning, as human behavior, strategy, or tactic, is something that affects their lives regardless of affiliation or identification with religion. It is all around them all the time. Religioning may be a process that they can identify with, and see at work in their world, even if they do not consider themselves religious. Thinking about religion as religioning might also reveal the strategical power of religion in navigating and even shifting dominant power structures. For example, we might consider the ways in which minority groups claim religious rights as a way to compel their inclusion into a structure that does not want to make space for them. Instead of asking about the validity of their claims or whether they are involved in an authentic religious practice, we might instead ask how and why a group is religioning and what is at stake in the process. The verb form, in other words, can create space for students to imagine religion differently, to see the processes of religion at work in their personal and public lives.

Religioning in America

The project of teaching American religions as a history, a concept, and a process is quite daunting. The introductory course challenges me every semester. I try to balance content and form, and I rely on paradigms (of religion, religious literacy, tolerance, American identity, and more) to guide the class, even as we seek to disrupt them. The class examines American religion from three perspectives, based on three different answers to the question "what is American religion?" We start with Protestants (the notion of a Christian nation), move to minority traditions (to think about the pluralist framework), and then finish with American-made religions (indigenous traditions and new religious movements). Each unit relies upon—and pushes back against—ways of thinking about "American religion."[3]

To do this I use the notions of tolerance and intolerance as a way to initially engage my students. I am not "teaching tolerance" as much as I am hoping to teach how religious tolerance is a strategy of what Smith calls religioning. So I talk about Protestants, Catholics, Jews, Muslims, Mormons, and more (fairly standard examples of what my students would recognize as discreet religious traditions); for each group we think about tolerance and intolerance in American history. We examine historical examples of intolerance against each discreet group, and how that intolerance positioned the group as un-American, inauthentic, and either not *real* religion, or *bad* religion. So again, I risk the chance that my students will fall into the trap of reifying each of these traditions. However, I hope that instead the evidence will show them just how tenuous the category of religion can be, and

---

3. This three-part formula is based on Catherine Albanese's well-known textbook, *America: Religions and Religion* (Albanese 2013). It is my own loose interpretation of her three categories of manyness and oneness: original cast, expansion and contraction, and newmade in America. Instead of an historical lens, I apply a thematic one, organizing along the lines of cultural hegemony.

that some of the groups seem today to be obviously real religions were not always considered legitimate.

Teaching about tolerance instead of teaching tolerance thus means examining classificatory power at work- the denial of religious status to some groups, the lack of recognition as legitimate religion, and how that changes over time in the US. For example, we study colonial violence against Quakers, a group most students today have no trouble identifying as real religion, and as one whose members they can't imagine being persecuted and killed for not practicing legitimate religion. The trick in these conversations, and by trick I mean the really hard work, is not to let this slide into a sort of easy critique of past ignorance of what we today know are real or legitimate religions. This is, of course, not what I am trying to convey. My goal is to show the negotiations of power involved in being recognized as a legitimate religion in the US, the benefits that can be gained by claiming religious identity, and the Protestant templates that are often at work in our legal and everyday notions of what counts as religion. It is actually quite easy for students to assume at first that the lesson is one of cultivating tolerance for all religions in contemporary pluralist America, in contrast to the intolerance of the past. Instead, again, I try to use positionality to show that they too do not accept all claims to religious legitimacy (this usually becomes clear when we get to Islam, LDS, and Scientology). While on the surface my students are quite accepting of any and all claims to religion, it turns out that many of them are also are pretty skeptical of some of the stories in the book of Mormon or the tech of Scientology. Recognizing the ways contexts shape our perception of who is granted religious tolerance is key. But to making this shift in the classroom and getting students into this metacognitive mode of analysis is a challenge.

Pedagogical Examples

Early in the semester I do several in-class activities meant to draw students' attention to their own conceptions of what counts as religion and why. None of these activities are unique or original, and I am sure many colleagues have used versions of these as well. My goal here is to break them down a bit and consider whether or not they are successful in illustrating the ways in which religion can be conceptualized as a process or verb.

One of the first ways I do this is an activity I call "Is it religion?" In this exercise I show video clips of different human activities, and ask students to answer two questions about each:

1. Is it religion, yes or no?

2. Why or why not?

Students watch the videos, decide if they think it is religion, and then give a few reasons for their choice. I use the videos, which move from practices that my students may recognize as religious to less traditional ones (eucharist, Buddhist chanting, hula hooping), as a way for students to think about where they recognize religion in the world. What do they see and identify as religion and why? What do they exclude from that category? As we move through the videos, I take notes on the board and a list takes shape, a sort of family resemblance or cluster definition of religion, that highlights what my students decide counts as religion or not. Students often claim that the activities in these videos are recognizable as religion because of things like ritual activity, clothing and accoutrements, recognizable traditions and symbols, organization of leaders and laypeople, and more. As we proceed, we add to the list and start to see patterns. Subsequent videos disrupt the pattern a bit.

For instance, a video of whirling dervishes is quite confusing at first (many of my midwestern students do not see religion there). Some students say it is religion because of the highly choreographed group movement, the matching elaborate clothing, or the sense that there are bodily postures, like bowing in reverence toward a person who appears to be directing the dancers, that are familiar to them in religious contexts. Some students argue that none of these are enough to call this religion; it appears to them simply to be a dance performance. But inevitably someone in class knows they are Sufi Muslims, and then suddenly, almost everyone agrees it is a religious ritual. Here I take a moment to notice how knowing this activity is connected to something called "Islam" seems to be enough to qualify it as religion to the class, though not all Muslims agree that this practice would "count" as religion.

A video of hula hoopers dancing on a beach remains hard to categorize, despite strangely resembling the Islamic ritual they just decided was religion. Some students think dancing with a hula hoop is a spiritual practice, but not religious, because it lacks a certain decorum. The final video is the national anthem at a Tennessee football game.[4] Here, my students almost unanimously agree that, no, this is not religion. Instead, it is just the anthem. Or just a football game. When I take us back to our list, it actually seems to meet a lot of the criteria of ritual behavior and prescribed bodily movement, distinctions between leaders and laypeople, group activity of singing together, notion of a higher power, sacred symbols, clothing and accoutrements, and more. But even considering all of these commonalities between their working definition of recognizable religion and the human behaviors documented on the video, I can rarely convince them that it is religion. And I am not trying to, of course.

The question is not what is *really* religion and what is not, but rather, what do you *recognize* as religion and why? I want students to start to see the preconceptions they bring to the study of religion, the ideas they have about it being visible in the world and a stable and easy object to identify. After mulling over these

---

4. I know that many of my colleagues have done their own version of this exercise, so I do not claim to be the originator of this activity. In fact, several of these video examples, including that of the Tennessee football game, were borrowed, with permission, from Jenna Gray-Hildenbrand, and have been essential to my version of this lesson ever since. I am greatly indebted to her generosity as a colleague and interlocutor.

videos a bit, the final discussion questions for the class are centered around what distinguishes these activities as religion or not religion. We discuss cultural context and familiarity with certain traditions, and the ways that our socio-historical positionality influences our perceptions of what religion is or should be. We also begin questioning what kind of work calling something a religion does in the world. Why might it be important for your human activity to be seen by outsiders as religion, or not? What kind of power is inherent in being recognized as religion, or being able to decide what counts? These are the beginnings of our semester's discussions about religion in relation to the discursive construction of a category of power.

However, this is not easy to teach. I sometimes wonder if half of the class leaves this lesson thinking the goal was to show them that the performance of the national anthem at a sporting event is religion. I hope that as the semester goes on, it becomes clear that we are not actually looking to discover new or surprising examples of religion in the world, but rather, that we are interested in what gets classified as religion in the world and why. And particularly, what gets classified as religion in the United States, and what this tells us about the power of classification in American culture. In order to do that, I start with religion as a noun in this exercise: Is it religion? I do not imagine this to be a type of "gotcha" scholarship, as I actually believe that students need to be aware of the ways that religion is unconsciously and easily nominalized, and how they have taken that for granted. I hope then to start moving their understanding of religion toward plurals, adjectives, and eventually, verbs.

After considering our own preconceptions about what counts as religion in the video exercise above, I have two other class activities that investigate the ways in which the process of classification happens on multiple levels, including the personal, cultural, and institutional. I utilize the Pew Research Forum's online data and two of their open quizzes to help with this.[5] Both of these quizzes offer possibilities for "aha" moments in terms of understanding religion as a classificatory process, and not simply an objective reality in the world. The first quiz that we take is the "US Religious Knowledge Quiz." Based on a nationwide research survey, the quiz has fifteen questions designed to let the participant know how literate they are about the world's religions: "How much do you know about religion? And how do you compare with the average American? Here's your chance to find out" (Pew Research Center 2020b). I have students take the quiz and record their scores (either online before class or in class with a printout of the questions). The first thing we do is go over the answers to the questions, note how many questions they got right, how their results compare to other participants nationwide, and a few other basic descriptive elements about the quiz and the results of the broader findings included in a report, "What Americans Know About Religion," found on the Pew website (Pew Research Center 2019).

---

5. Pew has an option to create quiz groups for your class as well, which can be a great way to look at results (see Pew Research Center 2020a).

That first round of the discussion is primarily descriptive, and assumes that the PEW quiz is doing what it claims, testing religious literacy. Many of my students do poorly on the quiz, and so we discuss which questions were most difficult and why. The next part of the activity, however, asks students to dig a bit deeper into the quiz as not just reflective of religious literacy but as actively constructing it. I ask them to think about what counts as religion in the quiz. What kinds of knowledge is the quiz testing? Which religious traditions are included? In other words, what do you have to know to qualify as religiously literate? Again, I take notes on the board as we start to describe the "religion" of the quiz. Many questions refer to texts, rituals, figures in religious traditions, holidays, and historical events. Most of the questions are centered on traditional world religions with a focus on Jewish and Christian traditions (10 of the 15 questions relate to these two traditions) and American legal frameworks.[6] The questions ask for very standard institutional interpretations of these traditions, nothing too obscure or controversial. The questions, it seems, are not just telling us if we meet the mark for literacy, but they are actively constructing and reinforcing what counts as religion in American culture.

When our discussion goes well, students notice that to be religiously literate, they did not have to know much about lived religious practices, minority religious traditions, religious violence, and a plethora of other traditions and topics that might also qualify as religion. This quiz is measuring their knowledge of a very specific representation of religion. If I were to use Smith's terminology here, I would say the Pew quiz is a form of religioning as well. By creating a particular kind of pluralistic, world religions model of what counts as religion, Pew is participating in the process of defining and developing a public understanding of religion in America. As a class we start to see not what religion really is, but what Pew says religion is. I ask students to think about the negotiations of power at work in these classifications and the ways in which some traditions fit more easily into the category of religion, and some are not mentioned at all. Much like the "Is it religion?" video exercise, the goal here is to get students thinking about the foundational assumptions that inform the category of religion in American culture. Religion should look less like an existing object in the world, and more like a discursive construction, a negotiated selection of particular characteristics that become so familiar to us that we rarely question their validity, or the ways in which they come to wield power in society. I am attempting to demystify the stable, nominal notion of religion and replace it with a much more complex, active, processual form of religion here: religioning, in Smith's formulation.

In addition to the religious literacy quiz that tests Americans' knowledge through "fact-based, multiple-choice questions about topics related to religion" (Pew Research Center 2019), Pew also has a "Religious Typology" quiz

---

6. The version of the quiz I have used in classes through fall of 2019 included questions about the First Amendment and the legality of teaching religion in the public school classroom. The newest version of the quiz, however, seems to have gotten rid of these questions, replacing them with new questions about Sikhism, Hinduism, and Buddhism (see Pew Research Center 2019).

that classifies the participant along an axis of religious to non-religious, which is, according to the website, "a new way to categorize Americans by religion" (Pew Research Center 2018). The typology quiz thus labels participants into their religious type not by discreet religious identities or traditions (e.g., Christian, Buddhist, etc.), but rather in terms of how *religious* they are. Here, we see Pew also making a move away from nouns and toward adjectives and verbs. However, ultimately the lesson here is not in how much better or worse this classification is, but rather, how the adjective form is still beholden to particular notions of religion that draw upon dominant protestant frameworks in the US. When we complete this quiz, I ask students to think about their own results and how the labels fit or do not fit their perceived religious identities. Even if their results seem to fit, most students soon begin to see some problems with what counts as religion. As we deconstruct the seven categories, it becomes apparent that the notions of religiosity are actually quite loaded. The most religious are called "Sunday Stalwarts," "God-and-Country Believers," and "Diversely Devout." There are middle-of-the-road categories of "Relaxed Religious" and "Spiritually Awake," and the least religious fall into two final types, "Religion Resisters" and "Squarely Secular." All of these types reflect particular protestant American templates of what counts as religious belief and practice (e.g., church attendance, prayer, and belief in god). Many of my international students immediately see this, and they are the first to suggest that American notions of religion and religiosity are not natural or universal, but culturally specific and historically contingent. Students who practice traditions outside of Christianity, even if they see themselves as very religious, tend to find that the quiz does not categorize them as such. Their religioning may fall outside of the quiz's classifications.

Conclusions

These three class activities set the stage for students to begin to think about religion in new ways by highlighting the contingent nature of the category, as well as the ways in which religioning is also about positionality. What counts as religion or religiosity is reliant upon socio-cultural norms as well as the familial histories and personal choices that happen within and in relation to these broader contexts. As we contemplate these gaps, religion seems to be less of a recognizable object in the world, and more of a process of making sense of the world, a process that has implications outside of personal identity. My aim is to show the value of religion in the university while avoiding recreating or slipping into the "ambivalence" that Russell McCutcheon describes as "moving from studying why we call generic things religious—to somehow knowing that there are a variety of worthwhile and interconnected religion-like things in the world, whether we call them religion or not" (McCutcheon 2012: 239). This is the essentialism I try not to reinforce or reify in my classes, even as I find myself calling upon it from time to time in the name of conveying value. I recognize the ways that this pedagogy is itself a negotiation of power, a strategy that utilizes dominant frameworks in attempts to challenge them. This strategy, no matter how tactical and subversive, risks reinforcing essentialist notions of religion. Paying attention to the grammar of religious studies offers us an opportunity, as Smith argues, to revitalize our field and to challenge our students to reconsider the value of religion by religioning on multiple levels.

Martha Smith Roberts is assistant professor of religion at Fullerton College. Martha's teaching covers all aspects of religion in culture and the diversity of religious traditions around the world. Her research and writing focus on North American religious diversity and pluralism, race and ethnicity, new religious movements, and religious studies pedagogy. She has written articles on hula hooping, communities of practice, antiracist pedagogy, and religious diversity and pluralism in the United States.

References

Albanese, Catherine. 2013. *America: Religions and Religion*. Andover: Cengage Learning.
American Academy of Religion. 2019. "AAR Religious Literacy Guidelines." Retrieved from www.aarweb.org/aar-religious-literacy-guidelines#academic%20approach (accessed May 26, 2020).
Denison. 2020. "Vision and Values: What Matters Most at Denison." Retrieved from https://denison.edu/campus/about/vision-values (accessed May 26, 2020).
Eck, Diana L. 2002. *A New Religious America: How a "Christian Country" Has Become the World's Most Religiously Diverse Nation*, 2nd edition. San Francisco, CA: HarperSanFrancisco.
Ennis, Ariel. 2017. *Teaching Religious Literacy: A Guide to Religious and Spiritual Diversity in Higher Education*. New York: Routledge.
Gallagher, Eugene V., and Joanne Maguire. 2019. *The Religious Studies Skills Book: Close Reading, Critical Thinking, and Comparison*. New York: Bloomsbury Academic.
Gray-Hildenbrand, Jenna, and Rebekka King. 2019. "Teaching in Contexts: Designing a Competency-Based Religious Studies Program." *Teaching Theology and Religion* 22: 191–204.
Jacobsen, Rhonda Hustedt, and Douglas Jacobsen. 2012. *No Longer Invisible: Religion in University Education*. New York: Oxford University Press.
McCutcheon, Russell T. 2012. "A Tale of Nouns and Verbs: Rejoinder to Ann Taves." *Journal of the American Academy of Religion* 80(1): 236–240.
Moore, Diane L. 2007. *Overcoming Religious Illiteracy: A Cultural Studies Approach to the Study of Religion in Secondary Education*, 1st edition. New York: Palgrave Macmillan.
Nye, Malory. 2000. "Religion, Post-Religionism, and Religioning: Religious Studies and Contemporary Cultural Debates." *Method & Theory in the Study of Religion* 12(1): 447–476.
Pew Research Center. 2018. "The Religious Typology: A New Way to Categorize Americans by Religion." Retrieved from www.pewforum.org/2018/08/29/the-religious-typology (accessed May 26, 2020).
Pew Research Center. 2019. "What Americans Know About Religion." Retrieved from www.pewresearch.org/quiz/u-s-religious-knowledge-quiz (accessed May 26, 2020).
Pew Research Center. 2020a. "Typology Group Quiz Help Center." Retrieved from www.pewresearch.org/typology-group-quiz-help-center (accessed May 26, 2020).

Pew Research Center. 2020b. "US Religious Knowledge Quiz." Retrieved from www.pewresearch.org/quiz/u-s-religious-knowledge-quiz (accessed May 26, 2020).

Prothero, Stephen R. 2007. *Religious Literacy: What Every American Needs to Know—and Doesn't*, 1st edition. San Francisco, CA: HarperSanFrancisco.

Part II

The History of the Field

Chapter 6

The Enduring Presence of Our Pre-Critical Past; or, Same as it Ever Was, Same as it Ever Was

Russell T. McCutcheon

> I think a lot of people still believe in the sacred.
> —Aaron Hughes, "Reflections on 'Thinking with Jonathan Z. Smith'" (2019)

When invited to deliver a paper to the 2019 meeting of the North American Association for the Study of Religion (NAASR) on the topic of the history of the field, I accepted, though with some small degree of trepidation; for I felt the need to say something a little different from what I've already put into print, on a variety of past occasions, concerning problems found in the history of the study of religion—a history that may seem rather distant to some of us now, given that it was situated in, say, the height of nineteenth-century European colonialism (see, for example, McCutcheon 2000) or, more recently, in the Cold War politics of two generations ago (see McCutcheon 2004). For, as those two citations make evident, I have already discussed the practical implications (both inside and outside of the academy) of how prior scholars approached the study of religion—approaches that were, in the earliest years, grouped together and called either Comparative Religion or the Science of Religion. To state it simply, my argument has been that, given my understanding of the requirements for studying human beings from within the modern research university, some of those approaches are more fitting than others. In fact, as I've also argued, some of the approaches adopted by our colleagues actually undermine the field, at least as I understand it to be properly constituted, despite being offered by their supporters as but one more viable alternative. I therefore contest the position that holds that virtually any use of the word "religion" in a post-secondary setting, or as part of a piece of research, qualifies as but another instance of the so-called big tent that some think we all inhabit.[1] As with how I discuss definitions in my own introductory classes, then, when it comes to an academic pursuit I would argue that what some now see as the admirable desire to include as much as possible (often accomplished by means

---

1. Readers would not be incorrect to understand this, in part, as a commentary on the structure, expanse, and self-understanding of the American Academy of Religion (AAR), the world's largest professional association for scholars of religion (to which I have belonged for almost 30 years). It equally well applies, however, to a variety of other organizations within the international field today.

of what, on a past occasion, I characterized as the virtually limitless "religion and ..." genre) actually hampers the field; instead, when it comes to scholarship, the more precision the better.[2]

So, having made plenty of such claims in the past about all of this, I felt that this occasion presented an opportunity to say something new. Recollecting both Roland Barthes's views on authorship and that strategically brief piece that I've often used in classes, "Borges and I" (Barthes 1999: 324), I could say that, *qua scriptor*, I certainly know how to write like the author that shares my name, so this—or so I reasoned—might be an ideal moment to go against the grain, just a bit, and to offer something a little unexpected, perhaps in hopes that those who, at least as I see it, so often stereotype my work as a means to dismiss it might be surprised, just a little. For along with their surprise there might be a temptation actually to read it for a change and not, as I've seen on many past occasions, assume that a little bit of such older books as *Manufacturing Religion* (1997) or *Critics Not Caretakers* (2001) told them all that they needed to know about either the trajectory or current shape of my work. But, sadly, despite this earnest desire, I've decided that I see little new to say when I look again over not just the much older work that helped to establish our field (whether first in Europe or then, later, in North America) but, more importantly, also the work that now characterizes large segments of our field, much of it coming from a newer generation of scholars; for, in both cases, I find myself returning to the same old unresolved themes, since many of the problems that I find with past practices and the criticisms that I have offered on previous occasions strike me as being *just as relevant today*, when applied to the work that some consider to be at the field's cutting edge.

And so, because it seems to me that old problems endure, I have no choice but to use this opportunity to reiterate and thereby reinforce what I have said in the past, such as when William Arnal and I concluded several years ago that, "after looking a little more closely at the work of some of those who are now rethinking their use of the category 'religion,' it has become clear to us that troublesome assumptions persist despite the so-called advances" (Arnal and McCutcheon 2012: 7). Although there is a risk of some reading all that follows as being redundant—a risk that I am willing to take, given what I see to be the perennial nature of the challenges that greet critical scholarship on religion[3]—my goal here is simply to exemplify what are longstanding problems of the field at a site that I have not previously discussed in print. So, as should by now be clear, despite the title of this part of the book, this chapter is *not* about the past at all. (But, come to

---

2. Although one might hope that this goes without saying, the either vague, multiple, or even non-existent definitions of religion that often guide scholarship in our field should make evident that this point bears repeating—something that, thankfully, frequently takes place via Craig Martin's social media presence.

3. Revising this paper for publication, immediately after the meeting at which it was first presented, I can't help but recall the speaker immediately behind me at a reception one evening who, presumably, was unaware that I was there, and who complained loudly to several others about how redundant my work was and how Aaron Hughes had written far more than me.

think of it, *when is the past ever about the past?*)⁴ For, despite a wide variety of contemporary writers, notably some who now identify their work as post-critical or post-theoretical,⁵ claiming to have left flawed earlier practices and assumptions behind—after all, who even reads Eliade anymore, one might justifiably ask⁶—the practices and assumptions that drive much of the field today are, I argue, little different from those that did decades ago.

So, despite what some consider to be advances in the modern field—consider Daniel Dubuisson, for instance, in the opening sentence to his latest English book, celebrating "a veritable scientific revolution" taking place in the study of religion over the last two decades (2019: 1)—it seems to me that an effective and always ready rearguard action has undermined many of those gains by domesticating theory, thereby ensuring that, to use Bruno Latour's title (1993), but for my own purposes, *scholarship on religion has never really been modern*;⁷ for despite many scholars saying that they've read the critical work, by and large they continue to pursue their studies with colonial era tools in the pursuit of normalizing their own group's self-interests.⁸

Dubuisson's conclusion that the results of what he describes as a revolution "are so considerable that one must here and now envisage new ways to think of the History of Religions" notwithstanding, many in the field today are instead falling back on lightly revised versions of long familiar (and, I argue, troublesome) approaches. In writing this chapter I am therefore in strong agreement with Leslie Dorrough Smith when she notes that "although the field itself is now populated by scholars who ... claim a focus on more theories and methodological concerns ...

---

4. See Touna (2017) for one of the more thoroughgoing applications of this principle to the study of so-called ancient religion.

5. I take this position to be one that, for instance, highlights the importance of critiques of the category religion yet which nonetheless laments how what is judged to be an excessive focus on such critiques prevent us from just getting on with the work of actually studying religion (a stance examined throughout Hughes 2017). It is a sentiment that I also find in the work of so-called critical realists in the field today (see McCutcheon 2018a: 95–120 for an extended discussion of critical realism in our field).

6. On a past occasion my work was criticized as being aimed at outdated straw targets, inasmuch as, or so it was phrased to me then, "no one reads Eliade anymore." I replied by asking if people instead now study the thing they call religion as utterly reducible or at least akin to any number of other mundane elements of human practices. Lacking evidence of such an approach being in any way widespread—for, sooner or later, at least in my reading, religion often turns out to be a special case requiring some sort of special attention—the focus on Eliade's work as exemplary of wider and continuing trends struck me, and strikes me, as still having utility.

7. By claiming that we've never been modern I also do not have in mind the sort of argument put forward by Josephson-Storm (2018); interested readers can see my own thoughts on his recent book (McCutcheon 2018b).

8. This shortcoming has long been apparent to some in the field, such as when they considered (i) how frequently the work of the late Jonathan Z. Smith is cited appreciatively in the field despite (ii) how rare it has been for the critical impact of his work to be operationalized in a programmatic way, in either scholarship or teaching. Concerning Smith's contributions to the field, see the pieces collected in Crews and McCutcheon (2020).

there is a widespread, uninterrogated, essentialist impulse still remaining in the research of many who claim theoretical savvy" (Chapter 1, this volume). To put it in simple but still significant terms: it is remarkable just how many people in our field still routinely talk about those two supposed things that they call "the west" and "the east," or western as opposed to non-western religions (let alone still dividing things up between Christian and non-Christian religions); this is done despite all of us having apparently read (and understood?) our Edward Said, who, readers may recall, argues in detail that such terms are socially formative and self-referential and are therefore *not* descriptive of actual regions, agents, mentalities, or items at large in the world.[9] So significant are these shortcomings that I am hardly the first to observe them; for example, consider how Naomi Goldenberg (herself a one-time NAASR President and strong advocate for the governance role of the rhetoric of religion) has described this problem:

> My department colleagues ... are a highly intelligent, accomplished group of religious studies scholars. They are familiar with the substantial body of critical scholarship in the discipline that, for the past two decades at least, has argued ... that "religion" is a modern concept that operates as a distorting anachronism when applied to the study of earlier epochs ... [and] that "religion" has roots in European colonial ambitions and intellectual history.... I do not expect my colleagues to refrain from disagreeing with some or even all of these general tenets of the sub-field of "critical religion." Rather, what I find disconcerting is their choosing to ignore critical approaches to fundamental terms when they are describing religious studies as a discipline.
>
> (Goldenberg 2018: 80)

And, as Ian Cuthbertson observes, in a reply to Goldenberg's above-cited NAASR presentation:

> Colleagues in the religious studies department where I teach will often listen attentively whenever I insist that religion is not a self-evident thing in the world and then shrug their shoulders and proceed with the serious academic business of studying various individuals, tests, and practices in an attempt to determine what these might reveal about religion as a coherent object of study or thing in the world.
>
> (Cuthbertson 2018: 103)

So, to elaborate on my thesis concerning what my one-time colleague, Emily Crews, has called "a rash of scholarship that operates blindly when considering 'religion,' failing to parse the many layers of problematic meaning the category religion has accrued" (2018: 117), what Matthew Baldwin, in an earlier NAASR paper of his own, characterizes as a "given ... that many of our colleagues do ignore and dismiss or minimize" what he also terms "critical scholarship on 'religion' as

---

9. That the discourse on "the east" and "the west" has practical results that run the gamut from what many would judge to be benign to grievous or even catastrophic, is, of course, something that I recognize (contrary to dismissive caricatures of my work); such a recognition, however, does not mean that one's interest in studying discourse and its effects is diminished.

a category employed in human thought" (2019: 76), as well as what Craig Martin's own recent NAASR paper describes as the sort of "cavalier dismissals" that cause him "anger and frustration" (2019: 152; sentiments shared by Touna in her own work: Touna 2019: 175), let's briefly examine the now popular linkage between the study of religion and advocating for increased religious literacy, seeing it as but one, exemplary site where well-known difficulties reappear.[10]

While we could begin with Stephen Prothero's book on this topic—whose publisher's web page phrases the point of the book as follows:

> "We have a major civic problem on our hands," says religion scholar Stephen Prothero. He makes the provocative case that to remedy this problem, we should return to teaching religion in the public schools. Alongside "reading, writing, and arithmetic," religion ought to become the "Fourth R" of American education.[11]

—we could instead cite more recent instances, such as the AAR's just completed three-year initiative (begun 2016 with a $160,000 grant from the Arthur Vining Davis Foundations)[12] to "produce consensus guidelines on religious literacy that administrators and faculty nationwide can draw upon to help shape college curricula."[13] Along with that project we could also draw attention to Harvard Divinity

---

10. From the outset of this analysis I must cite Wolfart's important forthcoming essay (pre-posted online by the journal as an advance publication, done so while the present chapter was being copyedited); it concerns not just the historical roots of all such literacy campaigns but their always hopeful basis (i.e., the utter lack of empirical evidence to support their aims and claims). Although the main text of the present chapter has not been revised with Wolfart's careful analysis in mind (which reinforces my own work here), anyone interested in the many current scholarly and institutional initiatives based on enhancing religious literacy would be well advised to read his paper carefully, to consider what else might be happening in such discourses—in his words—a "strong residual theology of hope."
11. From www.harpercollins.ca/9780060859527/religious-literacy. Prothero's interest in this topic continues, e.g., his public lecture at the University of Kansas on April 6, 2018, advertised as being on "Religious Literacy in an Age of Religious Nationalism."
12. The foundation, established in 1952, and which has a program specifically to fund interfaith leadership as well as religious literacy, is driven by its "founder's principle that religious diversity is essential to civil discourse within a democracy and that leaders in all walks of life are more effective through an appreciation for the religious views of others" (quoted from www.avdf.org/Programs/InterfaithLeadershipReligiousLiteracy.aspx, accessed September 15, 2019). Davis (1867–1962), the one-time president and chairman of the board of the Aluminum Company of America (Alcoa), was also a large land developer in the Bahamas and Florida before establishing the foundation.
13. The committee, which also involved a team of respondents and which holds public sessions annually, was led by Eugene Gallagher and Diane L. Moore (according to www.aarweb.org/about/religious-literacy-guidelines-for-college-students, accessed September 15, 2019). The October 3, 2019, press release announcing the completion of their work was found at www.aarweb.org/the-aar-publishes-religious-literacy-guidelines-for-college-graduates (accessed October 10, 2019). Its guidelines, while also focused on issues of method (e.g., "Distinguish confessional or prescriptive statements made by religions from descriptive or analytical statements"), predictably also focused on acquiring the descriptive details that comes with acquiring the world religions discourse (e.g., "Discern accurate and credible knowledge about diverse religious

School's current Religious Literacy Project,[14] along with Diana Eck's much earlier (begun in 1991) but not unrelated Pluralism Project,[15] or even mention the Open University, in the UK, and its free online short course, "Why Religion Matters: Religious Literacy, Culture and Diversity."[16] In fact, we could even refer to the wide variety of Departments of Religious Studies throughout the US, whose members now see the topic of religious literacy as a thematic engine capable of driving, to whatever extent, their programing initiatives, institutional identity, and thus success. To name but a few: (i) Northwestern University grounds its major in the context of Prothero's work on religious literacy (notably citing his March 19, 2007, appearance on *The Daily Show with John Stewart*);[17] (ii) Stanford's Department of Religious Studies' home page claims that "[r]eligious literacy is key to global citizenship in the 21st century";[18] (iii) the chaplain's office at Brown University (the proper place for such an endeavor, I contend) sponsors a Religious Literacy

---

traditions and expressions") (see the executive summary of the report: American Academy of Religion 2009: 2). At the public session I attended, near the start of the group's project, many audience members were frustrated by the manner in which the Department of Religious Studies could be undermined by what then seemed like the committee's interest also to advocate for acquiring knowledge about religions in almost any other disciplinary or course setting—a move that, or so some in the audience argued, could provide warrant for administrations not to support the work of scholars of religion. This made it into their final report nonetheless: "In addition to religious studies courses, religious literacy can also be promoted in other disciplines including (but not limited to) anthropology, archeology, art, biology, criminal justice, economics, education, film, geology, history, humanities, journalism, literature, languages, media studies, music, neuroscience, nursing, philosophy, political science, psychology, social work, sociology, speech, and theatre," as written in the report (ibid.: 4). Ironically, perhaps, as one committee member responded on that occasion, the organization's mission, to promote the public study of religion, does not necessarily require that it promote the academic field of Religious Studies. It may be worth noting that the AAR's head office in Atlanta currently has an opening for a fulltime Advocate for the Study of Religion (though it took an earlier social media backlash to prompt them to consider adding training *in our own field* as a legitimate background for applicants).

14. This initiative was founded, and is led by, Diane L. Moore, cited in the previous note; the project "advances the public understanding of religion with special attention to power, peace, and conflict. Through resources and training for educators and other professionals we explore the complex roles religions play in society" (the project's self-description at https://rlp.hds.harvard.edu/about, accessed September 15, 2019). The site now (May 2022) states "The Religious Literacy Project (RLP) has now joined Religion and Public Life (RPL) at Harvard Divinity School. Visit the new website at rpl.hds.harvard.edu to engage with this exciting new chapter in Harvard Divinity School's work to advance the public understanding of religion." The equivalent page on the new site is https://rpl.hds.harvard.edu/about but the copy has been revised.

15. Learn more at http://pluralism.org/about/our-work/history (accessed September 15, 2019).

16. See www.futurelearn.com/courses/why-religion-matters (accessed October 17, 2019) for information on the Open University's online course.

17. See www.religious-studies.northwestern.edu/undergraduate/first-year-focus.html (accessed September 14, 2019).

18. See https://religiousstudies.stanford.edu (accessed September 14, 2019).

Project;[19] (iv) San Diego State University's Department of Religious studies offers a 15 credit hour Global Religious Literacy Certificate; and (v) The University of Vermont offers REL 105 Religious Literacy, described as follows: "Religious literacy entails understanding the history and contemporary manifestations of religion, including the central texts, beliefs and practices as they are shaped within specific contexts. Introduces ways of thinking about the public expression of religion and profession-specific engagements with religion."[20] (UVM also celebrated October 2019 as religious literacy month and find #RelLitUVM on social media for a list of programing events associated with their religious literacy month.) And even the current American Religious Sounds Project (a project which seems not to define religion, as far as I can tell) seems to be part of this initiative, inasmuch as "the need for understanding religious pluralism has arguably never been greater. Given the remarkable diversity of American religious life and the increasing polarization of our politics, building a civic culture that is inclusive and valuing of all peoples constitutes one of the most pressing challenges we face today."[21]

These examples should all make plain that one would not be incorrect to understand the effort to increase the public's knowledge of religions—doing so both inside and outside of our classrooms—as now being one of the major rationales of the academic study of religion.[22]

But just what is entailed in this widespread initiative? As phrased in a 2015 article in *The Chronicle of Higher Education*, this turn toward teaching religious literacy recognizes "the urgency to make our campuses successful models of communities of diversity and global citizenry that do not ignore but recognize—and draw on—the significance, beauty, and complexity of religion" (Rosenhagen 2015). That the just-quoted essay was written weeks after the November 2015 terrorist attacks across Paris and in the more immediate context of candlelight vigils held on the author's campus (University of Wisconsin at Madison)—attended, as he describes it in his opening paragraph, by students of a variety of faiths (as well as the religiously unaffiliated)—cannot go unnoticed; for the desire to arrive at a civil and inclusive public square (civil and inclusive as judged by specific and usually undisclosed and thereby naturalized standards, of course—*this* is the issue that needs attention) is the driving force behind the religious literacy initiative.[23] Or, as the

---

19. See www.brown.edu/campus-life/spiritual-life/chaplains/office-chaplains-and-religious-life/religious-literacy-project (accessed September 14, 2019).
20. See the course description at www.uvm.edu/courses/rel_105 (accessed September 15, 2019).
21. See http://religioussounds.osu.edu/about-faq#whyReligion (accessed September 15, 2019).
22. It should be noted that the AAR's mission statement itself reads as follows: "to foster excellence in the academic study of religion and enhance the public understanding of religion"; to that end it has as Committee on the Public Understanding of Religion, which, among other initiatives, annually awards the Martin E. Marty Public Understanding of Religion award as well as an award to journalists (from www.aarweb.org/about/committee-public-understanding-religion, accessed September 15, 2019).
23. In November of 2015, 130 people were killed and 494 people injured as part of attacks in the French capital, involved a bombing at a sports stadium and attacks on the streets, restaurants, and a night club.

author, Rosenhagen—himself an ordained pastor in the Evangelical Lutheran Church in America who also holds a PhD from the University of Heidelberg and who was the Associate Director of the one-time Lubar Institute for the Study of the Abrahamic Religions while now being the Director of the University of Wisconsin at Madison's Center for Religion and Global Citizenry[24]—phrases it:

> Colleges need to invest more in their students' religious literacy—not proselytizing, not affirming any particular faith—but simply teaching vital competence about religion and its impact on global affairs that will prepare students for their future while enlightening our civic discourse along the way.
>
> (Rosenhagen 2015)

Or consider how Moore's Harvard project defines religious literacy:

> Religious literacy entails the ability to discern and analyze the fundamental intersections of religion and social/political/cultural life through multiple lenses. Specifically, a religiously literate person will possess:
>
> - a basic understanding of the history, central texts (where applicable), beliefs, practices and contemporary manifestations of several of the world's religious traditions as they arose out of and continue to be shaped by particular social, historical and cultural contexts
> - the ability to discern and explore the religious dimensions of political, social and cultural expressions across time and place[25]

So, not only do we see in this discourse on religious literacy a normative and uncritical notion of religion as a beneficial (i.e., peaceful, beautiful, and civil)

---

24. Although it closed in June of 2016, as described on their now out-of-date website, "The UW Lubar Institute for the Study of the Abrahamic Religions opened in July 2005, testimony to the vision and benefactions of Sheldon and Marianne Lubar of Milwaukee, Wisconsin. Concerned about rising religious tensions worldwide and believing Jews, Christians and Muslims to be capable of prolonged and honest inquiry into both their common heritages and varying perspectives, they imagined a center that would advance mutual comprehension by mingling scholars with the general public, clergy with laity, and members of different faith communities with citizens of Wisconsin, the United States, and the world. Through encouraging people belonging to and/or interested in the Abrahamic traditions to engage each other and to find out more about both of these several traditions and their intersections, the Lubar Institute is dedicated to strengthening the values of religious pluralism so vital for sustaining American civil society and peaceful international discourse." Interestingly, this unit was an institute in the College of Arts & Sciences at the University of Wisconsin at Madison, a public land-grant university in the US (https://lubar.wisc.edu/welcome/mission.html was the source of this description, accessed September 21, 2019). The Center for Religion and Global Citizenry was established on the same campus in August 2017, explicitly as a revised version of the Lubar Institute (see https://religion.wisc.edu/about, accessed September 21, 2019). Aaron Hughes's critique of the category of Abrahamic religions (2012) as a socially formative devise used by liberal religious pluralists to establish the basis for interreligious dialog, and thus a category of no analytic power for scholars of religion, deserves mention at this point.

25. Quoted from https://rlp.hds.harvard.edu/our-approach/what-is-religious-literacy (accessed September 15, 2019).

force in human affairs, as well as a politically and theologically liberal understanding of diversity and inclusion (something already addressed in *Critics Not Caretakers*, by the way; McCutcheon 2001: ch. 10), but we also find traditional or what we might better call pre-critical notions of religion as a socio-politically autonomous force that is merely "shaped" by history while "manifesting" itself (or its various "dimensions") in a variety of discrete locales; in this way, seemingly positive practical effects are said to be achieved by one or more of the so-called world religions or what are often termed faith traditions, effects enabled or promoted by our correct understanding of the religions...—*all of which flies in the face of a variety of critical gains made in the field over the past generation or two of scholars.*

First off, in an effort to recover some critical intelligence in our field, consider that suspicion from the political left (rightly, I would argue) usually greets the discourse on civility when it is wielded by those on the right of contemporary politics, for in such cases it is (again, rightly, I would argue) recognized to be a strategic way to promote *a certain sort of order* and thereby *to suppress resistance to it* (by ruling such resistance as being out of bounds, because it is "uncivil"). For example, consider the reaction by some to the recently founded program for civil public discourse at the University of North Carolina, Chapel Hill, established by its Board of Governors—a board that is understood by some current UNC faculty to be at odds with the idea of shared faculty governance.[26] The irony, however, is that when the same term, "civility"—which I assume *always* to be a rhetorical term with socially formative effects, regardless who uses it—is employed by those on the political left it is often left unscrutinized by them, as if it only now just means what it naturally says and is no longer the strategic front for other, undisclosed claims. The first problem, then, with religious literacy initiatives in our field is that I see little if any critical analysis of the links between these projects and claims that it somehow enhances some untheorized notion of civility.

But what concerns me even more is the uncritical manner in which the discourse on world religions makes its reappearance by means of such initiatives. To name but a few examples that might have already come to the reader's mind, the work of such scholars as Tim Fitzgerald (1990), Tomoko Masuzawa (2005), and Suzanne Owen (2011), not to mention about half of the authors collected together in Cotter and Robertson 2016)[27]—work specifically on the manner in which the discourse on world religions not only was, from the start, intertwined with very specific colonial governance efforts but also on the ways in which it remains invested in a variety of modern political projects—strikes me as going completely unrecognized and thereby ignored in the religious literacy literature. What is fas-

---

26. See http://publicdiscourse.web.unc.edu, or for a more recent article on the program and faculty reactions, see www.insidehighered.com/news/2019/09/12/program-civic-virtue-unc-chapel-hill-raising-concerns-about-secrecy-and-funding (accessed September 12, 2019).

27. I say this because, as elaborated in the Afterword that I wrote for the volume, about half of the contributors to the book are devoted to using the world religions category better (e.g., adding more traditions that have been, in the estimation of such scholars, inappropriately ignored in the past, such as pagan or indigenous traditions) while the other half wish to dispel with the category all together.

cinating in all this, then, is that, despite the critical work of these and other writers, and the way that their research on the links between categories, methods, and power politics has driven much of the conversation in the modern field, the main problem with the world religions discourse today, at least according to yet others also working in the field today, is apparently *that people do not know it, and thus use it, well enough*; in other words, the problem is *not* that scholars and the general public at large continue to divide the world into a number of so-called faith traditions (thereby perpetuating a sort of apolitical idealism and individualism, each of which have, or so some have argued, profound socio-political implications) but *that we all don't sufficiently know the descriptive ins and outs of each*.[28] Recall that, as quoted above, among the goals of Harvard's religious literacy initiative is to enhance "a basic understanding of the history, central texts (where applicable), beliefs, practices and contemporary manifestations of several of the world's religious traditions." What's more, if we add Fitzgerald, Masuzawa, Owen et al.'s critique of the discourse on world religions to the work of those engaged in the wider critique of the category religion itself (the genus of which world religions could be said to be but a species), and its practical effects in modern liberal democracies, then we arrive at the curious moment when a critical portion of the field is working to historicize and thereby limit our attraction to naming something *as* religion or *as* a world religion while much of the rest of the field seems to be working to revive and secure an undefined notion of civil society by ensuring that the population can—to put it crassly, but in a manner in keeping with the goals of this initiative—properly distinguish a Sikh from a Muslim from a Hindu from a Jain from a ... all in hopes, I gather, that a deference to *certain sorts of differences* will become apparent to those sufficiently articulate in the use of this taxonomy.

And voila: the critical gains made over the past decades in studying how the discourse on religion or on world religions helps to make certain sorts of social worlds possible and persuasive is lost in the effort to normalize but one of those very worlds.

While we might easily think of other recent developments in the field where a disciplinary past that some of us had thought we had left far behind turns out, upon closer inspection, to be far more current than we had thought,[29] the

---

28. While I agree that we ought to be careful in the description of other people's claims and actions (with a nod toward Wayne Proudfoot's once widely quoted criticism of what he termed descriptive reductionism, as opposed to his support for explanatory reductionism; Proudfoot 1985: 196–197), this agreement has not prevented me on a variety of occasions from also reminding scholars (with a nod to a point demonstrated long ago by reflexive anthropologists), that our very questions, assumptions, and categories frame the conversation in ways that often predetermine what our so-called informants or interlocutors say in reply to us (as I elaborate later in this paper); our nuanced or sensitive description of others' claims therefore does not prevent our (perhaps unwitting) determining of how others are understood in our work.

29. The longer version of this paper (McCutcheon 2021) examined recurring problems at such other sites as: material, lived, or embodied religion; the notion of public religion; as well as studies on religion and law.

contradiction here between, on the one hand, the prominence of contemporary religious literacy initiatives, championed by some of the leading or most influential (or at least well-funded) aspects of the field and, on the other, critical scholars of religion who treat the study of religion as no different than the study of any other domain of human life, should cause us to pause and ask a few questions about just how modern this modern field of ours actually is. For the colonial-era world religions discourse that many in our field think they've left far behind turns out to be as relevant as it ever was, whether or not world religions courses continue as the so-called bread and butter classes of Departments. (My assumption is that they still are, by the way—this would be an interesting study to tackle.)[30] What's more, the notion of religion as unique and irreducible—a stance associated by many with what many consider to be the now out-of-date though once prominent Chicago school of thought (though it was never just about Chicago, of course)—remains, I contend, as invigorated and consequential as ever, for it turns out to be the assumption that drives the use of the term religion in these literacy efforts;[31] for, as in pollsters collecting voter data outside polling stations and thereby trying to determine how religious beliefs inform voting patterns (i.e., religious sentiments are presumed to be primary and thus causal), religion, belief, faith, experience, or any other of their analogues, are still generally assumed by such scholars to be a pre-social, non-political disposition that merely has political and social "dimensions" and cultural "expressions" (as per the Harvard Religious Literacy project, cited earlier). Here, as I've identified before, the etymology and modern uses of "express" are both helpful to keep in mind, inasmuch as it connotes "speaking one's mind" or putting something nonverbal "into words"— thereby reproducing the common "ghost in the machine" model of the human, whereby a dynamic, prior, and private inner consciousness and meaning is, by means of some secondary and invariably flawed step, said to be conveyed into the public by means of a symbol system that exists at a distance from the original intention ("That's not what I meant!" is sure evidence of this model, also making plain its agonistic role.) And thus, despite longstanding protests to the contrary, the old Cartesian dualism is, as alive as it ever was in the study of religion—something evident from the very beginning of another now popular subfield (i.e., studies of material religion), as in when one of its founders, Colleen McDannel (though we could easily quote the work of other influential figures, such as Robert Orsi), noted that her topic was "[t]he physical *expressions* of religion" and, in particular, "the material *dimension* of Christianity," thereby prompting her research to have

---

30. Studying the credit hour production that comes through such courses—a key indicator of a department's vitality—along with obtaining sales information on still thriving world religions textbook genre, would provide insight into this. On the enduring influence of Huston Smith's still in-print 1958 textbook, originally entitled *The Religions of Man* (including its unwavering sales over the years), see McCutcheon (2018a: 46).
31. Aside: there's even an annual world religions day, established in 1950 by the Spiritual Assembly of the Bahá'ís of the United States, and which is celebrated around the world (see Goldenberg 2018: 85 for a description of a Canadian celebration of the day).

"ranged broadly over many *expressions* of material Christianity" (McDannel 1995: 1–2, 276; emphases added).

Taking all of this into account suggests to me that, despite the ease with which many in the field now claim to have read the critical work and taken it into consideration, the field has actually changed very little in the past 150 years; for, citing but one scholar who has already been mentioned above, the distance between Goldenberg's critical approach to the category religion as a tactical governance device of nation-states, whereby what she terms marginal, vestigial states are created and policed by dominant populations (2015), on the one hand, and, on the other, contemporary religious literacy initiatives—which, by the way, Greg Alles has recently described as "not a particularly robust justification for the study of religions" (Chapter 10, this volume)—is so great that the latter can be understood to be but one more data point in need of the former's analysis.[32] If anything has changed at all, over this time, it is perhaps the political causes supported by the same old devices. I think here of the widespread notion of strategic essentialism and the manner in which a form of essentialism, hotly critiqued by scholars in many cases (recall here Smith's comments quoted above), can nonetheless be seen by some to be allowed or even embraced as long as it is in support of causes or interests which they support; or, as recently phrased by M Adryael Tong, in an article concerned with how scholars can "encounter the [historical] archive *on its own terms*" (2019: 40; emphasis added), "sometimes it is politically expedient—perhaps even necessary—to adopt essentialist language in order to effect one's political goals" (ibid.: 43). That one's adversaries are just as likely to adopt this technique, arguing just as vehemently for its legitimacy in helping them to achieve *their* practical goals by means of their scholarship and teaching, ought to be enough reason for scholars of religion to reconsider how to establish an institutional space where such work is excluded.

Before closing, I feel that I should be clear on the reason for offering the preceding critique. Although I may be incorrect, of course, I have the impression that some members of a younger generation for whose work recent critical gains are important have sometimes naturalized the contemporary place where they do their own work, thereby failing to recognize or appreciate that their institutional and disciplinary space is historically contingent, meaning that its establishment and maintenance was hard won, i.e., gained only by previous scholars tackling the work of their predecessors and peers in order to make plain how it was lacking or how it therefore led to a study of religion that was out of step with what they understood to be the usual requirements of scholarship. While I do not share Luther Martin and Donald Wiebe's despair over what they described as their delusion about the field's future as a scientific enterprise (2012)—and neither do I share their narrow understanding of science—I admit to being concerned that without scholars at all career stages being willing to stand up and make strong

---

32. See the last chapter to McCutcheon (2003), "Religion and the Governable Self," for an example of my own analysis of the political function of the category religion—an approach certainly related to but by no means coterminous with Goldenberg's approach.

statements about what they consider to be inadequate work in the field, the critical gains that some of us value will, within a surprisingly short time, be lost. For, as just argued, despite many of us apparently all agreeing that the world religions genre is an antiquated relic from a prior era, I would conjecture that it is now as vibrant and influential as it ever was.[33]

Now, I recognize that there are always prices to be paid in critically engaging the work of others, those whose scholarship strikes one as problematic—prices that vary widely based on, among other factors, the place of the critic and the place of the one being critiqued. This is what I meant by the *hard won* gains that we risk taking for granted today. I think here of the earnest warning that my own doctoral supervisor once offered to me, just a short time into my own tenure-track career (in fact, just after he had read my book, *Critics Not Caretakers*), concerning the behind-the-scenes work of some of those who were then (and who still are) well-placed in the field—efforts, as he characterized it, to undermine those with whom they disagreed concerning the shape and effects of the study of religion. I also recall a variety of incidents and interactions in my own career (some of which had administrative and thus institutional force behind them while others were more akin to polite warnings from no doubt well-meaning colleagues)[34] but, far more than this, I also recall the experiences of scholars in the generation ahead of my own, for whom firings (due to what I can only interpret as disciplinary disputes) were not an unusual part of the career for those who thought the study of religion could be something more than interreligious dialog. There are always things at stake, after all, and one would be naïve to ignore that; though the spoils are not that great (at least by some measures), there are spoils nonetheless, and, like all professions, there is an economy of status, rank, and perks that governs our institutions (everything from gaining admission to a graduate program to obtaining employment, let alone a full-time tenure-track position, to finding a position in certain schools, supervising doctoral students, gaining lighter teaching loads, or being recognized for awards). So I admit to having concerns for where all this might be going in the near future, a concern which drives

---

33. Aside: at the University of Alabama, where I've worked since 2001, my colleague, Steven Ramey, teaches this course but does so in a way that ultimately problematizes the idea and the course itself for his students.

34. This varies from once being called on the carpet by a department chair, at the insistence of a school's associate provost and also being denied tenure, to being advised by a senior colleague to use the word "approaches" rather than "theories" in a course title (so as not to alienate others), being told by another to place the work of Peter Berger on a syllabus so as to satisfy yet another senior colleague who saw in Berger the pinnacle of theoretical work in the field, having work rejected by a peer review journal for being too critical (cue the policing function of the discourse on civility), being likened to a small dog that has learned a new trick in an article on my work published in that same journal, and having my work trivialized as being mere journalism. Related to this, see Hughes and McCutcheon (2019) for a critical analysis of the discourse on collegiality (an article previously rejected by the *Journal of the American Academy of Religion* because, as we were told at the time, it was not about world religions or methods for studying world religions—the only topics the journal apparently published.

my effort to persuade you today that the field (as some of us understand it) is not as far along or as secure as some of us might imagine it to be. What's more, all this is heightened now, for, as almost everyone likely knows, changes over the past decades in how public higher education is funded (i.e., significant cuts in government support) have led to a situation in which university administrations have not only increasingly relied on tuition revenue but have also opted to employ far greater numbers of (cheaper and less protected) non-tenure-track faculty (i.e., contingent faculty). Although the detrimental effect of this policy on young scholars' individual careers certainly deserves our attention, I maintain that it has also not helped the situation in the study of religion as a field and as a node within those institutions; for it means that far greater numbers of early career scholars remain in significantly exposed settings (under-employed or employed just course-by-course and year-by-year), thereby denying them the privileges of the tenure system and thereby providing them with little incentive (because of little protection!) to critically tackle the work of their elders and their peers, with an eye toward the health of the field at large.[35]

For, should my analysis of the socially formative role played by the category religion be persuasive (a topic on which I have written on a variety of past occasions), then we would be well advised to consider that no critical gain will ever be widely influential, let alone permanent. For just as with each new crop of students entering our classes, every new academic generation will bring with it their own long entrenched habits of thought and action concerning what religion is and does, habits that will continually require re-examination and, in some cases, undoing. For, as I have also noted on other occasions, the introductory class is a place where we would do well to make our students curious, as soon as they arrive in our classes, of their own taken-for-granted practices and knowledge, making their presumptions about the world and habits in the world their eventual objects of study. Or, to borrow J. Z. Smith's language, gains in such courses, let alone the field as a whole, often result from defamiliarizing the material that we study and the tools that we use to go about those studies. But though pre-critical problems inevitably endure—ensuring that they will reappear, in some new guise, no sooner than they are critiqued (I think here of Mary Jane Rubenstein's apt comparison of the discourse on experience to a carnival game in which toy moles keep popping up out of their holes no matter how many times you've whacked them; see Rubenstein 2012)—I'm hopeful that a critical self-consciousness among those who see these gains as worth fighting for will be just as wily and even more resilient. For, in agreement with what Peggy Schmeiser (2019: 127) argued, this very sort of "self-reflection and critique is imperative to the survival of our field and discourses."

---

35. As far as I can tell, no one has yet explored in any detail the disciplinary conservatism that more than likely results from universities increasingly relying on contingent faculty labor.

Acknowledgements

Out of deference to the requirements of the published version of the conference, this chapter is a significantly shortened version of the paper that was originally pre-distributed to the respondents (for the full version see McCutcheon 2021); it retains but one of the original examples in support of its thesis (i.e., religious literacy initiatives). My thanks to all of the respondents who worked with that lengthier original and also to Aaron Hughes and Craig Martin for their feedback on an earlier drafts of that paper.

Russell T. McCutcheon, who has served as NAASR's executive secretary/treasurer (2004–2007), as its president (2014–2017), and, for a total of eleven years, as either co-editor or editor of its journal, *Method & Theory in the Study of Religion* (1990–2001), is university research professor and chair of the Department of Religious Studies at the University of Alabama.

References

American Academy of Religion. 2009. *AAR Religion Religious Literacy Guidelines: What US College Graduates Need to Understand About Religion*. Atlanta, GA: American Academy of Religion.
Arnal, William E. and Russell T. McCutcheon. 2012. *The Sacred Is the Profane: The Political Nature of "Religion."* New York: Oxford University Press.
Baldwin, Matthew C. 2019. "Objects and Objections: Methodological Reflections on the Data for Religious Studies." In Leslie Dorrough Smith (ed.), *Construction "Data" in Religious Studies: Examining the Architecture of the Academy* (pp. 73–100). Sheffield: Equinox Publishers.
Borges, Jorge Luis 1999. "Borges and I." In Jorge Luis Borges, *Collected Fictions* (p. 324). Trans. Andrew Hurley. New York: Penguin.
Cotter, Christopher R. and David G. Robertson (eds). 2016. *After World Religions: Reconstructing Religious Studies*. New York: Routledge.
Crews, Emily. 2018. "Perhaps Action Enough." In Brad Stoddard (ed.), *Method Today: Redescribing Approaches to the Study of Religion*, 114–118. Sheffield: Equinox.
Crews, Emily, and Russell T. McCutcheon (eds). 2020. *Jonathan Z. Smith: A Career and its Consequence*. Sheffield: Equinox Publishers.
Cuthbertson, Ian Alexander. 2018. "Preaching to the Choir? Religious Studies and Religionization." In Brad Stoddard (ed.), *Method Today: Redescribing Approaches to the Study of Religion* (pp. 96–105). Sheffield: Equinox.
Dubuisson, Daniel. 2019. *The Invention of Religion*. Trans. Martha Cunningham. Sheffield: Equinox Publishers.
Fitzgerald, Timothy. 1990. "Hinduism and the 'World Religion' Fallacy." *Religion* 20: 101–118.
Goldenberg, Naomi R. 2015. "The Category of Religion in the Technology of Governance: An Argument for Understanding Religions as Vestigial States." In Trevor Stack, Naomi Goldenberg, and Timothy Fitzgerald (eds.), *Religion as a Category of Governance and Sovereignty* (pp. 280–292). Leiden: Brill.
Goldenberg, Naomi R. 2018. "Forget About Defining 'It': Reflections on Thinking Differently in Religious Studies." In Brad Stoddard (ed.), *Method Today: Redescribing Approaches to the Study of Religion* (pp. 79–95). Sheffield: Equinox.

Hughes, Aaron W. 2012. *Abrahamic Religions: On the Uses and Abuses of History*. New York: Oxford University Press.
Hughes, Aaron W. 2017. *Theory in a Time of Excess: Beyond Reflection and Explanation in Religious Studies Scholarship*. Sheffield: Equinox Publishers.
Hughes, Aaron W. 2019. "Reflections on 'Thinking with Jonathan Z. Smith'." *Religious Studies Project*, November 11. Retrieved from www.religiousstudiesproject.com/podcast/reflections-on-thinking-with-jonathan-z-smith.
Hughes, Aaron W., and Russell T. McCutcheon 2019. "Epilogue: The Gatekeeping Rhetoric of Collegiality in the Study of Religion." In Leslie Dorrough Smith (ed.), *Constructing "Data" in Religious Studies: Examining the Architecture of the Academy* (pp. 267–290). Sheffield: Equinox.
Josephson-Storm, Jason. 2018. *The Myth of Disenchantment: Magic, Modernity, and the Birth of the Human Sciences*. Chicago, IL: University of Chicago Press.
Latour, Bruno. 1993. *We Have Never Been Modern*. Trans. Catherine Porter. Cambridge, MA: Harvard University Press.
Martin, Craig. 2019. "'The Thing Itself Always Steals Away': Scholars and the Constitution of Their Objects of Study." In Leslie Dorrough Smith (ed.), *Constructing "Data" in Religious Studies: Examining the Architecture of the Academy* (pp. 151–174). Sheffield: Equinox Publishers.
Martin, Luther H., and Donald Wiebe. 2012. "Religious Studies as a Scientific Discipline: The Persistence of a Delusion." *Journal of the American Academy of Religion* 80(3): 587–597.
Masuzawa, Tomoko. 2005. *The Invention of World Religions Or, How European Universalism Was Preserved in the Language of Pluralism*. Chicago, IL: University of Chicago Press.
McCutcheon, Russell T. 1997. *Manufacturing Religion: The Discourse on Sui Generis Religion and the Politics of Nostalgia*. New York: Oxford University Press.
McCutcheon, Russell T. 2000. "The Imperial Dynamic in the Study of Religion: Neo-colonial Practices in an American Discipline." In C. Richard King (ed.), *Postcolonial America* (pp. 275–302). Champaign, IL: University of Illinois Press.
McCutcheon, Russell T. 2001. *Critics Not Caretakers: Redescribing the Public Study of Religion*. Albany, NY: State University of New York Press.
McCutcheon, Russell T. 2003. *The Discipline of Religion: Structure, Meaning, Rhetoric*. New York: Routledge.
McCutcheon, Russell T. 2004. "'Just Follow the Money': The Cold War, the Humanistic Study of Religion, and the Fallacy of Insufficient Cynicism," *Culture & Religion* 5(1): 41–69.
McCutcheon, Russell T. 2018a. *Fabricating Religion: Fanfare for the Common e.g.* Berlin: Walter de Gruyter.
McCutcheon, Russell T. 2018b. "On the Myth of Disenchantment." *Harvard Theological Review* 111(4): 610–617.
McCutcheon, Russell T. 2021. *On Making a Shift in the Study of Religion and Other Essays*. Berlin: Walter de Gruyter.
McDannel, Colleen. 1995. *Material Christianity: Religion and Popular Culture in America*. New Haven, CT: Yale University Press.
Owen, Suzanne. 2011. "The World Religions Paradigm: Time for a Change." *Arts and Humanities in Higher Education* 10(3): 253–268.
Prothero, Stephen. 2008. *Religious Literacy: What Every American Needs to Know—And Doesn't*. New York: HarperCollins.
Proudfoot, Wayne. 1995. *Religious Experience*. Berkeley, CA: University of California Press.
Rosenhagen, Ulrich. 2015. "The Value of Teaching Religious Literacy." *The Chronicle of Higher Education* (December). Retrieved from www.chronicle.com/article/The-Value-of-Teaching/234393 (accessed September 16, 2019).

Rubenstein, Mary-Jane. 2012. "The Twilight of the Doxai: Or, How to Philosophize with a Whac-a-Mole Mallet." *Method & Theory in the Study of Religion* 24(1): 64–70.

Schmeiser, Peggy. 2019. "Governance and Public Policy as Critical Objects of Investigation in the Study of Religion." In Leslie Dorrough Smith (ed.), *Construction "Data" in Religious Studies: Examining the Architecture of the Academy* (pp. 127–135). Sheffield: Equinox Publishers.

Tong, M Adryael. 2019. "Categorization and its Discontents." In Leslie Dorrough Smith (ed.), *Constructing "Data" in Religious Studies: Examining the Architecture of the Academy* (pp. 38–47). Sheffield: Equinox Publishers.

Touna, Vaia. 2017. *Fabrications of the Greek Past: Religion, Tradition, and the Making of Modern Identities*. Leiden: Brill.

Touna, Vaia. 2019. "Scholars and the Framing of Objects." In Leslie Dorrough Smith (ed.), *Constructing "Data" in Religious Studies: Examining the Architecture of the Academy* (pp. 175–182). Sheffield: Equinox Publishers.

Wolfart, Johannes C. Forthcoming. "'Religious Literacy': Some Considerations and Reservations." *Method & Theory in the Study of Religion*.

Chapter 7

The Vocation of a Scientist of Religion

D. Jamil Grimes

> [A] variety of roles [beyond historian or scholar of religion] are available: some perfectly respectable (amanuensis, collector, friend and advocate), and some less appealing (cheerleader, voyeur, retailer of import goods). None, however, should be confused with scholarship."
> —Bruce Lincoln, "Theses on Method" (1996)

By the evening of October 26, 2020, those who usually would not have noticed a US Supreme Court confirmation had been given several reasons to do so. Amy Coney Barrett was highlighted for being only the fifth woman to serve in the high court's long history, for being an evangelical Catholic with religious affiliations (i.e., People of Praise) some found curious, and for being an ardently avowed originalist. The last attribute—especially Barrett's rhetoric around it—evoked the memory of another judge, the late Antonin Scalia. Barrett pledged to interpret the law according to the meaning of enacted texts and *not according to the desire for certain social or political outcomes*. On the evening of her confirmation, Barrett's remarks were brief, but she did not fail to address this distinction and to describe the latter kind of interpretation as a "dereliction of duty" (Barrett 2020). Scalia would have certainly approved. He routinely lambasted judges who disregard a text's meaning by imposing one they prefer. And he likened this to the "disreputable" practice of scriptural *eisegesis*, a comparison that I, a biblical scholar by training, cannot help but note (Scalia and Garner 2012). Elsewhere, in words Barrett would undoubtedly apply to herself, Scalia described judicial restraint as the primary distinction for the vocation of a judge: "The good judge must suppress [her] personal views and must decide each case as the law dictates, not as [she] would have resolved the matter if [she] would have drafted the law or constitutional provision at issue" (Scalia 2017: 282).

Why this anecdote about Barrett and Scalia, about judgeship and jurisprudence? I admit my deep interest in legal matters, but, more than this, I also see a parallel between the sort of vocational understandings that have long divided public and professional opinions about judges and those that divide the field of religious studies. To put it simply, there are many who ultimately want judges to be—who believe that *to be a judge is to be*—a force for implementing desirable outcomes, and the meaning of legal texts should be subordinated to this higher pursuit. Likewise, there are those who ultimately want scholars of religion, even ones purportedly scientific and non-theological, to be a force for certain social and political values, e.g., gender equality, anti-racism, anti-militancy, environmentalism, etc. (A related issue is that religion—if only the light of its true purpose is allowed to shine undimmed—is *expected* to facilitate moral transformations and, as Jonathan Culler says of one approach to literature, is treated "as an aesthetic object that could make us 'better people'"; Culler 2000: 37) In this higher pursuit, any meaning of religion(s) as described, analyzed, explained, or otherwise interpreted, is ultimately in service to these goals. That this sentiment is frequently a rule rather than exception is reflected in one of McCutcheon's very important notes where he says there is "no clear definition of what counts as scholarship on religion and thus what ought to be included or excluded from the pages of peer review journals in the field" (Chapter 6, this volume).[1] While methodological questions are also implicated here—something I will return to below—a more fundamental question concerns what it means to be a particular sort of scholar; that is, what it means to be a scientist of religion. This is perhaps a rather abstract and philosophical issue, but wrestling with it supports the demarcations for which McCutcheon appropriately calls. At the very least, *we*, those insist on clear and self-critical definitions, should be adamant about what defines appropriate scholarship and should assess the implications.

At the risk of overstating, I want to clearly voice my belief that a scientist of religion—*qua* scientist—interprets their data to provide empirical explanations. Moreover, their critical engagement in this interpretation is controlled by a deliberate effort to be independent and objective, to resist the potential impact of passionately held social, political, and other morally loaded views on a fair reading of the data. This vocational understanding of a scientist of religion would not permit, as in McCutcheon's given example, a scholar using their status and work to reform a religious community that opposes same-sex interests (Chapter 6, this volume). Nor would it permit, to give an example more resonant with my work, a black scholar either denouncing a black church for not having enough "liberation" in its theology or selectively researching black religiosity in a way that excludes unsavory representatives. To riff on Scalia, who disagreed with a colleague's good-natured opposition to capital punishment, "If [a religious studies scholar has] moral objections to what [a scientific interpretation] requires ... [their] proper course is to resign ... and perhaps lead a revolution" (Scalia 2017: 287). Yet, religious studies scholars regularly allow if not encourage a mode of interpretation that is shaped by their understandable desire to resist homophobia,

---

1. The problem of "what counts as scholarship" is not unique to religious studies. Beyond the legal field, where the similar question of what counts as judging remains quite lively, historians have wrestled with identifying both the proper "tools of the trade" and their uses. Wendie Schneider engages the legal case involving David Irving's Holocaust denial as an interesting and instructive occasion when "historical methodology [was] on trial." What analogous moment has taken place or might take place for religious studies is anyone's guess. But perhaps Schneider's effort demonstrates how moments of acute methodological awareness experienced by those outside of a discipline can be opportunities for those within to articulate and defend a "code of conduct." See Schneider (2001).

overturn patriarchy, or rescue Islam from terrorist associations. Advancing moral revolutions in the seats of the academy raises no vocational contradictions for them. "Seats" and "streets" are blurred by an activism that knows no bounds: not even the hard sciences are untouched (Krauss 2020). That the vogue hyphenation of "scholar-activist" is a feather in one's professional cap rather than a chink in one's scientific armor further illustrates the problem. We need more religious studies scholars who ably articulate a vocational understanding of our scientific profession, one that is governed by objectivity and independence. The need for such an articulation, and for such an articulation to take root in the "younger generation of scholars" McCutcheon repeatedly calls upon, is one of the things that makes histories of religious studies so valuable.

Of course, one might still groan, "Yet another diatribe about the history of religious studies." Like the lukewarm subjects of "method and theory"—or the "scrutiny of a specific scholarly situation and practice" that McCutcheon has elsewhere distinguished properly as "methodology" (McCutcheon 2015: 30–31)— critical disciplinary histories are deemed drudgery. Worse, they get waved off as overzealous investigations that see in almost every present shape a shadow of the past. Yes, many will concede that the occasional history is needed when an authoritative version has become stale, but they will also say that repeated forays into the makings of a field—however dressed up by quixotic battles with Eliadean windmills—are not as productive as they make themselves out to be. In fact, they are counter-productive, because they direct precious time and effort away from doing the *real* work of religious studies: describing, interpreting, explaining, etc. religion.

It is ironic that scholars of religion, many of whom use history to expose for their students the constructed nature of religion and its dependence on material conditions, often discount the value of applying history self-reflexively, as a critical tool for analyzing *themselves* and their *own* work. Especially when prized values like "justice" and "diversity" are at stake, we give short shrift to J. Z. Smith's oft-quoted dictum that "the student of religion ... must be relentlessly self-conscious. Indeed, this self-consciousness constitutes [their] primary expertise, [their] foremost object of study" (Smith 1982: xi). Scholarly identities and practices that are related to popular political positions become shrouded in an aura of self-evidence, not unlike the phenomena of religionists. Because of this, the "irreducible strangeness" of scholars and their work—the contingent *why* of what they study and *how* they study it—is not strange at all but is instead taken for granted (Moore and Sherwood 2011: x). Critical disciplinary histories serve us well as they provoke an otherwise absent curiosity, one that might question the field's dominant "aetiological saga" or the "myth of origin" that "powerfully predetermines its practice" (ibid.: x, 130). Histories are far from inconsequential accounts of the past. Exploring a discipline's history enables us to identify, in the apt language of Sam Gill, its "heritage"—the collection of valued scholarly traditions that are scrupulously authorized, performed, and *handed down* (Gill 1994: 968).

Thinking in terms of heritage is helpful because, as McCutcheon rightly points out, "every new academic generation will bring with it their own long entrenched habits of thought and action concerning what religion is and does" (McCutcheon, Chapter 6, this volume)—along with the more vocational matter of *why and how religion is to be studied*, I add. Professional identity—understanding what it means to be a scientist of religion—is also heritage. As one among this new generation, I benefit immensely from ongoing talks about our discipline's terrain, its evolution and persistent fault lines, particularly the line that *should* divide religious studies from theology. If we take social formation in our discipline seriously, as we should, then it is important to recognize the value of history for new members who would become "one of us." Younger scholars need to gain clarity about their vocational identity and about where they stand in relation to the several kinds of religious studies scholarship. This is all the more pressing if we uphold with McCutcheon that "some of the approaches adopted by our colleagues actually undermine the field" and are not "but one more viable alternative" (ibid.). In an age when hyper-postmodernism explains away bedrock scientific standards like objectivity as *total* illusions and admits—if not encourages—multiple, even contradictory perspectives as equally valid, there is a lot at stake in supporting younger scholars of religion as they search out approaches suitable for a truly scientific discipline. Taking social formation seriously might also remind us that no identity, including scholarly identity, is formed once and for all, but is successfully maintained through repeated reinforcement and adaptation; a success largely involving the stories we tell *over and over again* (McAdams 2019: 4–5). Tradition is for young and old alike. Seasoned scholars, too, need their dose of disciplinary history and a reminder of what it means to be a *scientist* of religion.

With all that being said, what kind of critical exploration of disciplinary history does McCutcheon present to us and how does it fit into my earlier statements about the vocational identity of religious studies scholars? McCutcheon's sobering essay strikes me, most of all, as one that throws scholarly independence and objectivity into doubt. Most scholars see themselves and, by extension, their work as having some degree of independence. Even when academic efforts are overtly political, such efforts are imagined as free, conscious, and deliberate, insofar as said scholars *know* and *choose* the political goals they are advancing. Perceived independence does indeed vary according to, not least, one's institutional and professional context, with some academics being more limited in their ability to determine research and/or teaching objectives, a circumstance to which I will return later. Still, the most constrained of religious studies scholars would stop short of considering the possibility that their work was not simply critically deficient but also unwittingly complicit in an international political movement. McCutcheon's essay is a push to make this very consideration.

This is one of the sharpest points, I think, of McCutcheon's argument—another biting critique, I appreciatively note, in his career as disciplinary gadfly. I worry, though, that some will miss the forest for the trees by focusing on the several instances of "pre-critical notions of religion"—ahistorical, metaphysical, essentialist, etc.—cited by McCutcheon (Chapter 6, this volume). What is worth emphasizing over these is his framing of the connection between the popular goal of religious literacy and the seldom questioned "modern political projects" that influence how said literacy is both imagined and implemented; a connection that privileges globalist presuppositions, such as an "undefined notion of civil society" and interreligious cooperation (ibid.). It is not simply that religious studies remains tormented by the pre-critical ghosts of figures like Eliade and that the scholars presently possessed by such ghosts echo—in sometimes novel but fundamentally unchanged reverberations—otherworldly descriptions of religion. These understandings of religion are subordinate to larger, more looming interests. "If anything has changed at all, over this time," writes McCutcheon, "it is perhaps the political causes supported by the same old devices" (ibid.). The oversimplifications of religion that served colonialism before serve globalism today.

Because globalism, like any other frequently and popularly used term, can easily dissolve into a semantic haziness, with everyone and yet no one knowing precisely what is meant, let's agree on a basic definition. Perhaps most would follow the *Oxford* explanation that globalism means a way of thinking and being that stresses the "dense interconnections and interdependencies that tie nations together," connections that have serious implications for, not least, political and economic success. Accordingly, globalism has at its core an interest in subordinating local differences, especially where said differences would result in conflict rather than pro-social behavior, particularly for the sake of cooperation across boundaries. That we live in a global world, increasingly linked by a proliferating internet and by worldwide threats like global warming—and, more recently, COVID-19—seems so obvious that the temptation is to unquestioningly accept both this and *whatever might be premised* on a "One Earth" point-of-view. "As globalization becomes institutionalized as a program not only in the academy but in corporate policy, politics, and popular culture," says Anna Tsing, we neglect to ask what "projects of globalization *do* in the world—and what else goes on with and around them" (Tsing 2000: 329). This additional step of inquiry is all the more necessary because, again, scrutinizing presuppositions—here the romantic sentiments of globalism or what Tsing describes as its "charisma" (ibid.)—is much harder when we associate such presuppositions with a better, morally preferable world. McCutcheon's prodding of religious literacy shows that globalism, like any other political project, comes with costs and pressures that challenge our work as critical scholars and *scientists* of religion. And scientists are not immune to charisma.

Of course, with religious literacy and the associated tolerance being such unquestionable goods, many might ask why we should problematize religious literacy by considering its political influences. To put it another way, why should we fuss about the science of religion and its professionals being influenced by socio-political values that are so obviously good? After all, who would question living in a world with greater understanding and peaceful acceptance of religious differences? By itself this might be a worthwhile reality, but the fact that religious literacy and tolerance are rarely, if ever, worked out apart from the governmental and commercial environments in which they exist, makes the matter more complicated and ought to make religious studies scholars more wary. Historical attention to the politics of religious literacy and tolerance shows that these common aspirations, a part of which is being able "to properly distinguish a Sikh from a Muslim from a Hindu from a Jain from a ..." (McCutcheon, Chapter 6, this volume) have routinely been politicized. Religious liberty, a cognate of religious tolerance, has, since its earliest incarnations, been driven by numerous interests, especially those that are religious, economic, and political, and this includes the interests of government officials in "their political survival (i.e., ability to get reelected or stave off a coup), the need to raise government revenue, and the ability to grow the economy" (Gill 2008: 7–9). Religious tolerance is similarly complicated. Historians have traced its formulation during the Enlightenment and troubled the view of tolerance as something primarily prized for its distinct moral rightness. Sylvana Tomaselli, for instance, shows tolerance was not always or even most often advocated as "a good in itself" or "because it would make [individuals] better human beings," but rather for the sake of civil stability and commercial prosperity (Tomaselli 2000: 86). Whatever lofty ideals of civic virtue might be present, it is often the case that the drivers of religious tolerance, literacy, etc. are far baser and more pecuniary. Civic virtues regarding religion are likely to be subsumed by the larger interests of national governments, global corporations, etc.

These voices and still others, along with McCutcheon, should stir us to ask how religious literacy and tolerance today exist in a network or constellation of interests, several of which see less critical understandings of religion as easily worth the cost of their satisfaction. So, before we eagerly enlist as scientists of religion in the service of some greater good, should we not ask, "For what parties is it desirable that Sikhs, Muslims, and so forth be able to appreciate and presumably tolerate their religious differences? What is at stake for these parties? How do they seek to achieve this and what is our relation to that effort? *What kind of researching and teaching about religion accompanies such a goal?*" Asking these and other such questions might expose the impetus behind and blind spots regarding pre-critical notions of religions. For instance, it might drive us to interrogate essentialist understanding of world religions based on some common denominator, an ethical ideal like the "Golden Rule" or Suzanne Owen's "peace and harmony" (Owen 2011: 263). Globalist markets might eagerly employ these ideals in the effort to maximize cooperation among diverse workforces and to encourage commercial relationships, both items of premium value in a globalist framework.

Again, all of this should sober our understanding of how scientific objectivity and independence are indeed challenged. But, lest I be seen as naïve, let me be clear: I would not suggest that we jettison religious literacy and other such discourses. I do not think we can or must. First, and I take courage here from McCutcheon's pragmatism, ditching these discourses—even for noble scientific aims—simply is not practical for most of us. McCutcheon's many examples show that there are religious studies departments, programs, and faculty whose work is in no small part legitimated on a basis that is very much associated with the sort of globalist political interests mentioned above. I hazard to suspect that a primary value of religious studies at many educational institutions is not its theoretical or explanatory power as a scientific discipline. Religious studies is rarely treasured because, as Hans Penner said, it "removes something puzzling, indicates causes, or supplies reasons" about or for religion as a *natural phenomenon*. Rather, ever-present if not explicit, there are hopeful expectations that parallel those associated with religious education in the UK—with which, on this matter, we ought to be more in conversation. These expectations concern increasing religious and cultural appreciation of others as well as learning from the presumed ethical wisdom—humanistically translated or secularized, if necessary—of different religions. Like religious education across the pond, religious studies in America is often a "huge over-filled bucket," weighed down by concerns quite remote from those we profess at NAASR (Lawson 2018: 33).

My own colleagues, Jenna Gray-Hildenbrand and Rebekka King, have recently demonstrated an effort to work productively with the challenges to scholarly independence, and they highlight the tension between speaking the "language" of institutional stakeholders, among others, while also trying to retain the critical dimension of our discipline. The authors indicate the practical necessity to achieve "alignment," which is an "essential" integration of demands associated with students, institution, profession, and discipline into "program goals, structure, and competencies" (Gray-Hildenbrand and King 2019: 192, 194). Importantly, this alignment reflects both the accountability of religious studies to a multitude of stakeholders—where a scientific discipline and its standards are easily overwhelmed—and a commitment to "holistic education" (ibid.). It is worth asking if the accountability and legitimacy of disciplines like physics and other natural sciences involves any commitment to holistic education: to shaping "civically engaged and globally responsible citizens" and "creat[ing] opportunities for cross-cultural interactions which have been demonstrated to contribute to self-confidence, motivation, cultural awareness, and *an appreciation of equality for all*" (ibid.). Or is this a special burden for religious studies and disciplines associated with the liberal arts and humanities? Burden or bane, many religious studies scholars serve at the behest of very interested stakeholders not objective scientists.

Beyond the sheer impracticality of jettisoning religious literacy, there is the possibility of engaging these discourses more on our terms. When McCutcheon bemoans "see[ing] little if any critical analysis of the links between these projects and claims that it somehow enhances some untheorized notion of civility" (Chapter 6, this volume), it seems that he stops short of calling for a complete moratorium. Rather than saying that any discourse associated with globalism or another political project is anathema, McCutcheon calls attention to how our present relation to religious literacy—which privileges religion as a "beneficial ... force in human affairs" and a "socio-politically autonomous force" conditioned but not finally dependent on history (ibid.)—undermines critical principles in our approach to the academic study of religion. We can interrogate these ideas, and perhaps subvert them, even as we engage them in our courses.

McCutcheon himself speaks to this when he mentions that Steve Ramey's teaching of world religions, a subject typically fraught with problematic paradigms and categories, "ultimately problematizes the idea and the course itself for his students" (Chapter 6, this volume). We can turn to this greater scrutiny instead of what some might say is a more appropriate level of resignation before such powerful globalist interests, including those espoused by our own well-intentioned institutions. However, to be more critical and questioning requires that we more fully count the costs of what it might take "to establish an institutional space where such work is excluded" (ibid.). The risks enumerated by McCutcheon challenge us to anticipate confrontations with scholars and institutional forces, and the latter deserve special attention because it turns out that globalism is not simply embodied by fellow scholars and researchers. Scrutiny of world religions, religious literacy and tolerance, and other problematic topics within our discipline is likely to stress an already tense relationship with the educational institutions many of us call home.

Perhaps McCutcheon would agree that the adoption of religious literacy as a "thematic engine" (Chapter 6, this volume) by religious studies departments and programs is likely often a result of both internal and external pressures. Sure, many scholars of religion sincerely believe in religious literacy and would advocate for it before administrators. This is unnecessary, however, when university and colleges themselves have incorporated notions of global citizenship and tolerance of diversity into their mission statements. I fear that, because of insufficient legitimacy on scientific grounds, religious studies must reckon with the fact that advancing religious literacy, religious tolerance, civil society, etc. is just how we have sold ourselves. Casting doubt on these discourses will likely involve renegotiating the basis on which we are justified; *A basis that never took seriously our vocation as scientists.* This is unsurprising given that the public understanding of the scientist of religion is no better than the public understanding of religion. But such a renegotiation would be no small task. Faustian pacts are not easily broken. And it is likely that, because this is not easily remedied, the need for a fuller and less burdened scientific study of religion will be best met by *alternate* institutional spaces, which might function like harbors and harbingers. In many scholarly situations, this will be outside of the universities and colleges where we belong. The very organization of NAASR comes immediately to mind.

That there are so many pressures, driving and shaping how we both imagine and implement our work as scientists of religion, and that these pressures can be as obscure as they are large should make us more vigilant and questioning. It is in this spirit that I want to use the rest of my response to explore—beyond religious literacy, tolerance, etc.—an additional and enduring political influence centered in one sub-field of the study of religion. My experience as a scholar of black religious studies (sometimes called African American religious studies or, in a time of increasing attention to diasporic communities, Africana religious studies) has demonstrated that a certain kind of progressive racial politics predominates scholarship. I illustrate what this means exactly in more detail below by briefly exploring an often overlooked layer in the history of religious studies.

Histories of religious studies are often limited by their broad brush strokes. As a result, the distinctive trajectories and genealogical nuances of sub-fields within the larger discipline are omitted. Historical observations about the field of religious studies, like those offered by McCutcheon, usually emphasize the role and legacy of nineteenth century European colonialism. They do so deservedly. A result of this legitimate focus, however, can be a truncation of the historical narrative that elides events that are important for the trajectories of particular areas. (Even some histories of the study of religion that are narrower in their purview do not include how the study of black religion underwent major shifts within the context of the racial politics of the 1960s; see Alles 2010: 39–55.) I agree with Robert Orsi's statement "that scholarship in *any area of religious studies* must be alert to its genealogy, to the history of the making of its terminology, to the cultural and religious values inscribed in its account of the past, and to the broader social and political context of its judgments" (Orsi 2012: 2–3, emphasis added).

I want to be clear before I proceed, however. My examination of how racial politics has affected the study of religion is an *expansion on* and not digression from McCutcheon's argument that religious studies has become an instrument of modern political projects. The progressive racial politics that, in an American context at least, has a very long lineage, is of a piece with the globalist insistence on cultural literacy, appreciation of diversity, and tolerance of difference. Globalism has as a goal—superficially if not substantively—an easing of both religious tensions and racial tensions. If there might be any doubt about how progressive racial politics, in the form of, let us say, anti-racism discourse, racial justice activism, and indigenous rights, is a global phenomenon, then that should be put to rest by considering the many varied and widespread international political responses to recent instances of police brutality in the US. Progressive racial politics, like religious literacy, is yet one more feature of the globalist landscape that religious studies must carefully navigate. And like religious literacy, progressive racial politics influence scholars to teach about religion in uncritical ways.

Attention to black religious studies requires looking closely at America's historical and contemporary racial struggle. Over the course of this struggle, black religion has functioned as a contested discursive site, a subject of heated discussion and debate insofar as black religion was a proxy for black (in)humanity. Condemnations of black religion as primitive, superstitious, and irrational supported similar conclusions about the inherent—and, relative to whites, inferior—nature of black people. Conversely, positive appreciations of black religion as deeply moralistic, authentically Christian, or politically progressive have encouraged better appraisals of African Americans. A central thought of the latter appraisal has been that winning the case of black humanity in the court of public opinion, in which black religion was exhibit "A," was prerequisite to more favorable treatment under the law and greater acceptance in society. Curtis J. Evans insightfully says that black religion "groaned under the burden of a multiplicity of interpreters' demands ranging from uplift of the race to bringing an ambiguous quality of 'spiritual softness' to a materialistic and racist white culture" (Evans 2008: 5). This burden has complicated engagements with faulty categories and dichotomies, like the "slave religion" of the antebellum south, the "black cults" of the twentieth century urban north, and the never-ending battle of "prophetic-vs-pietistic" traditions largely spurred by the influence of liberation theology.

What this has meant for many scholars of black religion is a loss of greater intellectual freedom and scientific objectivity, insofar as research questions have been driven by overriding concerns about how black religion assists or hinders the representation of African Americans, as well as their push for better treatment in a racially troubled society. Even when a line of inquiry, such as the anthropological question about the survival of African traditions among American descendants seems scientific, it in fact remains weighed down by racial interests. In the dispute between Merville J. Herskovits and E. Franklin Frazier, in which the preceding question was at issue, answering this question—at least for Frazier, the black scholar—is intimately connected with the "project of exposing the *social* [rather than biological] causes of 'deviant' behaviors among African-descended people in the United States" (Diakité and Hucks 2013: 32). Dianne Stewart Diakité and Tracey Hucks further explain Franzier's desire to prove, "The Negro's Africanness could not be blamed for her deviancy because there was no influential African heritage left to blame" (ibid.). Franzier went looking to disprove African survivals because he wanted to exonerate African Americans from some kind of transmitted inferior essence. While the details have shifted, today's black religious scholarship remains deeply enmeshed in the larger issue of racial injustice. As a result, teaching and research about black religion often focuses on black religion insofar as one form or another is seen as politically activist or revolutionary vis-à-vis oppression. A recent and supposedly "critical" black studies volume has as its singular contribution on religion a theological diatribe against the "silence" of the black church "in the face of certain injustices, especially ... police brutality" (Wiggins 2017: 189). For such a judgment to pass as scholarship is not exceptional but continuous with trends established decades ago.

When religious studies was being bolstered in the mid-twentieth century, particularly by the *Abington School District v. Schempp* judicial decision that upheld teaching about religion in public education, seismic race-related shifts were also occurring. Various expressions of black economic and cultural nationalism became louder, gained greater audiences, and soon displaced the more conservative wing of the civil rights movements. In the late 1960s, a younger generation of black students challenged the values and principles of higher education institutions. They demanded learning experiences that were race-conscious; that appreciated the cultural heritage of African Americans and concretely targeted the oppressive conditions in which so many of them lived. In 1968, San Francisco State was one of the first of several American colleges and universities to create a black studies program (Ferguson 2015: 21–29). Shortly thereafter, the 1969 publication of James Cone's *Black Theology and Black Power* was a product of this evolution vis-à-vis the discipline of theology. Although Cone was far from the only factor in the historical development of black theology as an academic discipline, he had a powerful influence on black religious scholarship (Gonzalez 2014: 54). In the racially turbulent period of the mid-twentieth century, as religious studies generally was gaining its footing as an academic discipline within public higher education, black religious studies was experiencing its own formative developments, as impacted by the advances of black studies and black theology. The legacy of these advances is frequently and clearly discernible in the discourse of black religious scholarship then and now. When Gayraud Wilmore, a leading figure in black theology, arranged an anthology, a volume in which historians and sociologists of religion like Charles H. Long and Hans A. Baer are featured, he stated the purpose for black religious studies as "authenticating and enriching personal faith and preparing both clergy and laity for a ministry in the Black Church and community ... in behalf of God's mission of liberation for all people" (Wilmore 1989: xiii). That Wilmore could arrive at such a purpose is understandable once you have noted his earlier rejection of "the epistemological split that often characterizes much of what is called religious studies in the prestigious white theological schools and university departments of religion," a rejection he bases on the very *nature* of black religion (ibid.: 12)—which makes, I suppose, an oxymoron out of "scientist of black religions." Black religious scholarship, Wilmore continues, is "'believing scholarship,'" not "a dispassionate, armchair science of religion" (ibid.).

There have been several attempts to correct Wilmore's confessional and Christocentric limitations.[2] Few, however, challenge the notion that black religious studies ought to interrogate its racial politics, even though such politics have been guilty of re-essentializing African Americans, albeit with a more favorable nature. Black religious studies remains at many points seemingly inseparable from concerns about social justice, anti-racism, etc. What I have described is not discordant with Sam Gill's incisive diagnosis that sub-fields are often intentionally sequestered from "the larger discourse of the academic study of religion" and their professionals "study [their own specific area] primarily because it has religious and political importance to their personal religious, racial, ethnic, or gender connection and whose studies are evaluated more on the authority granted by religion, race, gender, or ethnic identity than upon academic performance" (Gill 1994: 973). Gill's criticism is accurate.

All of this is to demonstrate just how fraught is the commitment to scientific independence and objectivity, for the religious studies scholar in general and for certain area specialists in particular. Perhaps readers can see in my own relation to black religious studies that I well understand the desire to employ scholarship for achieving political ends. I know how much can be at stake. It is also my understanding, however, that good science—the kind that exposes faulty essentialism rather than strategically deploying it—depends on objectivity and independence. As McCutcheon points out and as I have further shown, keeping these vocational values is perhaps no easier today than it has been in our field decades ago. In ways, it is harder. But it is worthwhile to try.

---

2. In addition to the above-cited essay by Diakité and Hucks, see also Corel West and Eddie S. Glaude, Jr.'s *African American Religious Thought: An Anthology* (West and Glaude 2003).

D. Jamil Grimes is adjunct instructor of religious studies at Middle Tennessee State University, Murfreesboro, TN. His current research interests include: religious studies methodology, particularly where this concerns the study of black or Africana religions; the construction and use of religio-racial identities by the African Hebrew Israelites of Jerusalem and other twentieth century black religious movements; the comparative study of religion and popular music to situate the former as a cultural production with common rather than sui generis functions; and criticism of the historiographic use of the Bible in public school education, especially in histories of ancient Israel and its religion.

References

Alles, Gregory. 2010. "The Study of Religions: The Last 50 Years." In John Hinnells (ed.), *The Routledge Companion to the Study of Religion*, 2nd edition (pp. 39–55). London: Routledge.

Barrett, Amy Coney. 2020. "Amy Coney Barrett Gives Speech After Supreme Court Confirmation." *NBC News*, October 26. Video, 4:20. Retrieved from www.youtube.com/watch?v=EmbdNtBD8Fg.

Culler, Jonathan. 2000. *Literary Theory: A Very Short Introduction*. Oxford: Oxford University Press.

Diakité, Dianne M. Stewart, and Tracey E. Hucks. 2013. "Africana Religious Studies: Toward a Transdisciplinary Agenda in an Emerging Field." *Journal of Africana Religions* 1(1): 28–77. https://doi.org/10.5325/jafrireli.1.1.0028.

Evans, Curtis J. 2008. *The Burden of Black Religion*. New York: Oxford University Press.

Ferguson II, Stephen C. 2015. *Philosophy of African American Studies: Nothing Left of Blackness*. New York: Palgrave Macmillan.

Gill, Anthony. 2008. *The Political Origins of Religious Liberty*. Cambridge: Cambridge University Press.

Gill, Sam. 1994. "The Academic Study of Religion." *Journal of the American Academy of Religion* 62(4): 965–975.

Gonzalez, Michelle A. 2014. *A Critical Introduction to Religion in the Americas: Bridging the Liberation Theology and Religious Studies Divide*. New York: New York University Press.

Gray-Hildenbrand, Jenna, and Rebekka King. 2019. "Teaching in Contexts: Designing a Competency-based Religious Studies Program." *Teaching Theology and Religion* 22: 191–204.

Krauss, Lawrence. 2020. "The Ideological Corruption of Science." *Wall Street Journal Online*, July 12. Retrieved from www.wsj.com/articles/the-ideological-corruption-of-science-11594572501 (accessed May 2, 2022).

Lawson, Clive A. 2018. "Time to Abandon Religious Education: Ditching an Out-of-Date Solution to an Out-of-Date Problem." In Mike Castelli and Mark Chater (eds), *We Need to Talk about Religious Education: Manifestos for the Future of RE* (pp. 21–35). London: Jessica Kingsley Publishers,

McAdams, Dan P. 2019. "'First we invented stories, then they changed us': The Evolution of Narrative Identity." *Evolutionary Studies in Imaginative Culture* 3(1): 1–18.

McCutcheon, Russell T. 2015. *A Modest Proposal on Method: Essaying the Study of Religion*. Leiden: Brill.

Moore, Stephen D., and Yvonne Sherwood. 2011. *The Invention of the Biblical Scholar: A Critical Manifesto*. Minneapolis, MN: Fortress Press.

Orsi, Robert. 2012. "Introduction." In Robert Orsi (ed.), *The Cambridge Companion to Religious Studies* (pp. 1-13). New York: Cambridge University Press.

Owen, Suzanne. 2011. "The World Religions Paradigm: Time for a Change." *Arts and Humanities in Higher Education* 10(3): 253-268.

Scalia, Antonin. 2017. "The Vocation of a Judge." In Christopher Scalia and Edward Whelan (eds), *Scalia Speaks: Reflections on Law, Faith, and Life Well Lived* (pp. 279-295). New York: The Crown Publishing Group.

Scalia, Antonin, and Bryan Garner. 2012. *Reading Law: An Interpretation of Legal Texts*, Kindle edition. St. Paul, MN: Thomson West.

Schneider, Wendie Ellen. 2001. "Past Imperfect." *Yale Law Journal* 110(8): 1531-1545.

Smith, Jonathan Z. 1982. *Imagining Religion: From Babylon to Jonestown*. Chicago, IL: University of Chicago Press.

Tomaselli, Sylvana. 2000. "Intolerance, the Virtue of Princes and Radicals." In Ole Peter Grell and Roy Porter (eds), *Toleration in Enlightenment Europe* (pp. 86-101). Cambridge: Cambridge University Press.

Tsing, Anna. 2000. "The Global Situation." *Cultural Anthropology* 15(3): 327-360.

West, Cornel and Eddie S. Glaude Jr. 2003. *African American Religious Thought: An Anthology*. Louisville, KY: Westminster John Knox Press.

Wiggins, Linda A. 2017. "When the Church Sins: The Violence of Silence." *Critical Black Studies Reader*, edited by Rochelle Brock et al., 189-196. New York: Peter Lang.

Wilmore, Gayraud. 1989. *African American Religious Studies: An Interdisciplinary Anthology*. Durham, NC: Duke University Press.

Chapter 8

Historicizing Endurance

Andrew Durdin

For a chapter notionally intended to set the tone for a discussion on the "History of the Field," Russell McCutcheon's piece (Chapter 6, this volume) actually has little to say about history and doesn't reflect much on the past. This is not an oversight on McCutcheon's part, but by design. In a brief sentence at the end of his introductory remarks, he states quite explicitly, "as should by now be clear, despite the title of this part of the book, this chapter is *not* about the past at all. (But, come to think of it, *when is the past ever about the past?*)." Both emphases in this sentence are McCutcheon's and both are worth pausing on for a moment. First, McCutcheon is emphatic that his essay is not a discussion of the "History of the Field" based on usual assumptions and expectations readers might bring to the table: that is, his paper does not engage in an imaginative reconstruction of any particular past moment from the history of the study of religion nor does he reflect on a certain past moment's implications for how contemporary scholars of religion do their work. As McCutcheon notes in his opening paragraph, he has done this elsewhere. Rather, McCutcheon's essay resolutely pursues an analysis of the present state of theory and method in religious studies.

However, the second emphasis McCutcheon marks in his parenthetical evokes precisely historiographic issues. Indeed, I take this qualifying remark as a nod to a presentist position toward the past and the scholarly practice of history.[1] That is, to a position held in some version by a range of scholars (from Hayden White to Roland Barthes to R. G. Collingwood, among others), which argues that historiography is neither a neutral nor disinterested affair of recovering the past. Rather, it is always an effort informed by present concerns at imaginatively inferring, (re)constructing, or (re)creating the vanished past, which is no longer subject to verification on its own terms and for its own sake (to paraphrase Dominick LaCapra). Presentists further insist that since histories are synthetic narratives of imagination constructed by particular historians, they tend to reveal more about the interests of the historians who construct them than they do about a clear, unobstructed vision of the past—especially as based on Leopold von Ranke's famous dictum, *wie es eigentlich gewesen* ("as it actually happened"). At least two methodological implications follow from this position: first, a base line question

---

1. McCutcheon elaborates in more detail on his view of the past and history in McCutcheon (2018: 33–42).

in assessing all histories must be "for whom" and "to whom" a given history is written; and second, historians must become as much a part of the data to be studied as the texts they write.[2]

I emphasize McCutcheon's passing references to the past, and the issues they cue, not simply to highlight how they allow him to shift attention to his own interests, but also because they invite what I think is a particularly revealing way of reading and responding to his essay. Namely, that despite what McCutcheon says, his essay is very much about the past, or at least a certain vision of it. Put another way, if, for McCutcheon, the past is never simply about the past, I would contend that his diagnosis of the contemporary terrain of religious studies isn't *just about the present*. In the brief space I have here for my response, I want to reflect on what I perceive to be the historical and methodological implications of McCutcheon's essay for thinking about the history of the study of religion. In particular, I want to suggest that McCutcheon's framing of his essay around the endurance of the "same old devices" in the contemporary study of religion at once creates a theoretical and methodological position useful for McCutcheon to critique the current academic study of religion while also committing him to a rather specific interpretation of the history of the study of religion. In other words, encoded in McCutcheon's critique of religious studies—"same as it ever was," he says, borrowing from the Talking Heads—is an implicit historical emplotment of the field as well as the proper place of its critic. The thoughts I offer here are admittedly spontaneous, incomplete, and provisional, but they pursue a very specific line of questioning: how can we historicize McCutcheon's claims regarding the endurance of the field's pre-critical past in the present? Noticing historical endurance and repetition is one thing but accounting for them is something else. The latter is what I'm interested in here.

And You May Ask Yourself: "Well, How Did I Get Here?"

In order to answer this question, it's worth getting a sense of the temporal rhythms that frame McCutcheon's larger argument. I begin with McCutcheon's introduction, in which he responds to and redirects criticism that his work has become redundant. McCutcheon devotes his first two and a half pages to expressing his "need" to say something "new" or at least "a little different," not just to expand on matters on which he's already written, but also in hopes of disrupting the views of those critics who "stereotype" and "dismiss" all his work based on partial (mis)readings of his older work. Yet, McCutcheon ultimately leaves aside his "earnest desire" to say something novel, lamenting that there is really nothing new to say since scholars of religion have not really moved on to new issues. Instead, the same "unresolved themes" continue to (re)emerge in the study of religion albeit sublimated into different forms and misrecognized as fresh "critical gains." These so-called gains, McCutcheon argues, remain premised on the

---

2. For a longer discussion of these issues see Clark (2004: 9–28).

same old phenomenological fixtures of previous generations, now with a new veneer. Such a situation leaves McCutcheon "no choice but to use this opportunity to reiterate and thereby reinforce what I have said in the past," with criticisms "offered on previous occasions… being *just as relevant today*, when applied to the work that some consider to be at the field's cutting edge" (all quotes from Chapter 6, this volume).

Put like this, McCutcheon effectively flips the charge of redundancy back onto his critics: it is not he who is redundant, but rather the field of religious studies and the scholars who comprise it. A further implication is that whatever redundancy one might perceive in his oeuvre should not be interpreted as a tired, out-of-touch critical refrain on the category of religion. Instead, McCutcheon's criticisms might be seen as the result of an ongoing and careful analysis of his privileged data set; namely, the academic study of religion itself. Put simply, the field has—over the last century-plus—persistently converged on, solidified around, and returned to a deeply problematic and self-serving set of themes. Much like a romantic symphony's *ideé fixe*, the academic study of religion has been composed of different variations on these persistent themes, and while they might be recapitulated in specific forms, their underlying essentialist and ahistorical logic remains unchanged. Therefore, as an analyst of the field of religious studies, for McCutcheon to say something "new" in this situation, bound as he is to report faithfully on his data set, would only be to "exemplify what are longstanding problems of the field at a site that I have not previously discussed in print" (Chapter 6, this volume). And through engaging the present vogue of religious literacy models, this is precisely what he does, even at the risk of "being redundant" (ibid.).

To be clear, I agree with McCutcheon's lucid characterization of the growing prominence of religious literacy models and his compelling analysis of the political and ideological underpinnings of these models. My point of departure is not with McCutcheon's datum, but the way McCutcheon frames and motivates the importance of his datum around a specific view of the history of the field. For McCutcheon, religious literacy models are constituted as evidence of scholars of religion returning *once again* to the task of enshrining pre-critical notions of religion at the heart of their field of study. However, to say that religious literacy paradigms are simply more of the same in the study of religion, or that they are a recent manifestation of a set recurring themes that have endured for more than a century, is to offer a historiographic (and analytic) model based on some version of the familiar platitude that, at least in the study of religion, history repeats itself. As I read it, the entire punch of McCutcheon's argument in this essay is premised on the claim that the underlying theoretical and methodological problems of the contemporary field of religious studies are *essentially* and *actually* the same as they were in the past, only now rebranded as new, different, and exciting critical gains. In other words, McCutcheon's historiographic framing in this paper is not operating simply, as one historian puts it, on the "silent preface: (this incident/ phenomenon/pattern makes it seem as though) nothing has changed," but on the conviction that at a fundamental and demonstrable historical level, the study of religion hasn't changed (Reed 2018: 105).

I tend to be suspicious of notions that ideas, concepts, themes, narratives, traditions or even larger ideational entities like mentalities, epistemes, and paradigms are self-sustaining and unproblematically replicate themselves across time and space. To assume such about intellectual contrivances presumes a certain philosophical idealism that underlies an old (and now discredited) view of the "history of ideas" where psychic units float across time and in and out of certain moments but are ultimately unencumbered by, and bear no necessary attachment to, a specific moment's social and material circumstances. Rather, I would judge—in keeping with a presentist historiographic view—that perceived patterns of historical endurance and recurrence are generated through specific historiographic practices, not found *in situ* in the historical record, and further, that those who perceive such things, whether as self-proclaimed inheritors of said ideas or as critics or observers of these ideas, are making a claim about the historical record rather than simply noting a fact of it. And, as always, such claims have certain interests at stake.

McCutcheon's rendering of the field's enduring past is undoubtedly idealist. He sees scholars' stubborn reliance on pre-critical ideas of religion in their work as the main point of continuity that persistently cycles through and threads together various moments of the field, and thus provides a backdrop for his present articulation of religious literacy as distilling past problems of theory and method. McCutcheon defines the pre-critical notion of religion as "a socio-politically autonomous force that is merely 'shaped' by history while 'manifesting' itself (or its various 'dimensions') in a variety of discrete locales" (Chapter 6, this volume). It's this perpetual and underlying conception that, for McCutcheon, is shared by a motley crew of scholars, across different times and places regardless of different social and material factors. While McCutcheon is not particularly clear about his chronology and what he means by the past ("then") or present ("now"), he nonetheless sees those producing "much older work" from "decades ago" and even "the past 150 years" (ibid.) (so perhaps the usual suspects like Mircea Eliade and Friedrich Max-Mueller?) and those producing work now (he foregrounds Stephen Prothero and Diana Eck in his discussion of religious literacy), who see themselves (wrongly for McCutcheon) as having moved on from earlier outdated modes of analysis to more critical and self-conscious modes, as implicated in fundamentally the same set of problems, regardless of their specific of context. Thus, what seems to define the history of the study of religion for McCutcheon is the continuity through time and space of an "essentialist impulse" (to borrow Leslie Dorrough Smith's phrase, cited by McCutcheon) that persists as an irresistible force impervious to changing social, cultural, and institutional factors. For McCutcheon, the perennial desire to continue to "bedazzle" old phenomenological approaches is itself simply a given here. In other words, the perseverance of a pre-critical impulse, disposed to essentialism, is itself essentialized in McCutcheon's rendering of an enduring past and operates in ahistorical terms as a causal agent: i.e., scholars persistently adopt sui generis notions of religion, build theories of religion based on these, and ignore critical insights *because of* this perennial impulse. Indeed, when McCutcheon comments that "[i]f anything has changed at all, over this time, it is perhaps the political causes supported by the same old devices" (Chapter 6, this volume), I read him as marking a dynamic between the constant "devices" set against the variable "political causes." Yet, as I'll argue below, this obdurate disposition and its intellectual expressions are themselves in need of further historical explanation.

A Little Ditty about the Futility of Criticism

Admittedly, my considerations so far might seem odd to anyone familiar with McCutcheon's work. Indeed, some version of "historicizing" is a veritable watchword across McCutcheon's writings, and a term which I have understood in his work to signify a method devoted to upending more providential accounts in/of our field. So, it might be worth asking: given McCutcheon's long-held commitment to historicization, what is he up to here in situating the broader impact of his detailed analysis of religious literacy models within an ahistorical narrative of recurrence and endurance?[3] At least one way of answering this question is to take a closer look at the sort of narrative McCutcheon coordinates by invoking such a vision of religious studies' enduring past. As McCutcheon has noted elsewhere, scholars now live in a "post-Hayden White world of historiography" (McCutcheon 2018: 36), so it might repay analysis to explore the aesthetic, explanatory, moral, and even ideological dimensions of McCutcheon's implicit historical narrative within his essay.

I'm not really intent on pursuing this issue in any length here but, in brief, I do think that reading McCutcheon's emplotment of the field's enduring past in conjunction with his concluding exhortation to "young scholars" regarding his hopes and fears for its future sets into relief a particular kind of narrative with particular ideological emphases. Specifically, McCutcheon's concern for the future of the field adds a tragic dimension of potential loss to his otherwise comedic narrative of the endurance of religious studies' pre-critical past. Set against the endurance of pre-critical notions of religion, McCutcheon contrasts legitimate "critical gains" over the last two generations: i.e., moments of meaningful disruption to enduring and chameleonic pre-critical conceptions of religion. Yet, on McCutcheon's telling, it would be a mistake to see these critical interventions as having effected some fundamental change in the study of religion—nor should

---

3. In raising these critical comments, I anticipate at least one kind of response: namely, various recommendations for further reading that point me elsewhere within McCutcheon's oeuvre to examples of his longstanding concern with historicization, denaturalization, and unsettling taken-for-granted conceptions. I'd read all such recommendations with great interest and I'm open to being persuaded that my critical remarks may not be relevant beyond this single essay. However, none of this is necessarily helpful in explaining why McCutcheon chose this particular framing in this particular essay in order to motivate the broader impact of his chosen exemplar. In fact, it would increase the need for an explanation! If McCutcheon is diligently historical at other points in his work, why the lapse into ahistoricism here? It's worth pointing out that McCutcheon has made a similar sort of argument in McCutcheon (2014).

they be expected to. For McCutcheon, these "historically contingent" spaces of critique can never be "widely influential, let alone permanent" (Chapter 6, this volume). And indeed, without proper custodianship and maintenance by the up-and-coming generation of critically minded scholars, these precarious and provisional openings ("hard won" by McCutcheon's and a previous generation) will not only be necessarily and inevitably swallowed up into the pre-critical status quo, but they will also likely become new disguises for pre-critical notions of religion to hide in plain sight.

McCutcheon's narrative of the field's past, present, and potential future is likely a familiar one to those committed to "critical theory" and its accompanying vision of society. On this vision, themes of power, domination, and exploitation (as well as a variety of other "dark" theoretical themes) are taken as the fundamental structural components of the social order, and by excavating beneath the surface of quotidian social relations, these components can be revealed as operating at all levels of human subjectivity, practice, and interaction (see Ortner 2016). Further, insofar as these components are ubiquitous and comprise a totalizing system with no "outside," it follows that there are also no obvious avenues of meaningful resistance. Thus, would-be challenges to these pervasive mechanisms of power must start from an inherent position of begrudging acquiescence, accepting that any incursion against the status quo will be trivial and temporary and will likely fail. Such skirmishes are not only futile in terms of effecting structural social change, but Power—in addition to employing coercive violence to crush resistance—also more subtly reverses and redeploys forms of resistance back into fortifying its hegemonic status. As one anthropologist sums it up: critical theory has made "power and domination so fundamental to the very nature of social reality that it became impossible to imagine a world without it" (Graeber 2001: 30).[4] If the Talking Heads lyric "same as it ever was" sums up McCutcheon's temporal view of the history of the study of religion, I would suggest adding a further ideological emphasis neatly summarized by John Mellencamp's famous line: "I fight authority, authority always wins."

Though critical theory surely has value, it may not be particularly useful as the framework for a pep talk intended to marshal young scholars of religion to take

---

4. In general, I find compelling David Graeber's comments on the class dynamics informing the theorizing of those academics variously called critical theorists, postmodernists, poststructuralists, etc.: "[P]ost-structural theory—particularly as enshrined in what might be termed the 'vulgar Foucauldianism' that came to dominate so many ostensibly oppositional academic disciplines at the time [1980s and 1990s]—came to enshrine the particular class experiences of the professional-managerial class as universal truths: that is, a world of networks and networking, where games of power create social reality itself, all truth-claims are merely stratagems, and where mechanisms of physical coercion are made to seem irrelevant (even as they became ever more omnipresent) because all the real action is assumed to take place within techniques of self-discipline, forms of performance, and an endless variety of dispersed and decentered flows of influence. As a description of academic life, or for that matter professional life in general, such descriptions are often spot on. But it's not what life is like for most people on earth and never has been" (Graeber 2014: 80).

up a principled stance in defense of the critical study of religion. In the service of McCutcheon's narrative, the field's enduring past set against his aspirations for the future actually paints an indelibly bleak and jaundiced view of things. Insofar as McCutcheon's historical imaginary in this essay conforms to the social model above, it offers no good reason—other than principle alone—for young scholars (or anyone else really) to pursue the work of the critical study of religion. And I'm not convinced, given the larger academic structures in which early career scholars work, that principle is sufficiently inspiring.

Historicizing Endurance: The Case of the World Religions Paradigm

Yet, as I said, I'm not interested in pursuing this line of inquiry (at least not here). I think there is a more constructive way to engage McCutcheon's argument over and above the internal discursive dynamics of his essay. That is, if we take McCutcheon's view of historical endurance at face value, then it's worth asking why—over the course of about 150 years—have scholars returned to and reinvented *ad nauseum* such pre-critical devices? That scholars do return to such pre-critical notions of religion is clear enough from McCutcheon's argument in this volume (and arguments he has made elsewhere).[5] But why scholars do this, and continue to do so, especially given the plethora of critical scholarship on the category of religion, is not clear. And it's not just McCutcheon that has noticed the trend of an enduring essentialist impulse. As he points out, several other critically minded scholars of religion have also highlighted and expressed "anger and frustration" (Craig Martin) at "a widespread, uninterrogated, essentialist impulse still remaining in the research" (Leslie Dorrough Smith) where scholars "shrug their shoulders" (Naomi Goldenberg) and "ignore and dismiss or minimize" (Matthew Baldwin) approaches that problematize the category of religion. I would observe further that in recent critical scholarship it is has become fairly common procedure to unmask and expose the various machinations of this operative impulse. In practice this has amounted to an exercise in tallying and cataloguing not just the various ingenuities of uncritical scholars of religion in disarming critical approaches, but also those who adopt such approaches but are not judged critical enough; that is, those who affirm the critical study of religion but nevertheless are seen as sidestepping the full brunt of critical approaches as they reinvent and

---

5. See Arnal and McCutcheon (2013). But see especially McCutcheon (2014), where he makes a similar argument to what he writes here in his introductory essay titled "Introduction: Plus ça Change ..." McCutcheon's criticism is directed specifically against "material" or "embodied" approaches to religion. For McCutcheon, these approaches, like religious literacy approaches, rebrand what is essentially an old Eliadian phenomenology. Yet, McCutcheon also goes back even further to Ernest Troeltsch's "The Dogmatics of the 'Religionsgeschichtliche Schule,'" arguing that Troeltsch's liberal Protestant pluralism, which insulates a singular (Christian) core of religious experience against historically varied religions, is still "the overwhelmingly dominant preoccupation of scholarship on religion" (ibid.: 15).

redeploy sui generis ideas of religion in new forms.[6] Yet, how might one explain this persistence of a compulsive commitment to such essentialist notions among scholars? What are the specific historical circumstances—social, cultural, economic, and institutional—that might explain, at different times and places, and in different contexts, the formation of such an essentialist impulse, one that subtends and continues to make appealing to scholars of religion sui generis ideas of religion and phenomenological approaches? Rather than simply seeing it in various manifestations and forms *alongside* different social, cultural, and institutional contexts, how can we explain its production and reproduction as itself an effect of different social, material, and institutional contexts?

Elsewhere, McCutcheon and William Arnal make a similar point to what I'm getting at here, but about the category of religion, namely that:

> the *invention or manufacture of religion* is not something that happened one day in the 1600s (or 1300s, or 1500s, or 1700s), and that forever haunts us. The tradition of all the dead generations may indeed weigh like a nightmare on the brain of the living, but in this case, the living are complicit. Religion is manufactured over and over again in the modern and even postmodern West... [T]he sociopolitical functions of creating and defining the category of "religion" are continually active. The demarcation and segregation of religion are not merely relics inherited from the past.
>
> (Arnal and McCutcheon 2013: 57)

In posing my interest in historicizing the dogged recurrence of an essentialist impulse, I'm similarly asking after those persons, practices, intuitions, and attendant interests that were "complicit" in particular times and places across what we call the "history" of the field in constructing and normalizing forms of essentializing at the root of much theorizing in the study of religion. In a recent introductory essay critiquing "material" approaches to religion, McCutcheon argues, as he does here, that this purportedly novel form of method is underwritten by a tired phenomenological theory that sees material artifacts as simply "physical expressions" of an "animating faith" that "is not itself an historical, social, material artifact but is, instead, already there, simply needing external reminders,

---

6. I take this unmasking procedure to be one of animating premises of Arnal and McCutcheon (2013). Craig Martin has also written in a similar vein noting how a handful of recent books "incorporate recent poststructuralist criticisms of the field of religious studies, but, simultaneously, their work walks back away from the radical poststructuralist conclusions" (Martin 2017: 317). While I have my own issues with the books Martin reviews, I ended up with the impression that Martin's main problem was not that the authors weren't being critical, but that they weren't being critical in a very specific and narrow poststructuralist manner that Martin prefers. In the same essay, Martin says: [R]eligious studies is nevertheless perpetually afflicted with new, more sophisticated forms of perennialism under different guises—perennialism is, I would argue, the perennial philosophy of religious studies" (ibid.: 318). And this is my point. If phenomenological perennialism is the perennial problem of the study of religion, so much so that critical scholars of religion *perennially* return to it in order to expose its essentialist and ahistorical logic, then perhaps it's worth discussing more concertedly the various historical conditions under which it continues to be a problem.

public venues for its expression" (McCutcheon 2014: 13). Yet, for my money, critical scholars often mirror this dynamic in returning to and thematizing the field's essentialism and ahistoricism with no (or at least few) concrete discussions of the social and material circumstances that animate these essentialist commitments at various times and places. When McCutcheon writes in Chapter 6 of this volume, "If anything has changed at all, over this time, it is perhaps the political causes supported by the same old devices," I would modify the sentiment so it's expressed not as a conjunction of shifting political realities set against the "same old devices" but rather a question posed as: how have shifting material and sociological factors at different historical moments generated, hardened, and naturalized certain devices and dispositions, and even given them the appearance of being part of a coherent disciplinary tradition, thus in continuity with how previous scholars (e.g., "founders" or "giants in the field") have done things? To my mind, it is such questions that offer useful analytic leverage in accounting for the pre-critical persistence that McCutcheon (and others) perceive over time.

Another way of putting my point is to say that claiming continuity, endurance, and recurrence in the field of religious studies in order to set into relief critiques of the field will likely eclipse important historical specificities of past and present alike in constructing any history of the field. Indeed, I very much second McCutcheon's sentiment that "when it comes to scholarship, the more precision the better" (Chapter 6, this volume). But for all that critics of the field have usefully denaturalized and provincialized the category of religion, they often rely on superficial constructions of the past as a crutch for contemporary critiques of the field. These studies sometimes give the historical impression that certain problematic paradigms related to the category of religion were produced, as McCutcheon and Arnal say, "one day" in the late nineteenth or early twentieth centuries, and that most scholars of religion today are simply passive inheritors of the these "relics" rather than active agents involved in fashioning and normalizing these paradigms. In other words, that once the academic study of religion congealed its deeply problematic logic in the late nineteenth century then somehow this logic propelled itself in a long, continuous arc of dissimulated theologizing and lingering colonialist methods into the present where now the task of critical scholarship is to point out dutifully where these centuries-old assumptions still dwell.

As an example, take the notorious endurance of the world religions paradigm (WRP) from the late nineteenth century to now. Indeed, for McCutcheon, the obstinacy of this paradigm seems at various points in his essay representative of the larger problem of pre-critical endurance that concerns him. Of particular interest to me here is the history of the WRP as related in Christopher Cotter and David Robertson's introduction to their *After World Religions* volume (2016: 1–20). The history the editors construct is drawn from the best and brightest of recent critical scholarship on the historical development of the category of religion and its ramification into the WRP. Yet, what I find notable is that their history barely makes its way out of the nineteenth century, with the attempted construction of "The Victorian 'science of religion'," before it fast-forwards to the more recent critiques of the WRP in late twentieth and early twenty-first centuries. This is, of course, not a criticism of Cotter and Robertson, but rather a comment on how well their "potted history" (ibid.: 2) gives a clear indication of the current state of scholarship on this topic: namely, it reveals a yawning gap in historical investigations of the WRP between the vigorous late nineteenth and early twentieth century theorizers and the late-twentieth- and early twenty-first-century critics. Yet, one comes away with the impression that the WRP paradigm, constructed as it was around "Protestant norms" and fortified in various colonialist projects, was essentially locked into place in late nineteenth and early twentieth centuries. And other than a superficial dash of mid-century Eliade it has remained essentially unchanged until today.[7] The process is essentially "black boxed" where we understand point A (the origins of the WRP) and point B (its critique) but not how we get from point A to point B. But I would wager that critiques of the WRP will be more effective if we have a more detailed historical account of how we got into a situation where the WRP is the status quo. Without robust accounts of this kind, critiques of the WRP and those who are actively creating pedagogical alternatives to it risk swatting at anachronistic constructions while leaving the contemporary mechanics of power that continue to secure the WRP unexplored and unchallenged.

At least part of the problem, as I see it, is that very few scholars of religion have pursued or extended, to any substantive degree, Tomoko Masuzawa's quite suggestive avenues for future research on the WRP offered in her book *The Invention of World Religions* (2005).[8] Masuzawa is explicit that while her research explores the "rhizomatic growth" (ibid.: 11; 29) of the WRP in the nineteenth century, it leaves unexplored and unaccounted for "the efficient causes, so to speak, that finally brought about the new discourse of world religions" (ibid.: 27). There has been extensive work done on topics potentially relevant to the WRP (for instance, the World Parliament of Religions in 1893) but, as far as I know, not much on how it figures as part of a "transition" from nineteenth century (largely European) scientific debates over the universality of religion to the twentieth century (American) "populist world religions discourse" (ibid.: 269). The scholarship that has attempted to elaborate on Masuzawa's work has been slight and uneven (though not without interest), focusing again mostly on thinking through nineteenth and early twentieth century developments.[9] Indeed, while Masuzawa sees

---

7. Eliade serves as their only mid-century example of how religion and WRP were cast in terms of sui generis, which is then followed by a discussion of the ways WRP could be used by colonizing nations in order to manage colonial populations (Cotter and Robertson 2016: 6–7).
8. She gives brief discussions of these across chapters 8–9: the Sacred Books of the East series, the World Parliament of Religions, the role of private funding in the study of religion, non-Western participation, and discourses of pluralism.
9. As far as I've discovered, James Cox (2007) and Anna Sun (2013) are the only two scholars who have substantially attempted to integrate and expand Masuzawa's insights into their own work on the categories of, respectively, Indigenous Religion and Confucianism. That said, Jason Josephson-Storm (2012) and Alex Rocklin (2019) have also framed interesting historical analyses of, respectively, Japan and Trinidad more loosely around Masuzawa's work.

the time between the late nineteenth century and the 1920s and early 1930s—a period that begins with the apex of European colonialism and ends between world wars—as the period of explanandum, it seems to me that her initial inquiries would repay further analysis into the mid- to late twentieth centuries and the early twenty-first century in both academic and popular idioms.

Yet, over and above Masuzawa's particular suggestions for future research, her orientation toward historical method might also be worth emulating in constructing more detailed accounts of the WRP's development. A good place to start is Masuzawa's analysis of early world religions books worrying over impeding global crisis (e.g., the world wars), which she connects to the material effects of colonial exploitation, a larger sensibility of global interconnectedness in the "West," and, in the face of this connectedness, an uneasiness about the potentially unprecedented scale of change that such an intertwined world could produce. Equally useful is Masuzawa's contention that in the midst of these early twentieth century material and ideational developments, even Christian sensibilities, biases, and preoccupations became repositioned and re-signified in this historical conjuncture. That is, the advent of WRP did not do away with a European sense of Christian superiority to other religions but rather recast it in the emerging liberal Protestant vocabulary of pluralism and diversity. For all of their differences and distinctive flavors that WRP was meant to highlight, the religions of the world—of which Christianity was now notionally just a single species—were still defined and described on specifically Protestant Christian criteria.

Both of Masuzawa's above analyses have implications for analyzing other various historical moments where the WRP is adopted and installed in the mid- to late twentieth and early twenty-first centuries. For instance, the Cold War produced a sense of global conflict and pending catastrophe that helped justify and fortify the WRP.[10] It also arguably did so as it recalibrated accompanying Protestant Christian sensibilities of plurality and diversity, especially as the dominant global order came to be conceived as a likely nuclear battleground between the religiosity of American, capitalistic, Christians (but also monotheists) and the atheist Soviet communists.

But, more importantly, both of Masuzawa's analyses demonstrate that the historical circumstances around the advent of WRP were distinct, and later developments cannot be simply deduced or implied from earlier developments. On the one hand, extending a historical account of how WRP became installed as the dominant paradigm will involve mucking about in the weeds of particular historical moments, not reliance on some inherent persuasiveness or ideational power

---

10. In fact, McCutcheon has briefly discussed Huston Smith's teaching of officers at the Air Command and Staff College at the Maxwell Air Force Base near Montgomery, Alabama where what Smith sees as driving the importance of learning about "the religions of other peoples" is framed around knowing something about one's "allies, antagonists, or subjects of military occupation" (McCutcheon 1997: 179–180; see also McCutcheon 2018: 43–54). In terms of the category of religion, Arnal and McCutcheon have published an interesting and instructive piece on the emerging field of religious studies and government funding during the Cold War years (2013: 72–90).

within the model itself. For instance, James Cox is one of the few scholars who has made a serious effort to extend Masuzawa's initial work on world religions discourse. Yet, in tracing a purely intellectual line up through W.C. Smith's and Ninian Smart's work in the 1960s and 1970s, he ends his historical considerations, and segues into his critical discussion, by concluding:

> *It is no surprise then that the idea has persisted to the present day* that the religions of the world can be written about and taught according to the geographical regions where they are dominant, conceived, as Masuzawa asserts, largely along racial or ethnic lines, or under the conventional categories originally designated as the major traditions of the world, broken into a binary opposition between West and East.
>
> (Cox 2007: 44, emphasis added)

What I find problematic here is Cox's subtly attributing a sort of obvious self-propulsion to the WRP that gives it a push from where he stops his history to the "present day." For Cox, it is self-evident that the paradigm has enduring power in and of itself, over and above particular circumstances, which, at least in part, is evidenced by Smith and Smart's failed attempts at "uprooting the basic model associated with 'world' religions."

On the other hand, Masuzawa's historical method also denies the category "Protestant Christian" any monolithic critical power for critics of the WRP. As Cotter and Robertson rightly point out, that "the WRP constructs 'religion' according to an ostensibly Protestant Christian model" is one of the key points that critics emphasize. Yet, Masuzawa gives us pause to consider that historically the content of such denominations as "Protestant Christian," "Christian theological assumptions," "Protestant norms," or even what it might mean "to Christianize" something can and does change over time, and thus cannot be a one size fits all indictment of the WRP. The historically peculiar discursive content and rhetorical usage of these categories should be taken into account in any historical or critical investigation of the WRP. And so much more for critical approaches to the category of religion that posit the persistence of essentialist impulses. Indeed, if one were to explain the persistence of an essentialist impulse in the academic study of religion by seeing it as a function of residual Christian theological ideas, then one would need to be more precise about the historical contours of such assumptions at particular times and places, or even how specifically Christian, theological impulses give way to more generic, scholarly essentialist ones (cf. Cox 2007: 46).

Conclusion: A Political Economy of Endurance

In closing, and to return to McCutcheon's chapter, let me give a final example of the kind of historical arguments I'm getting at here. McCutcheon's final paragraphs regarding his concern for the field's future, I think, suggest a potentially useful context, and one that might help explain why contemporary scholars of religion gravitate toward and cultivate essentialists models (instead of critical models)—and perhaps more to the point, why they do so under the auspices of "critical gains." To dust off a perhaps overused and underdefined term, I take McCutcheon's passing concessions to risk-reward factors for critical work as raising the issue of academic "neoliberalization." It is well beyond the scope of this response to detail the ways that the larger political economy (from roughly the late 1970s to now) has transformed the structure of the university and affected the way scholars (of religion) do their work. Yet, McCutcheon's brief mention of the "prices to be paid" for critical work, the risks and stakes, and potential "spoils" involved, and the increasingly "exposed" positions of scholars all indicate how these larger shifts have defined, ordered, and prioritized academic consciousness and practice over the last thirty-plus years.

As McCutcheon notes, these trends are situated in and exacerbated by a material and institutional context marked by a widening gap between the tenured, the tenure-earning, and the precariat. Yet, there is more still to be said about the power dynamics implied in this disparity. The tenured and tenure-earning status groups presumably have some vested interest in protecting this field of study from the logic of the market. This includes resisting the bloated corporate-administrative apparatus, which has expanded while the humanities have declined. Unfortunately, for the growing underclass of "contingent" professors, they not only have "little incentive (because of little protection!) to critically tackle the work of their elders and their peers, with an eye toward the health of the field at large" (Chapter 6, this volume); they have quite justifiable reasons to *not* be critical and to toe the party line set out by the tenured and tenure-earning elect. The terms, interests, and priorities of the field are set by these scholars and establish the rules of the game. The only control that contingent instructors, graduate students, etc., have over their futures is to model themselves on their successful would-be peers. Simply put, this means presenting one's research as new, critical, and constructive without alienating the gatekeepers and career-killers.

This is just another way of getting to McCutcheon's point that what passes as *the cutting edge* is really just "lightly revised versions of long familiar ... approaches" (Chapter 6, this volume). I don't disagree with McCutcheon's assessment of the "stakes" involved in critical work. But I want to make clear that these stakes are the institutional and material conditions that explain why the old keeps dressing itself up as new. That scholars appear to be turning to the same old repertoire with a few novel embellishments is not simply because certain pre-critical ideas keep inevitably rolling over from one generation to another, but rather is due to conformist dispositions cultivated by present structural and institutional circumstances. The sort of explanation I'm proposing here is that the pattern McCutcheon identifies is a by-product of the academy's late-twentieth and early-twenty-first-century political economy. The nineteenth-century colonial world or the Cold War fears of global doom have very little to do with the matter at hand, at least directly. In other words, the *all-too-human* and *all-too-material* circumstances that condition junior scholars to adopt religious literacy models are historically distinct.

Thus, rather than taking it as a given that scholars of religion simply and stubbornly refuse to accept critical methods, it seems to me there are potentially more useful accounts. To see the history of the study of religion as repeating the same essentialist and ahistorical problems without situating these problems in their wider historical contexts and political economies presumes a rather procrustean view of pre-critical, sui generis notions of religion: that once deployed they come to take on a life of their own, becoming a staple for scholarly theorizing with their own predictable logic that operates seemingly independent of time and place.

Andrew Durdin is assistant professor in the Florida State University department of religion. His work focuses primarily on the religions of the Roman imperial period, ancient esotericism, and the modern historiography of ancient religions. Recently, he has also started thinking and writing about the issues of social class, identity, and the political economic contexts of the modern study of religion.

References

Arnal, William and Russell T. McCutcheon. 2013. *The Sacred is the Profane: The Political Nature of Religion*. Oxford: Oxford University Press.

Clark, Elizabeth A. 2004. *History, Theory, Text: Historians and the Linguistic Turn*. Cambridge, MA: Harvard University Press.

Cotter, Christopher R. and David G. Robertson. 2016. *After World Religions: Reconstructing Religious Studies*. New York: Routledge.

Cox, James L. 2007. *From Primitive to Indigenous: The Academic Study of Indigenous Religions*. Farnham: Ashgate Publishing.

Graeber, David. 2001. *Toward an Anthropological Theory of Value: The False Coin of our own Dreams*. Basingstoke: Palgrave.

Graeber, David. 2014. "Anthropology and the Rise of the Professional-Managerial Class." *Hau: Journal of Ethnographic Theory* 4(3): 7–88.

Josephson-Storm, Jason Ānanda. 2012. *The Invention of Religion in Japan*. Chicago, IL: University of Chicago Press.

Martin, Craig. 2017. "Yes, ... but ...": The Neo-Perennialists." *Method and Theory in the Study of Religion* 29: 313-326.

Masuzawa, Tomoko. 2005. *The Invention of World Religions: Or, How European Universalism Was Preserved in the Language of Pluralism*. Chicago, IL: University of Chicago Press.

McCutcheon, Russell T. 1997. *Manufacturing Religion: The Discourse on Sui Generis Religion and the Politics of Nostalgia*. Oxford: Oxford University Press.

McCutcheon, Russell T. 2014. "Introduction: Plus ça Change ..." In Russell T. McCutcheon, *A Modest Proposal on Method: Essaying the Study of Religion* (pp. 1–16). Leiden: Brill.

McCutcheon, Russell T. 2018. *Fabricating Religion: Fanfare for the Common e.g.* Amsterdam: De Gruyter.

Ortner, Sherry B. 2016. "Dark Anthropology and Its Others: Theory Since the Eighties." *Hau: Journal of Ethnographic Theory* 6(1): 4–73.

Reed, Adolph Jr. 2018. "Antiracism: A Neoliberal Alternative to a Left." *Dialectical Anthropology* 42: 105–115.

Rocklin, Alexander. 2019. *The Regulation of Religion and the Making of Hinduism in Colonial Trinidad*. Durham, NC: University of North Carolina Press.

Sun, Anna. 2013. *Confucianism as a World Religion: Contested Histories and Contemporary Realities*. Princeton, NJ: Princeton University Press.

Chapter 9

Intercepted Dispatches
A Speculative History of the Future of Religious Studies

Rebekka King

Agents of the Society for Pluralistic Tolerance intercepted the following letter. It was discovered on the body of an unidentified assailant who leaped to his death while being pursued on foot concerning suspected crimes against the public good. It is dated: April 4, 2157.

Dear Theomises,

I write to you to set down an orderly account of the events that have transpired since the founding of the Ministry of Religious Literacy and the Society for Pluralistic Tolerance. I have recently come into possession of competing reports from eyewitnesses at the early meetings of these societies, which occurred many years ago. These two societies were established following the dissolution of a former conglomerate of "scholarly societies" dedicated to the academic study of religion. That combination of words—academic study of religion—might sound foreign, as we now think of religious studies as a pragmatic field necessary for "civic health and well-being," to quote the most excellent AAR Religious Literacy Guidelines, which debuted in 2019 and changed the face of our field.[1] After investigating everything carefully, I have decided to write an orderly account for you, so that you may know the truth concerning the things about which you have been instructed.

There was a time when religious studies aspired to constitute a discipline dedicated to scientific, objective, and scholarly analyses of religion and its impact on social and cultural realms. As unbelievable as it sounds, in this era, the study of religion stood alongside other humanistic and social scientific fields pursued for intellectual curiosity and to better understand and question everyday presumptions and worldviews.[2] In those days, formal religious studies departments were not found at all colleges and universities. Those schools that featured religious studies programs often had only a handful of faculty and students. Such departments were sometimes combined with disciplinary cognates such as philosophy,

---

1. American Academy of Religion (2019).
2. As Richard Newton argues, "our attention should be on helping the student ask questions that make even us think twice" (Newton 2019: 242; cf. Smith 2007). See also Chapter 1, this volume, by Leslie Dorrough Smith.

history, or an antiquated area of study known as classics. It seems that many engaged in religious studies found interest in extinct traditions and ancient texts that bear little or no influence on current practices and policies nor the work of aiding people to choose the best religious affiliation for themselves. Such departments lacked any sense that studying religion naturally supported and encouraged civility and the public good. Instead, they promoted a form of study known as "critique," wherein they would undertake a theoretical evaluation of religious content deemed worthy for the mere sake of research and analysis.[3]

In those days, it was commonly perceived that students of religious studies would either pursue careers in religious ministry or further graduate education. There were fears that the discipline was unsustainable. Today, of course, those deemed most prolific in their aptitude to religious studies are rewarded in the esteemed role of analysts who tirelessly collect, scrutinize, and disseminate survey data in the Department for Empirical Research of Attitudes and Activities Empirically Reported through Empirical Measures (DERAAEREM). But in the past, many worried about whether graduates would find any form of work, let alone something related to their studies. I know this prospect sounds laughable today when even the most incompetent religious studies graduate can earn a decent living as a tutor for the pluralistic values test or as instructors at the Prothero Center for Co-Opted Awakening. But this was well before the Prothero Center began training instructors as guides for choosing one's religious affiliation. It even predates the mandated pluralistic values license, which, as you know, since its implementation in the year 2042, all citizens aged 29–70 are required to renew every ten years. Its directive to ensure a population of "informed citizens [who] interact effectively at work [and] foster good relationships with diverse people, as well as understand local, national, and global events" is lifted directly from the aforementioned Religious Literacy Guidelines.

But I digress, dear Theomises. I do not mean to dwell on the diplomatic and vocational labor that we, as scholars of religion, take as our sworn duty. I am near the end of my life, and I remember early on in my career, rumors of when things were different. As shocking as it sounds, in the early days of the twenty-first century, there was little government recognition that understanding religion was an essential component of workplace productivity and an indispensable social good. No doubt, you have paused to reread my earlier statement about the period. Yes, Theomises. I wrote, "twenty-first," not "first." One did not decide their religious affiliation through college training programs, but instead, people typically adopted the religious identities of their parents and extended family. Can you imagine? Choosing to be Hindu or Methodist, simply because your mother had made a similar choice!

During this era, a genuinely bizarre hypothesis developed. Some claimed that religion was not a self-evident entity, that instead, the category of religion required interrogation. They decried it as anachronistic to see religion as an essential and universal concept. Even going so far as to state that it was a modern invention,

---

3. See for example the previous NAASR Working Papers volume (King 2022).

brought about by particular colonial enterprises that emerged in what they called "the west."[4] In the early twenty-first century, some were sensible enough to see that religion references *a priori* transcendent experiences shared by all humans. A category that has currency for public understanding and accessibility. But even among those who clearly understood the benefits of describing religion as a concrete set of practices and identity markers, there remained some hesitancy about the longstanding and ubiquitous existence of religion. Indeed, well into the first two decades of the twenty-first century, a guileless group of scholars presumed religion was somehow a modern invention fabricated in the mind of a scholar.

Everything came to a head sometime around 2023. The history of these dark days of the discipline is covered in several prominent texts written in the late twenty-first century, such as:

- *From NABI to Nobody: The Necessary Disillusion of Scholarly Societies in the Study of Religion*
- *Resurrecting Religious Studies: The Final Return and Conversion*
- *Factual Terms for Pragmatic Descriptions of Religion*
- *Equating Map and Territory: All the Necessary Data for Religion*

Ideally, you should have read about these texts during your comprehensive exams, Theomises. But I know many students skip those works that chronicle what they see as a dry and disconnected history of a field that is related in name only. As a result, many details remain unclear. Indeed, a history of religious studies would garner little interest among most people other than a few outliers whose memories reach back to this era's aftermath. I say this because I think it may come as a shock to you that I have recently taken up as a hobby an investigation into what was known as religious studies in the first two decades of the twenty-first century.

There is little to work with. All I have is a list of professors, snippets from a biographical dictionary. I know this is not a serious venture. Merely something to dabble with as my career comes to a close. I think I like the challenge and the chase. Most written material was not well preserved. They had a penchant for recording their most crucial information on a type of cellulose fiber derived from wood. Even more bizarrely, they relied on a primitive electronic storage system known as "the cloud" (it was longer than I care to admit before I determined that this was a form of media that had nothing to do with the makeshift science of meteorology).

Now, despite these unenlightened times, some scholars had begun to make claims that foreshadowed our contemporary perspective. As early as 2015, Adam Dinham and Matthew Francis made the case that understanding religion was central to public policy.[5] Not long after, Kim Knott published an overview of the

---

4. See, for example, Chidester 1996 and Masuzawa 2005.
5. Dinham and Francis (2015) argue that the pervasiveness of religion necessitates learning about it and religious literacy is an imperative for participation in civic society (see also Dinham 2020).

partnerships between law enforcement agencies and security policymakers with scholars of religion in the UK, Canada, and the United States. Her findings, however, were oddly cautionary, suggesting that scholars might have reservations about the potential contribution of their work to anti-terrorist or other security measures.[6] Others, such as Naomi Goldenberg, looked at how religions mobilized claims to sovereignty which mirrored, and in some instances, provided fodder for nations to make claims about their own sovereignty.[7] Surprisingly, Goldenberg discusses the issue without a celebration of the obvious long-lasting positive impacts.

Regardless of the peculiar reservations on the part of the aforementioned scholars, the notion that the study of religion serves as a public good was well entrenched in the United Kingdom during the first Brexit era. Religious Education was a compulsory program in public schools. It fostered what key educators and policy experts brilliantly called a balance between "learning about" and "learning from" religion to pursue the larger goal of social tolerance.[8] In fact, in the fall of 2019, the Commission on Religious Education in the UK shifted their programmatic offerings "to reflect more diverse beliefs" and designated a change from "Religious Education" to a new and much more practical name: "Religion and Worldviews." Lest you worry about the impact of "worldview" as potentially too broad. The Commission evaluated particular worldviews, such as communism and capitalism, as not counting because they lack the ontological and epistemological claims necessary for classification as a religious worldview. This program took a critical step by introducing a "national entitlement statement," which would formally set out what all students were entitled to experience as part of their religious education. Schools were subject to regular inspections to ensure appropriate "themes and concepts" about religious education were "being taught by teachers with secure subject knowledge."[9] In doing so, they safeguarded what we all know to be crucial to studying religion—the edification of students' religious views must stand as our most important consideration.

Around the same time, across "the pond" (a term, for reasons I cannot determine, they used to mislabel the Atlantic Ocean), legislative developments linking religious tolerance to citizenship were emerging in what is now La Nation du Québec. As a province of the now-defunct Dominion of Canada, Quebec instigated a values test to evaluate immigrants' comprehension of democratic values embedded in Quebec's Charter of Human Rights and Freedoms.[10] Based on a now disproven premise that a secular workforce ensures the most productivity and democratic engagement, the values test followed on the heels of laws prohibiting

---

6. Beginning with the Branch Davidians standoff in Waco, Texas in 1993 consultations and collaborations between security agencies and scholars of religion have occurred. Knott (2018) raises some hesitation, but ultimately concludes that such relationships should be nurtured to sustain a productive and copacetic collaboration.
7. See Goldenberg (2018) and Stack, Goldenberg, and Fitzgerald (2015).
8. Chater and Erricker (2013).
9. Commission on Religious Education (2018).
10. CBC (2019).

public displays of religious affiliation. Such values tests and legal regulations were significant as they secured the public necessity for scholars of religion as we understand them today. However, despite the positive contributions they made toward evaluating what counts as markers of religious identity, the authors of the values test missed the mark in understanding their more noble purposes. They failed to see such tests as a vehicle to mobilize consensus-building beliefs, such as "religion makes people moral," "everyone has a faith," and "learning about religion leads to tolerance."[11]

The cases of Religious Education in the United Kingdom and Values Tests in Quebec paralleled shifts we saw in our own nation. The formidable work by those involved with the Religious Literacy Project stands as the most outstanding achievement of our discipline's early years. Undoubtedly, you are familiar with those accomplishments from your tenure at the Prothero Center for Co-Opted Awakening (I followed your career there with interest, Theomises, and was pleased to see that you set the record for the greatest diversity in religious traditions adopted by your trainees). The most excellent AAR Religious Literacy Report in 2019 paved the way for the development of legislative programs that required the teaching of religious literacy within college curricula as well as within "pre-professional, scientific, technical, and workplace programs." As that initial report claimed, such programs are essential to private and public industries, such as "healthcare, criminal justice, business, and hospitality."[12] The rest, as they say, is history. We enjoy continued economic growth, worker productivity, and civil obedience. These positive gains are undoubtedly linked to the inalienable right to choose one's own religion and the ability of all citizens to recite the core beliefs and practices of major religious traditions and follow proper etiquette when encountering religious differences. As a result, the need for professional experts remains high in all sectors of government, education, and private workplaces.

Today, the American Academy of Religion and the Society for Biblical Literature are recalled in history books as formidable institutions that brought us to our current circumstances. But in their early formation, they experienced opposition and hostility, which required quick wits and strategy to overcome. Until the mid-twentieth century, the study of religion was focused almost singularly on Christianity. In particular, they saw their task as acquainting students with the Bible's origin, content, and proper interpretation. Other faiths were usually studied in a way that lent further esteem to the importance of the Christian faith. We should not fault these early scholars too much. Like us, they held that it was necessary to understand the practices and ideals of the religious majority. Whereas we count several core traditions from which people typically choose, it appears they had but one. Their efforts were coordinated through a confessional society known as the North American Bible Institute (NABI), who prided themselves on

---

11. See chapters of the same titles by Jennifer Ely, James Dennis LoRusso, and Tenzan Eaghll in Martin and Stoddard (2017).
12. American Academy of Religion (2019).

having chosen an acronym matching the Hebrew word for prophet. Their mission, not unlike ours, was to "foster religion in education."[13]

A series of court cases in the mid-twentieth century forbid teaching the Bible and promotion of the Christian faith over others. At this time, the ideal of teaching about religion and religious history emerged. Universities and colleges began to offer Comparative Religion courses to train students in understanding different religious traditions.[14] The historical records that I have been able to find do not explicitly state that they were undertaking such comparisons with the aim of choosing one's religious affiliation. But I cannot imagine, given what we know to be true about human nature, vocational training, and religious identity, how it could have been anything other than precursory training for association purposes.

As I peruse the documents and historical materials—at least those that are readily available—they hint at strange and unexpected conflicts. There was an expression in those days that "history is written by the winners." On the surface, this adage seems understandable enough. Why would we care about anything other than winning? But from what I can gather, many saw this obvious virtue as problematic. While we have long held that the disbanding of the scholarly societies was a liberating lockstep in the march towards pragmatic and practical studies of religion for the sake of public good. It seems that there existed a dissenting opinion. One that has more or less been struck from the official record. It appears that in the last days of the American Academy of Religion and the Society of Biblical Literature, there existed competing tensions in the field of religious studies between, on the one hand, endorsing religion as an affective, precognitive sensory experience, and on the other hand, assimilating religiosity into the multiple dimensions of human culture and social arrangements.

We should be careful of anachronistic readings of the past. We cannot claim to thoroughly understand the perspectives and policies of former societies. As I lingered over the manifold praise directed toward the merger of several scholarly organizations into the Ministry of Religious Literacy and the Society for Pluralistic Tolerance, it occurred to me that we might try to read between the lines. I know, Theomises! It is so bizarre and unbecoming of a scholar to impose such a suspicious reading onto official documents. But I could not help myself! The more I read, the more I became convinced that these recommendations might be directed at someone or something that disagreed. I poured over the archives—searching through archaic bylaws and constitutions. Until finally, I found it.

---

13. It is noteworthy that "foster" has been retained in the AAR mission and motto. The history of the split is outlined in a chapter by Bruce Lincoln (2012: 131–136). It is further elaborated on and challenged in Imhoff (2016).

14. For further discussion of the development of religious studies in American higher education, see McCutcheon (2003). While often assumed to have germinated in a similar fashion to the American context, the development in religious studies in Canada followed a different trajectory, which has been delineated for the first time in a recent book by Aaron Hughes (2020).

During this same dark era, a resistance movement existed that appeared not to have a name but rather a geographic orientation. They called themselves the "North American Association for the Study of Religion" (NAASR). They drew membership from a wide variety of institutions that have long since disappeared from the historical records. The publications associated with the NAASR group that I have been able to track down are replete with references and citations to the great Jonathan Z. Smith. Naturally, Smith's work has been immortalized as the foundation of the pragmatic study of religion. For it is Smith who provided the justification by which we, as scholars, are able to regulate and reinforce the content and understanding of correct religious ideas and affiliations for the betterment of public life. It is to Smith that we owe the orienting framework of our discipline: "Religion is solely the creation of the scholar's study. It is created for the scholar's analytic purpose by his imaginative acts of comparison and generalization. Religion has no existence apart from the academy."[15] Truer words have never been spoken; it is hard to imagine it ever being anything but. From this premise, we know that scholars of religion have not only the capacity but also the duty to create a discipline that encourages civility and resourcefulness.

The NAASR reading of Smith appears to be quite unorthodox. One wonders if they were aware of their perverse custom of falsifying and magnifying his words. In contrast to ours, they see his work as emboldening a starting point for studying religion that is taxonomic, rather than focusing, as we do, on the importance of comparison and accurate classifications. They saw Smith's work as centered on explaining differences for the sake of explanation. It appears they feel that the more disparate, the better! As if, by "imagination," Smith meant unending possibilities instead of clearly delineated processes set forth by the disciplined mind of the religious studies scholar. Their focus was on the acts of classification and description as if some understanding of human activity and social practices could be gleaned from that process itself. They were not concerned with what counts as authentic religion, but more so with how people identified specific religions, practices, and beliefs as genuine or not. Can you even begin to imagine a world in which scholars of religion did not weigh in and offer insight into what is appropriate religiosity or not? It is almost as if they did not think that the sacred was real. I am sure you join me, Theomises, in a good chuckle at the very thought of such nonsense!

Despite thinking it nonsense, I need to get, at last, to the point of my writing to you. As I reflect on what the world would have been like had NAASR successfully convinced their peers to stop essentializing religion or relying on non-material assumptions concerning its nature. I think it is worthwhile to use them as a cautionary model for the ways that our interpretations can be devastatingly wrong when pursued outside of the codified and accepted lenses we so clearly impart in the contemporary study of religion. My investigation has consisted of false starts and unanswered questions. What happened to the NAASR group remains unclear.

---

15. Smith's ever-present, over-quoted adage (Smith 1982: xi) is best clarified by William Cavanaugh, who explains "religion is not simply found, but invented" (Cavanaugh 2009: 58).

I find myself lying awake at night, ruminating on their fate. I picture them huddled together in conference rooms disputing the merit of different theoretical lenses: cognitive sciences, poststructuralism, discourse analysis, and others. I envision them corresponding to one another with the handheld electronic devices that were pervasive during that era: sharing news of recent publications and job postings, commenting on political events, and exchanging oh so many photos of cats.

A few days ago a strange package arrived at my home. Inside was a single sheet with the words Working Papers and a list of titles. Nothing else. The best of my efforts cannot track down from where or whom it came. I've included that list here in hopes that you might help me to better understand their meaning. It begins:

> On the Subject of Religion: Charting the ...

The letter ends abruptly at this point, as if it has been truncated. It contains no closing remarks or signature. Scribbled in the bottom corner, almost illegibly, is written, "what a difference a difference makes."

Rebekka King is an associate professor of religious studies and honors faculty fellow at Middle Tennessee State University. She served as NAASR's vice president from 2017 to 2020, and is currently its president. Her term will end in 2023, just before the events forecast in this speculative epistle to Theomises.

References

American Academy of Religion. 2019. "AAR Religious Literacy Guidelines: What US College Graduates Need to Understand about Religion." Retrieved from www.aarweb.org/aar-religious-literacy-guidelines [accessed November 1, 2019].

Cavanaugh, William T. 2009. *The Myth of Religious Violence: Secular Ideology and the Roots of Modern Conflict*. New York: Oxford University Press.

CBC. 2019. "Quebec Will Make Immigrants Pass 'Values' Test." Retrieved from www.cbc.ca/news/canada/montreal/quebec-values-test-immigration-1.5340652 (accessed November 5, 2019).

Chater, Mark, and Clive Erricker. 2013. *Does Religious Education Have a Future?* New York: Routledge.

Chidester, David. 1996. *Savage Systems: Colonialism and Comparative Religion in Southern Africa*. Charlottesville, VA: University of Virginia Press.

Commission on Religious Education. 2018. "Religion and Worldviews: The Way Forward. A National Plan for RE." Retrieved from www.commissiononre.org.uk/final-report-religion-and-worldviews-the-way-forward-a-national-plan-for-re/ (accessed November 5, 2019).

Dinham, Adam. 2020. *Religion and Belief Literacy: Reconnecting a Chain of Learning*. Bristol, UK: University of Bristol Press.

Dinham, Adam, and Matthew Francis (eds). 2015. *Religious Literacy in Policy and Practice*. Bristol: University of Bristol Press.

Goldenberg, Naomi. 2015. "Forget about Defining 'It': Reflections on Thinking Differently in Religious Studies." In Brad Stoddard (ed.), *Method Today: Redescribing Approaches to the Study of Religion*. Sheffield: Equinox.
Hughes, Aaron W. 2020. *From Seminary to University: An Institutional History of the Study of Religion in Canada*. Toronto: University of Toronto Press.
Imhoff, Sarah. 2016. "The Creation Story, or How We Learned to Stop Worrying and Love Schempp." *Journal of the American Academy of Religion* 84(2): 466–497.
King, Rebekka (ed.). 2022. *Key Categories in the Study of Religion: Contexts and Critiques*. Sheffield: Equinox.
Knott, Kim. 2018. "Applying the Study of Religion in the Security Domain: Knowledge, Skills, and Collaboration." *Journal of Religion and Political Practice* 4(3): 354–373.
Lincoln, Bruce. 2012. *Gods and Demons, Priests and Scholars: Critical Explorations in the History of Religions*. Chicago, IL: University of Chicago Press.
Martin, Craig, and Brad Stoddard (eds). 2017. *Stereotyping Religion: Critiquing Clichés*. New York: Bloomsbury Academic.
Masuzawa, Tomoko. 2005. *The Invention of World Religions: Or, How European Universalism Was Preserved in the Language of Pluralism*. Chicago, IL: University of Chicago Press.
Newton, Richard. 2019. "Teaching in the Ideological State of Religious Studies: Notes towards a Pedagogical Future." In Leslie Dorrough Smith (ed.), *Constructing "Data" in Religious Studies: Examining the Architecture of the Academy* (pp. 235–245). Sheffield: Equinox.
Smith, Jonathan Z. 1982. *Imagining Religion: From Babylon to Jonestown*. Chicago, IL: University of Chicago Press.
Smith, Jonathan Z. 2007. "Afterword: The Necessary Lie: Duplicity in the Disciplines." In Russell T. McCutcheon (ed.), *Studying Religion: An Introduction* (pp. 73–80). Sheffield: Equinox.
Stack, Trevor, Naomi Goldenberg, and Timothy Fitzgerald (eds). 2015. *Religion as a Category of Governance and Sovereignty*. Boston, MA: Brill.

Part III

The Role and Influence of Private Funding in the Field

Chapter 10

Private Money and the Study of Religions
Problems, Perils, and Possibilities

Gregory D. Alles

> "It's the funders that drive things."
> —David Blight (Yale University, quoted in Alterman 2019).

The Museum of the Bible

On a hot, humid day in July 2019, I made my way to the Museum of the Bible in Washington, DC. It provided a good opportunity for people watching: the small but steady line of people, myself included, making their way from the L'Enfant Plaza metro stop to the museum, some of the elderly suffering in the heat; a woman on one side of an exhibit talking animatedly to (I presume) friends about what the devil is doing today and how we need to combat him; a child, maybe ten or eleven years old, wondering what was kept in the pantry at the back of a room in the reconstructed village of Nazareth (my guess: the room was a synagogue and the pantry an ark); the ease with which some people publicly acknowledged their difficulty in pronouncing unfamiliar terms such as Tanakh, Torah, Nevi'im, and Ketuvim; and the generally greater fascination with videos and digital displays than with printed Bibles themselves, a not unexpected sign of our times.

I chose to visit the Museum because I had already been asked to reflect on the role of private money in the study of religions, and the Museum seemed to present an interesting local case. Originally its funding came primarily from the family that owns the Hobby Lobby retail chain and the National Christian Foundation. I had my suspicions about what it would display, but I also tried to keep an open mind. I deliberately chose not to read any reviews before my visit.

To be honest, I found some parts of the museum surprisingly congenial. I did not expect to encounter an explicit consideration of what the Hebrew Bible shares with its ancient Near Eastern context: links on a digital display identified "flood stories," "law collections," "treaties, oaths, and covenants," "proverbs and wisdom [literature, I suppose]," and "birth accounts."[1] Nor did I expect to

---

1. Since I did not explore this digital exhibit, I am not sure what birth stories in the Hebrew Scriptures it referred to.

see so many examples of the figurines that people worshiped in ancient Judah, Israel, and surrounding areas, although I suspect that my attitude toward them was rather different from that of the run-of-the-mill visitor. The collection of old books was hardly unexpected, but I was surprised to find a copy of Thomas Jefferson's *Notes on the State of Virginia*, open to the beginning of the query on religion.[2] Most impressive to me was the special exhibit on the so-called "Slave Bible," published on behalf of the Society for the Conversion of Negro Slaves in 1807, an exhibit made possible by a public-private partnership with Fisk University and the National Museum of African American History and Culture. Two walls were filled with plaques highlighting what this particular Bible included and omitted, but I was drawn to the exemplar itself. It was opened to the page that jumped from Genesis 45 to Exodus 19. To include the account of the Exodus, the publishers feared, might have provoked a slave rebellion.

Such unexpected encounters notwithstanding, I found it hard to overlook the Museum's agenda. Although one room on the ground floor was devoted to the Vatican libraries, the Museum itself was clearly trying to communicate a message that was American, Protestant, and evangelical.[3] As visitors ascended higher and higher, they encountered the impact of the Bible on American culture, then the rest of the world (second floor), an opportunity to experience Bible stories and Bible lands (third floor), and then the history of the Bible: its birth (sort of) and its transformation from a local book into one translated into over a thousand languages (fourth floor). But as with the Slave Bible, what was missing conveyed a message, too. There was no serious consideration of how the biblical books came into being or their intertextual relationships (e.g., the documentary hypothesis of the origin of Torah, the Deuteronomic literature, the synoptic problem). Although the Museum acknowledged religious plurality in the time before Jesus, with the appearance of Jesus plurality seemed to disappear among Christians, at least initially. The Nag Hammadi codices were as absent as the Dead Sea Scrolls and to a lesser extent the Samaritan Pentateuch were present; visitors learned nothing about the diversity of early Jesus movements and early Christian texts. If the Museum said anything about processes of canonization, especially New Testament canonization, I missed it. I also missed any hint that the Bible has not always been interpreted literally. Where were the various other forms of interpretation, starting with the allegory so prevalent when the Bible was finalized in the fourth century?[4] To jump to the US: events such as the social gospel, the Scopes trial, the abolition movement, and the civil rights movement were mentioned but

---

2. But only to the opening page; the curious would not encounter passages like this: "The legitimate powers of government extend to such acts only as are injurious to others. But it does me no injury for my neighbour to say there are twenty gods, or no god. It neither picks my pocket nor breaks my leg."
3. As a parallel biblical tradition, Jewish traditions received more attention than did Catholic traditions; nevertheless, I found the video that presented Maimonides not as an extremely sophisticated thinker but as an actor doing a shtick somewhat offensive.
4. I did note a discussion of Talmud and Midrash, and there was a reader on the history of biblical hermeneutics hidden on a shelf in the book shop.

hardly explored. The closest the Museum got to contemporary biblical scholarship was a statement under the heading "Fundamentalist-Modernist Debates": "Today, debate about biblical interpretation continues to grow with a much wider spectrum of opinion. This discussion stands at the root of current differences between evangelical and mainline Protestants, as well as similar differences in Catholic and Jewish traditions." (Apparently the Bible is not a topic for academic discussion.) Mounted above and to the right of this statement was a large print of E. J. Pace's "Descent of the Modernists." It shows three male figures descending a set of steps from Christianity at the top to Atheism at the bottom.

In retrospect, the Museum seemed studiously designed to avoid provoking and problematizing (shall we say educating?) American evangelical visitors, and not just in terms of theology. A pillar bearing the heading "Work" contained a quote from Rabbi Jonathan Sacks: "The market economy is deeply congruent with the values set out in the Hebrew Bible." I, too, left with my prior views confirmed: private money presents perils for scholarship; does it also present possibilities?

Religious Studies in a Time of Crisis

News about the study of religions seems to have turned unrelentingly bleak. Granted, I am reading it through lenses tinted by my own recent institutional experiences. Despite having strong and increasing demand for our courses (two of my courses in spring 2019 were overenrolled), our institution has decided both to discontinue the major in religious studies—but retain the minor—and to eliminate one position upon retirement: mine. The hope is that if more courses are desired in the study of religions, they can be offered by adjuncts—or by a retired professor teaching for adjunct's pay.

I am not looking for pity or sympathy. Rather, there is little point in talking about resources—in this case private money—in an abstract, ideal realm divorced from the realities in which we live and work. At last year's meeting of NAASR and the AAR in Denver, I seemed routinely to encounter bad news, even when I was not looking for it: a reduction in general education requirements (for those schools where students are still required to take courses in "religion"), a reduction in the number of faculty teaching the study of religions, a reduction in support for small, intense classes even at small, arguably elite institutions, and an overall reduction in programs, the elimination of the major being only one possibility. One friend told me that, denied a sabbatical for two years, he finally obtained it by agreeing to eliminate the major in religious studies and replace it with a minor in interfaith studies.

One can, of course, read these developments within the context of a crisis of the humanities in the US. One only needs to recall the roller-coaster rides that the University of Wisconsin–Stevens Point and Hampshire College have been on this past year. But one can also read it as part of a more global trend pertaining to the study of religions. Consider this comment from a report by the British Academy published in May 2019:

> While the study and research of theology and religion[5] remains an attractive area for many, it has seemingly fallen foul of the many challenges faced by the higher education sector, and particularly since the reforms to fees and funding in 2012: the number of students studying Theology and Religious studies [*sic*; subsequently TRS] degrees has fallen by a third. Fewer students means additional pressures on schools and departments to demonstrate their worth or face closure.
>
> (British Academy 2019: 2)

The report goes on to note:

> the overall trend in enrolment onto TRS courses in UK higher education is downward, in contrast to other humanities subjects like philosophy and history. ... The drop in TRS student numbers in 2012/13 and beyond coincided with the introduction of up to £9000 annual fees for full-time undergraduate degrees. The increase in fees may have created both demand-side and supply-side effects leading to a collapse in enrolment.
>
> (British Academy 2019: 3)

Notice the roles of private money in these developments. On the one hand, figures from the Higher Education Statistics Agency (HESA)

> suggest that in 2007/08, as many as 40% of students on foundation degrees[6] in TRS had funding from charities or international organisations to cover their fees, but by 2016/17 the number of UK domiciled foundation degree students with their fees funded by charities or international organisations was effectively zero.
>
> (British Academy 2019: 3)

On the other hand,

> Around 2700 students are on TRS undergraduate programmes in alternative providers who submit data to HESA. Undergraduate enrolment at these providers increased by 14% between 2016/17 and 2017/18. This suggests that while we are seeing declining enrolment in public [Higher Education Institutes], this may be partly offset by an increase in the private sector.
>
> (British Academy 2019: 7)

The alternative providers referred to are primarily Christian, often evangelical, but they also include two Muslim institutions.

When queried about this report, British colleagues have told me that the difficulty lies specifically with theology, not with the study of religions. Be that as it may, there are clearly differences between the situation in the UK and that in the US. Whereas enrollments in history programs have been increasing in the UK, in

---

5. UK statistics lump theology and religious studies together, so it is difficult to know to what extent the effects the report discusses characterize the study of religions conceived more strictly.

6. According to the report, a foundation degree is "an undergraduate course which combines academic and vocational elements of learning, equivalent to two-thirds of a first (bachelor's) degree and usually studied over two years if full-time."

the US the greatest loss in number of majors—roughly a third—has come in history (unfortunately, the second greatest loss has come in what IPEDS data simply designate "religion") (Schmidt 2018). In an article in *The New Yorker*, Eric Alterman (2019) noted that at Yale the study of history seems to be bucking the national trend: the number of students studying history is increasing. Nevertheless, David Blight, director of the Gilder Lehrman Center for the Study of Slavery, Resistance, and Abolition at Yale, told Alterman that, in a meeting with a Yale administrator "he was told that individual funders were all looking to fund STEM programs." Blight's commentary is quoted above: "It's the funders that drive things."

A Very Brief History of Private Money

Like so much else, higher education seems to present a case of American exceptionalism. Toward the end of his massive history of American higher education up to the outbreak of the Second World War, Roger Geiger observes: "In most countries, the role and status of institutions of higher education would be determined largely by governments. This was the case for only minor parts of the American system ... In the main ... the American system of higher education was a fluid free market with multiple actors" (Geiger 2015: 537). In other words, in the US higher education has generally been inconceivable apart from private money. My very limited knowledge does not allow me to discuss higher education elsewhere, so this very brief history concentrates entirely upon the United States. Most of what I have to say is abstracted from Geiger's voluminous accounts (Geiger 1986, 2015, 2019; cf. Thelin 2014, 2019).

Most scholars who are active today may find the idea that government has had little to do with the American system of higher education to be somewhat odd. For most of us, even those who attended and then worked in private institutions, as I have, the federal and, to a lesser extent, state governments have seemed great fonts of funds. We tend, justifiably, to lament recent reductions in federal and state support for institutions of higher learning and the shifting of the financial burden for tertiary education onto future student earnings. Nevertheless, from a historical vantage point, the large role that federal and state funds played in American colleges and universities in the second half of the twentieth century was an exception to an exception.

Colonial colleges were largely established to train ministers and promote Christianity (also to create cultural capital for the elite). Their names attest to the importance of private money: John Harvard's bequest of his library and half of his estate; Elihu Yale's donation of books, saleable goods, and a portrait of King George I; the extensive patronage of the Brown family to what was originally Rhode Island College; funds donated into a trust overseen by the Earl of Dartmouth for the education of Native Americans (Geiger 2015: 2, 11, 68, 70, 114, 135). In something of a contemporary-sounding twist, King's College, renamed Columbia after the Revolution, was founded with the proceeds of a public lottery. Nevertheless, the college "was owned and operated by the powerful families that patronized Trinity [Church] and the Dutch Reformed churches" (ibid.: 40–42). In the early days, colleges may have been chartered by governments, but any financial support they received from them was spotty at best.

In the era immediately following Independence there was some interest in supporting higher education with public money, but it generally foundered on Republican (as opposed to Federalist) claims that tax revenues should not be used to subsidize the cultural pretensions of the wealthy (e.g., Geiger 2015: 112, 114, 118, 160–170).[7] After the turn of the century the Second Great Awakening initially promoted a general suspicion of educated ministers and so of the institutions that educated them. Eventually, however, Methodists decided to establish colleges by the droves, more as a means to provide a religiously proper education for laypeople than to create an educated clergy (ibid.: 134). The same period saw the establishment of generally unregulated and often proprietary (private for-profit) professional schools in medicine and law, but also of theological seminaries, such as Andover and Princeton, that were dependent upon donations because students often studied for free (ibid.: 124, 155).

During the nineteenth century American higher education underwent important developments, not the least of which was the opening of doors to women and African-Americans, starting with Oberlin College in 1834 (Geiger 2015: 200–201). Structurally, however, higher education was a hodge-podge of different kinds of institutions, many of them proprietary, but all devoted entirely to teaching (ibid.: 270–277)—until two momentous changes, both made possible by private money.

The first change was the introduction of the German tradition of the research university. It began the slow spread of the expectation, still not entirely uncontroversial, that the task of institutions of higher learning is not just to disseminate knowledge but also to create it. The first such American university was, of course, Johns Hopkins in 1876 (ibid.: 323). Soon other members of the wealthy elite recognized the social capital that derived from either creating new universities—Leland and Jane Stanford (1891), John D. Rockefeller II (University of Chicago, 1892), Andrew Carnegie (Carnegie Institute of Pittsburgh, now Carnegie Mellon University, 1900/1912)—or contributing to already existing schools—Washington Duke (to what was then Trinity College, 1895) (Geiger 2015: 326–350). When a handful of public universities embraced the research ideal, notably Cornell (a land-grant university), California, and Michigan, they, too, benefited considerably from private funds (Geiger 1986, 2015: 354–362).

The second major change that transformed American higher education was standardization, which resulted in the tiered system that we know today: high schools, followed by undergraduate studies, then graduate and professional studies. Inasmuch as politics at the time prevented the federal government from establishing meaningful national policies for education, this system, too, was the creation of private money (Geiger 2015: 479). Particularly important were activities of foundations established by John D. Rockefeller and Andrew Carnegie:

---

7. The University of Virginia and South Carolina College were exceptions to this rule (cf. Geiger 2015: 119, 167, 181).

Rockefeller's General Education Board (founded 1902), the Carnegie Foundation for the Advancement of Teaching (1905), the Carnegie Corporation (1912), and the Rockefeller Foundation (1913) (Geiger 1986: 45 and passim). Although Carnegie spoke disparagingly about the humanities and general education (Donoghue 2008: 3–4), both he and Rockefeller had an interest in fostering research, particularly in the natural sciences (e.g., Geiger 1986: 46, 143). After the Second World War, leadership among philanthropic organizations passed to the Ford Foundation (Geiger 2019: 99).

Public support of higher education was not, of course, unprecedented in the second half of the twentieth century. Lotteries and land grants had a long history. The latter was especially important in promoting agricultural studies and engineering in the form of the Morrill Land Grant Act of 1862, passed—significantly—when the Civil War removed many potential objectors from Congress (Geiger 2015: 166, 269–314). Additional funding for agricultural research came from the Hatch Act of 1887 and the second Morrill Act of 1890 (ibid.: 303–304). But it was the participation of universities in the military efforts of the Second World War that led to a massive expansion of federal involvement in higher education. Especially noteworthy has been support for research in the natural sciences, engineering, and medicine. Equally noteworthy is the manner in which federal funding transformed what had been a privilege of the elite into a product for mass consumption, from the GI Bill to tuition grants to what now seems to be an ill-conceived program of abundant student loans (Geiger 2019). Today over half of the funding for university and college research in the United States comes from the federal government. More than half of that funding comes from the Department of Health and Human Services, with the Department of Defense and the National Science Foundation each adding slightly under 15% more (Chronicle of Higher Education 2018a, 2018b). Federal programs that benefit the humanities, including the study of religions, are apparently easy to overlook. Neither the Fulbright Scholarship Program (1946) nor Fulbright-Hays Act funds (1961) nor the National Endowment for the Humanities (1965) nor the Woodrow Wilson Center (1968) merits mention in Geiger's account of *American Higher Education Since World War II* (2019).

The federal government may invest heavily in university research, but private money (including tuition revenue) still dominates research in the humanities. Of the one hundred institutions—fifty public and fifty private—that spent the most on research in the humanities in 2016 (the latest figures available at the time of writing), research in the humanities accounted for only 0.87% of the federal research funds received, and in aggregate, only 12.78% of the funds that these institutions devoted to humanities research came from the federal government. In only four of the one hundred institutions did federal dollars constitute more than half of humanities research funding: Brigham Young (89.20%), Johns Hopkins (81.10%), Virginia Commonwealth (79.2%), and Yale (71.20%). Twenty institutions reported receiving no federal funds for humanities research at all (figures calculated from Chronicle of Higher Education 2018c). When *The Chronicle of Higher Education* reported these statistics, however, it did run a story that highlighted a relatively well-funded humanities program at the University of Michigan—in the study of religions and directed by Donald Lopez (Adams 2018).

Knowledge about Religions—Who Needs It?

The preceding paragraph only begins to capture the role of private money in the study of religions. First, not all funding in the study of religions is funding for the humanities; for example, one should also count funding for social scientific and cognitive studies of religion. Second, the numbers do not identify what percentage of federal funding for the humanities supports the study of religions; they may be quite small compared to funds for fields such as literature and history. Third, the numbers do not distinguish between the study and the practice of religions. For example, Valparaiso University (my alma mater) ranks 36th overall in private universities that support the humanities, and 4th among all 100 universities in the percentage of research and development dollars devoted to the humanities. The associate provost for faculty affairs tells me (personal communication, August 5, 2019), however, that he thinks a large chunk of that funding might derive from the Lilly Fellows Program in the Humanities and the Arts, which "seeks to renew and enhance the connections between Christianity and the academic vocation at church-related colleges and universities."[8] Finally, the figures exclude faculty salaries, which, given the relatively low cost of doing research in the humanities, surely make up a sizable proportion of indirect research funding, at least in those institutions that expect their faculty to engage in research.

Rather than multiply examples of private money supporting the study of religions, it is perhaps more important as a springboard for discussion to identify structural tensions that interfere with this support. These tensions are widely familiar, but they are still worth identifying, especially when the commitment of colleges and universities to the study of religions, a major source of researchers' salaries, is diminishing. I will draw on ideas that Steven Brint has developed in his essay, "An Institutional Geography of Knowledge Exchange" (Brint 2018).

Brint begins from the premise that not all knowledge is produced in an academic setting. He writes, "Knowledge produced outside of academe can have a studied, systematic quality that, like academic knowledge, distinguishes it from folkways or mere opinion. Typically, its validity has been subjected to some degree of critical scrutiny—though usually not at the level that would pass muster at the highest levels of academe" (Brint 2018: 117). Indeed, in the geography of knowledge exchange academia occupies the central place; it is "the home of the

---

8. See www.lillyfellows.org/about/about-us. I have been unable to get clarity about the amount of funding from the Lilly Fellows program itself. Given the topic of this essay, and in the interests of full disclosure, I should perhaps acknowledge that I make a modest contribution every year to the particular college that runs this program—not to support the Lilly Fellows program but in gratitude for the education in critical thinking and the appreciation for the humanities that I received as a student.

ultimate cultural authority (and the privileged work space) that permits knowledge generated both in universities and elsewhere to be examined, proven, deepened, revised, or rejected on the basis of evidence" (ibid.: 137). Evidence is critical in this process, for knowledge is "based on more than assertion, convention, or opinion." It requires "the potential for verification." Without that potential, one may have a "conceptual structure," perhaps a very complex one, but not a "knowledge structure."[9] Illustrating the difference, he writes, "Religious systems, for example, are conceptual structures that are not subject to empirical verification" (ibid.: 120, 118).[10] In this regard religious systems differ from the study of religions. The latter seeks knowledge in Brint's strict sense of the term.

The topic of private funding for research is different from that of knowledge exchange. Knowledge exchange involves a bidirectional exchange of knowledge goods between academia and other organizations. Private funding refers to a unidirectional movement of money from sources outside of academia to support knowledge creation within it. The two do, however, share some characteristics. As Brint (2018: 131–132) observes, "All organizations have an interest in knowledge structures that lead to greater effectiveness in the achievement of valued outcomes." So, too, do donors. And both face what we might call barriers to trade. Brint identifies three such barriers in knowledge exchange. In order of ascending degree of obstruction, they are: corrupted knowledge goods, as when religious groups make misleading use of the results of academic research; failed exchanges, as when academic knowledge structures do not align with the objectives of outside institutions and vice versa; and complete blockages, as when conservative politicians and business leaders reject the results of climate science (ibid.: 133–135). Three similar barriers to trade impinge upon private funding for the study of religions.

First, several minority religious groups in the US have recognized that they have a vested interest in encouraging the academic study of their own religions. They may do so to counter a dominant narrative, whether Christian or ethnocentric, or they may do so out of a basic concern with self-preservation (consider the violence Muslims, Sikhs, and South Asians suffered in the wake of the 9/11 attacks).

Yet religious persons and organizations also make their own claims to knowledge. Some of them are quite open to adapting their conceptual systems and knowledge claims to accommodate the results of rigorous, critical academic investigation, but generally there are limits, sometimes severe. One relatively recent, relatively high-profile example concerns Rajiv Malhotra, his associates, and his

---

9. As distinct from knowledge, "knowledge structures" provide a framework of interrelated concepts, results, and procedures within which subsequent work is structured" (Brint 2018: 118).
10. But Brint allows that religious systems are not entirely divorced from knowledge. At the beginning of his chapter, he writes, "knowledge structures generated outside academe include … spiritual practices of Eastern religions insofar as they are tied to health benefits," and he notes that there is some overlap "between social-science evidence on marriage as a benefit and conservative religious institutions" (Brint 2018: 115, 133).

Infinity Foundation. Malhotra and the Infinity Foundation have in fact provided some funding for the study of religions. For example, they helped support the 2010 Congress of the International Association for the History of Religions. But they are best known for attacks on Indological scholarship, especially the study of Indian religions (e.g., Banerjee, De Nicolás, and Ramaswamy 2007; Malhotra and Neelakandan 2011; Malhotra 2016a, 2016b).[11] Malhotra's claims have provoked some discussion within the academy itself (e.g., Gier 2012; Larson 2012; Yelle 2012; Pennington 2013; Rambachan 2013), but I presume that most academics who take charges of academic Eurocentrism seriously give much more credence to in-house arguments advanced by scholars like Dipesh Chakrabarty (2009) and Philippe Descola (2013a)—at least Descola when he is critiquing anthropological categories like nature and culture (cf., too, Descola 2013b). By contrast, Malhotra is generally in the business of presenting "corrupted knowledge goods" to a more general audience.

To be fair, though, barriers to trade on the level of corrupted knowledge goods—a stance that supports academic scholarship in the study of religions only to the extent that it confirms rather than threatens the funders' own ideological agendas and commitments—is hardly limited to minority religious communities. Just recall my visit to the Museum of the Bible.

A second barrier to trade is analogous to Brint's notion of failed exchanges. It arises from a misalignment between the goals of funding sources and the aims of the academic study of religions. Among other places, potential for such misalignment is found in the relationship between foundations and scholars of religions.

Scholars have, of course, undertaken a very large number of successful research projects with foundation support. The first project that comes to mind, although it is not a project in the study of religions, is the multi-sited, collaborative ethnography of the Matsutake Worlds Research Group (cf. Matsutake Worlds Research Group 2009; Tsing 2015), which, on the initiative of the anthropologist Anna Tsing, received a sizeable award from the Toyota Foundation in 2007.[12]

As is well known, foundations generally frame competitions for funds in terms of themes that seek to advance their agendas. For example, in 2019 the theme for the Toyota Foundation's Research Grant competition was "Exploring New Values for Society," while the theme for its International Research Grant Competition was "Cultivating Empathy through Learning from Our Neighbors: Practitioners' Exchange on Common Issues in Asia." (The Toyota USA Foundation only supports projects in STEM fields.[13]) The Ford Foundation aims to combat inequality, which it attributes to five interconnected "drivers"—"entrenched cultural narratives,

---

11. Note that the Infinity Foundation provided some much-needed financial support for the 2010 Congress of the International Association for the History of Religions, held in Toronto, Canada.
12. See http://toyotafound.force.com/psearch/JoseiDetail?name=D07-R-0502.
13. See www.toyotafound.or.jp/english/research/2019; www.toyotafound.or.jp/english/international/2019; www.toyota.com/usa/community/grant-guidelines-applications/overview.html.

failure to invest in and protect vital public goods, unfair rules of the economy, unequal access to government, [and] persistent prejudice and discrimination;" it seeks to address these drivers with grants in "seven interconnected areas:" "civic engagement and government, creativity and free expression, future of work(ers), gender, racial, and ethnic justice, just cities and regions, natural resources and climate change, [and] technology and society."[14] The Henry Luce Foundation has two programs of potential interest to scholars of religions: Religion in International Affairs and Theology, the second of which "aims to advance understanding of religion and theology."[15] Much more limited is the Lilly Endowment, which states: "Our primary aim in religion is to deepen and enrich the religious lives of American Christians, principally by supporting efforts that enhance the vitality of congregations."[16]

There is no point in multiplying examples of foundations, and there is no justification for criticizing the orientations of the foundations just mentioned: people with money have the right to seek "greater effectiveness in the achievement of" whatever outcomes they value. The examples above do, however, illustrate potential misalignments between the goals of foundations and basic work in the study of religions. One way to deal with this misalignment is simply to frame one's own projects in the language of the foundation's agenda and themes. Such rhetorical accommodation will be more readily available to some projects than to others, but I wonder if it also exacerbates problems in the long run. First, to what extent should funding sources outside academia decide what research scholars of religions pursue? Second, to what extent does changing the frame for projects in the study of religions obscure the visibility and thus the perceived value of the knowledge that the study of religions creates?

A third, even more severe barrier to trade in support of the study of religions is analogous to Brint's blockage. One example is the refusal of fundamentalists even to consider critical scholarship on texts such as the Bible. Another is the pervasive, long-standing use of private money in higher education to promote one's preferred religious outlook.[17]

To some extent this use exhibits corrupted knowledge goods. For example, the chapter "Religion, Spirituality, and College Students" in the *Oxford Handbook of Religion and American Education* (Rockenbach and Park 2018) presents a rather enthusiastic account of the importance of religion and spirituality among college students, apparently as part of an agenda to encourage colleges to nurture spiritual development (ibid.: 406–407). The quite different survey of research published by Damon Mayrl and Freeden Oeur (2009), now ten years old, remains useful in exemplifying a significantly more balanced, nuanced approach to the subject (ibid.: 260; cf. more recently Hill 2017).

---

14. See www.fordfoundation.org/work/challenging-inequality.
15. See www.hluce.org/programs/religion-international-affairs.
16. See https://lillyendowment.org/our-work/religion.
17. Equally problematic, of course, but less common in the history of American higher education, is the donation of money in the interest of eradicating religion.

The agenda of promoting religion and spirituality is so typical of the *Oxford Handbook*, at least of the section on Religion and Higher Education, and so severe, that it constitutes a blockage to non-partisan research in the study of religions. In effect, the volume continues the project, begun in the 1990s, of attempting to re-establish within higher education the hegemony of Christianity, particularly of Protestantism, whether in evangelical or liberal form (interfaith studies, spirituality) (cf. Marsden 1994, 1997; Burtchaell 1998; Schwehn 1993; Sloan 1994; Palmer 1983; Cherry, De Berg, and Porterfield 2001; Schwartz 2001; Mahoney, Schmalzbauer, and Youniss 2001; Jacobsen and Jacobsen 2018: 315–320; Palmer 1998). Casual readers could be excused if, after perusing this section, they were completely unaware that there even is a serious, academic study of religions concerned with furthering knowledge about religions rather than with spiritual development.

Here are some examples: The Jacobsen's present the academic study of religion as an outmoded, naïve endeavor pursued by antiquated scholars unaware of postmodern epistemologies and occupying a minor place within a broader movement that seeks to destroy religion or at least to ignore it as unworthy of academic investigation (Jacobsen and Jacobsen 2018: 314–315). Eugene Gallagher (2018) at least acknowledges that there is disagreement about what teaching religious studies should entail, but he says precious little about what the academic study of religions actually is and does. A single quote should be sufficient to demonstrate the many missed opportunities in Robert Nash's chapter on "Teaching About Religion Outside of Religious Studies": "start the conversations with candid, personal disclosures on everybody's part concerning where they currently stand on their religio-spiritual journeys and where they would like to end up. Putting our religio-spiritual cards on the table early is a good way to set the stage for enlarging the conversational space for everyone" (Nash 2018: 446). In other words, Nash is teaching religion under the guise of teaching about religion. As far as an understanding of religion is concerned, scholars in anthropology, sociology, psychology, history, literature, political science, economics and so on apparently have nothing of value to offer.

It is clear, at least in principle, that persons or organizations who want to promote religious or spiritual development (the Lilly Foundation, the Louisville Institute, and so on) or skew research in a religious direction (e.g., the John Templeton Foundation) might donate money—in some cases a great deal of money—in the hope of achieving their valued outcomes. It also seems clear that in a variety of ways such contributors might be uninterested in or hostile to the critically sifted knowledge that the study of religions seeks to provide. As an article in *Zygon* on the significance of Huston Smith's *Why Religion Matters* (2001) and *The Purposes of Higher Education* (1955) puts it: "Verification belongs to the future" (Kenney 2015: 242). No; absolutely not. Verification—the testing of ideas on the basis of evidence, as well as the assessment of the adequacy of one's ideas and methods, including their political and moral "imbrications"—is a continuous, never-ending process, one that requires unceasing judgment in the present, not a deferred judgment that can only be experienced proleptically.

Let me put the question that underlies each of these barriers to trade bluntly. There are plenty of private interests that might find the critical assessment of knowledge in and about religions that the study of religions provides to be antithetical to—or at least misaligned with—"greater effectiveness in the achievement of [their] valued outcomes." Are there private interests that need this knowledge?

Can Private Money Save the Study of Religions?

My ultimate concern is with research, not pedagogy, the creation of knowledge rather than its transmission. The two are not, however, easily separated. Compared to the natural sciences, the major cost involved in research in the study of religions is generally an indirect labor cost: the ability to earn a living in a manner that allows enough time to read, think, and write and provides the wherewithal to have access to the data about which one writes and to communicate with one's colleagues. For most scholars of religions, this indirect cost is met in some way, shape, or form by teaching. That is the foundation upon which any special funds for research, even funds for research leaves, generally build. And while it may be tempting to fantasize about being independently wealthy and not dependent upon any institution for a living, I suspect that on the whole the financial benefits derived from such independence are outweighed by the intellectual costs of being removed from the give and take of the academic context—our "ultimate cultural authority (and [our] privileged work space)" for testing and refining knowledge.[18]

To be sure, a case can be made that governments should support the study of religions. For one thing, they need the critically sifted knowledge that the study of religions provides in order to establish "policies on religion ... shaped by research evidence" rather than based upon hunches, guesswork, and local prejudices (Stevenson and Aune 2017: 17). Furthermore, although I see no reason why governments should take an interest in nurturing (or impeding) religious or spiritual development, Stephen Prothero has made a well-known argument that a modicum of religious literacy is necessary for responsible citizenship, something in which democratic governments do have an obvious interest (Prothero 2007; cf. Gallagher 2018: 429). But religious literacy is a little like art appreciation: it provides precious little in the way of critical reflection and analysis. And besides, the United States has a long history of favoring teaching over research in subjects such as this. So religious literacy is not a particularly robust justification for the study of religions. In any case the question at hand concerns private money, not public.

There is one respect in which our colleagues who favor spiritual nurturing are correct. In a time of dwindling commitment to the humanities and to the study of religions in higher education, the case needs to be made that knowledge

---

18. In the interests of space, I have left to one side here research grants from private sources as well as the possibility of establishing research institutions, such as centers for the study of religions.

about religions is important. One way to make that case—a very pragmatic way, if it can be pulled off—is through private money, just as a century and more ago the Rockefeller and Carnegie Foundations made the case that American higher education needed to up its game. Clearly there are people with money who care about knowledge about religions; their willingness to support the study of religions would go a long way in helping to sustain it. Although in the current climate, dominated by funding for STEM fields, it seems like a hopeless fantasy, imagine what could be done with just the $100 million wasted in building the Ark Encounter theme park in Williamstown, Kentucky.[19] Invested as endowment in generous, $5 million blocks, the funds could provide income for twenty academic positions in the study of religions more or less indefinitely.

At the same time, in the interests of overcoming barriers to trade, scholars of religions need, carefully and patiently, to make certain points clear to those who raise and receive funds on behalf of academic institutions (essentially a process of cultivating long-term relationships[20]), to fellow members of the academy, and especially to donors.

First, from the recognition that all knowledge arises contextually and involves preconceptions it does not follow that all claims to knowledge are equally good. Otherwise, biologists should embrace creation science as well as evolution. Higher education is not about sharing, nurturing, and elaborating personal opinions, convictions, and traditions; it is about examining, proving, deepening, revising, and rejecting alleged knowledge—including cherished opinions, convictions, and traditions—on the basis of evidence. Second, pursuing such knowledge with the utmost seriousness does not mean adopting an outsiders' perspective that needs to be supplemented by the "involvement of religious practitioners in teaching religious studies" (Stevenson and Aune 2017: 17). It is a grievous error to equate the difference between theology and religious studies with the difference between an insider's and an outsider's perspective. As a scholar I am committed to taking the views of religious practitioners with whom I work as seriously as possible. And as a religious insider I still find the results of the study of religions compelling; they represent the best knowledge available. I also recognize that appeals to complex conceptual (rather than knowledge) systems, however traditional or emotionally compelling they may be, have evidentiary value only if I happen to be studying those complex systems. Third, to claim that "[e]ducation in Theology and Religious Studies should ensure both scientific detachment *and the personal attachment to one's own tradition*" (van Saane 2017: 182, emphasis added) is to abandon the academic pursuit altogether. Jonathan Hill may or may not be correct when he concludes that, "despite concerns about the secularising influence of higher education, college tends to have [at least at the present] a few positive (in the form of institutional belonging and practice), a few negative (in terms of certain super-empirical beliefs), but mostly no influence on religious

---

19. See https://arkencounter.com/press.
20. Or so I was told by a former student who worked in the principal-gifts office at the University of Chicago.

faith" (Hill 2017: 37). In any case, serious work in the academic study of religions pursues knowledge, come what may. The consequences for a person's attachment to her tradition are beside the point. Expecting—and funding—anything else is unacceptable.

My mind is drawn back to the Museum of the Bible. Not to overcome these barriers to trade and to allow academic study simply to affirm a religious tradition and to nurture spiritual development seems uncomfortably familiar. It is the twenty-first-century academic equivalent to producing a Slave Bible.

Gregory D. Alles is professor of religious studies at McDaniel College, Westminster, MD, USA. A past president of the North American Association for the Study of Religions and former editor on *Numen*, the journal of the International Association for the History of Religions, his current research focuses on Adivasis in India, specifically Rathvas and other Adivasis living in eastern Chhotaudepur District, Gujarat.

References

Adams, Liam. 2018. "The Humanities' Place in Research Spending." *Chronicle of Higher Education* 64(41): 40.
Alterman, Eric. 2019. "The Decline of Historical Thinking." *The New Yorker* 94(47).
Banerjee, Aditi, Antonio T. De Nicolás, and Krishnan Ramaswamy. 2007. *Invading the Sacred: An Analysis of Hinduism Studies in America*. New Delhi: Rupa and Co.
Brint, Peter. 2018. "An Institutional Geography of Knowledge Exchage: Producers, Exports, Imports, Trade Routes, and Metacognitive Metropoles." In Jal Mehta and Scott Davies (eds), *Education in a New Society: Renewing the Sociology of Education* (pp. 115–143). Chicago, IL: University of Chicago Press.
British Academy. 2019. *Theology and Religious Studies Provision in UK Higher Education*. London: The British Academy.
Burtchaell, James Tunstead. 1998. *The Dying of the Light: The Disengagement for Colleges and Universities from their Christian Churches*. Grand Rapids, MI: William B. Eerdmans.
Chakrabarty, Dipesh. 2009. *Provincializing Europe: Postcolonial Thought and Historical Difference*. Princeton, NJ: Princeton University Press.
Cherry, Conrad, Betty A. De Berg, and Amanda Porterfield. 2001. "Religion on Campus." *Liberal Education* 87(4): 6–13.
Chronicle of Higher Education. 2018a. "Research-and-Development Spending, by Source of Funds." *Chronicle of Higher Education* 64(41): 19.
Chronicle of Higher Education. 2018b. "Federal Support for Research and Development, by Agency." *Chronicle of Higher Education* 64(41): 33.
Chronicle of Higher Education. 2018c. "Colleges That Spent the Most on Humanities Research." *Chronicle of Higher Education* 64(41): 49.
Descola, Philippe. 2013a. *Beyond Nature and Culture*. Chicago, IL: University of Chicago Press.
Descola, Philippe. 2013b. *The Ecology of Others*. Trans. Genevieve Godbout and Benjamin P. Luley. Chicago, IL: Prickly Paradigm Press.
Donoghue, Frank. 2008. *The Last Professors: The Corporate University and the Fate of the Humanities*. New York: Fordham University Press.
Gallagher, Eugene. 2018. "Teaching Religious Studies." In Michael D. Waggoner and Nathan C. Walker (eds), *The Oxford Handbook of Religion and American Education* (pp. 425–437). New York: Oxford University Press.

Geiger, Roger L. 1986. *To Advance Knowledge: The Growth of American Research Universities, 1900-1940*. New York: Oxford University Press.
Geiger, Roger L. 2015. *The History of American Higher Education: Learning and Culture from the Founding to World War II*. Princeton, NJ: Princeton University Press.
Geiger, Roger L. 2019. *American Higher Education Since World War II: A History*. Princeton, NJ: Princeton University Press.
Gier, Nicholas F. 2012. "Overreaching to Be Different: A Critique of Rajiv Malhotra's Being Different." *International Journal of Hindu Studies* 16(3): 259-285.
Hill, Jonathan P. 2017. "Religion and Higher Education in the United States: Extending the Research." In Kristin Aune and Jacqueline Stevenson (eds), *Religion and Higher Education in Europe and North America* (pp. 25-38). Abingdon: Routledge.
Jacobsen, Douglas, and Rhonda Hustedt Jacobsen. 2018. "Religion in Mainline and Independent Private Higher Education." In Michael D. Waggoner and Nathan C. Walker (eds), *The Oxford Handbook of Religion and American Education* (pp. 311-327). New York: Oxford University Press.
Kenney, Garrett C. 2015. "Why Religion Matters and The Purposes of Higher Education: A Dialogue with Huston Smith." *Zygon* 50(1): 227-244.
Larson, Gerald James. 2012. "The Issue of Not Being Different Enough: Some Reflections on Rajiv Malhotra's Being Different." *International Journal of Hindu Studies* 16(3): 311-322.
Mahoney, Kathleen A., John Schmalzbauer, and James Youniss. 2001. "Religion: A Comeback on Campus." *Liberal Education* 87(4): 36-41.
Malhotra, Rajiv. 2016a. *The Battle for Sanskrit: Is Sanskrit Political or Sacred, Opressive or Liberating, Dead or Alive?* New Delhi: HarperCollins Publishers.
Malhotra, Rajiv. 2016b. *Academic Hinduphobia: A Critique of Wendy Doniger's Erotic School of Indology*. New Delhi: Voice of India.
Malhotra, Rajiv, and Aravindan Neelakandan. 2011. *Breaking India: Western Interventions in Dravidian and Dalit Faultlines*. New Delhi: Amaryllis.
Marsden, George M. 1994. *The Soul of the American University: From Protestant Establishment to Established Nonbelief*. New York: Oxford University Press.
Marsden, George M. 1997. *The Outrageous Idea of Christian Scholarship*. New York: Oxford University Press.
Matsutake Worlds Research Group. 2009. "Strong Collaboration as a Method for Multi-sited Ethnography: On Mycorrhizal Relations." In Mark-Anthony Falzon (ed.), *Multi-sited Ethnography: Theory, Praxis and Locality in Contemporary Research* (pp. 197-214). Farnham: Ashgate.
Mayrl, Damon, and Freeden Oeur. 2009. "Religion and Higher Education: Current Knowledge and Directions for Future Research." *Journal for the Scientific Study of Religion* 48(2): 260-275.
Nash, Robert J. 2018. "Teaching About Religion Outside of Religious Studies." In Michael D. Waggoner and Nathan C. Walker (eds), *Oxford Handbook of Religion and American Education* (pp. 438-452). New York: Oxford University Press.
Palmer, Parker J. 1983. *To Know as We Are Known: Education as a Spiritual Journey*. San Francisco, CA: HarperCollins.
Palmer, Parker J. 1998. *The Courage to Teach: Exploring the Inner Landscape of a Teacher's Life*. San Francisco, CA: Jossey-Bass.
Pennington, Brian K. 2013. "The Pitfalls of Trying to Be Different." *Journal of Hindu-Christian Studies* 26: 10-16.

Prothero, Stephen. 2007. *Religious Literacy: What Every American Needs to Know—And Doesn't.* San Francisco, CA: HarperSanFrancisco.
Rambachan, Anantanand. 2013. "The Traditional Roots of Difference." *Journal of Hindu-Christian Studies* 26: 2–9.
Rockenbach, Alyssa Bryant, and Julie J. Park. 2018. "Religion, Spirituality, and College Students." In Michael D. Waggoner and Nathan C. Walker (eds), *The Oxford Handbook of Religion and American Education* (pp. 397–410). New York: Oxford University Press.
Schmidt, Benjamin M. 2018. "The History BA Since the Great Recession: The 2018 AHA Majors Report." *Perspectives on History* 56(9): 19–23.
Schwartz, Arthur. 2001. "Growing Spiritually During the College Years." *Liberal Education* 87(4): 30–35.
Schwehn, Mark R. 1993. *Exiles from Eden: Religion and the Academic Vocation in America.* New York: Oxford University Press.
Sloan, Douglas. 1994. *Faith and Knowledge: Mainline Protestantism and American Higher Education.* Louisville, KY: Westminster John Knox Press.
Smith, Huston. 1955. *The Purposes of Higher Education.* New York: Harper & Brothers.
Smith, Huston. 2001. *Why Religion Matters: The Fate of the Human Spirit in an Age of Disbelief.* New York: HarperSanFrancisco.
Stevenson, Jacqueline, and Kristin Aune. 2017. "Introduction: Religion and Higher Education in Europe and North America: Historical and Contemporary Contexts." In Kristin Aune and Jacqueline Stevenson (eds), *Religion and Higher Education in Europe and North America* (pp. 1–21). Abingdon: Routledge.
Thelin, John R. 2014. *Essential Documents in the History of American Higher Education.* Baltimore, MD: Johns Hopkins University Press.
Thelin, John R. 2019. *A History of American Higher Education*, 3rd edition. Baltimore, MD: Johns Hopkins University Press.
Tsing, Anna Lowenhaupt. 2015. *The Mushroom at the End of the World: On the Possibility of Life in Capitalist Ruins.* Princeton, NJ: Princeton University Press.
van Saane, Joke. 2017. "From Cognitive Science to Personal Leadership: The Role of Religion and Personal Life Orientation in Curriculum Development Processes within the Domain of Religious Studies." In Kristin Aune and Jacqueline Stevenson (eds), *Religion and Higher Education in Europe and North America* (pp. 181–189). Abingdon: Routledge.
Yelle, Robert A. 2012. "Comparative Religion as Cultural Combat: Occidentalism and Relativism in Rajiv Malhotra's Being Different." *International Journal of Hindu Studies* 16(3): 335–348.

Chapter 11

Drugs, Dog Chow, and Dharma

Michael J. Altman

I would like to put three brief examples of private funding in the study of religion on the table and see what they might tell us about the past, present, and future of private funding in our field. These three examples are drugs, dog chow, and dharma.

I will begin with drugs. Eli Lilly, his father Josiah Kirby Lilly, and his younger brother J. K. Jr. founded the Lilly Endowment in 1937 through a $262,500 gift of stock in Eli Lilly and Company, a pharmaceutical firm. Eli Lilly was the first company to mass-produce the polio vaccine. More recently, it is the largest manufacturer of psychiatric medication. It produces Prozac, Dolophine, Cymbalta, and Zyprexa. In 2018, the Lilly Endowment grants in religion totaled $170.5 million dollars, 35 percent of the foundation's grant total. The Lilly Foundation has five aims for its religion granting: strengthening pastoral leadership, deepening Christian life, enhancing congregational vitality, strengthening religious institutions and networks, and improving the public understanding of religion (Lilly Endowment 2018).

Within those five aims, the Lilly Endowment has become one of, if not the, most influential funders of "religion in America" or "American religious history." As Thomas Tweed noted in a footnote:

> As far as I know, no one has done a thorough study of the effects of funding by the Lily Endowment and the Pew Charitable Trusts on scholarship about U.S. religion, though Wilson (87) also has noted its importance. To disclose my own debts, the collaborative project that led to *Retelling US Religious History* received funding from both Lily and Pew.
>
> (Tweed 2010: 252)

To Tweed's project one can add the Institute for the Study of American Evangelicals, founded by Mark Noll and Nathan Hatch at Wheaton College in 1982 and closed in 2014, and its successor in many ways, the Center for Religion and American Culture (CRAAC), founded in 1989 at IUPUI. The CRAAC runs the main journal within the subfield of religion in America and the popular Young Scholars of Religion in America program that has involved many of the most successful scholars in the field since its inception in 1991. These are just two of the many programs, fellowships, and research projects Lilly has funded. As Tweed's footnote (and it is a footnote!) reminds, no one has sat down and accounted for Lilly's full effect.

Insofar as the Lilly Endowment has funded the major shifts in method and historiography within the study of religion in America, and insofar as the Endowment's wealth has been generated by the success of Eli Lilly and Company, and insofar as that success has been driven by the market for psychiatric pharmaceuticals in the past forty years, one might argue, without judgement one way or another, that the field of America religion has been built on Prozac.

Now, dog chow. In 1927 William H. Danforth, the founder of the Ralston Purina Co., and his family established the Danforth Foundation with a gift of $100,000 in Ralston Purina stock and other securities. From its inception until 1996, the Danforth Foundation funded various education programs around the country. Beginning in the 1950s, Danforth funded a number of different fellowship programs in the study of religion and then in the early 1960s it turned to institutional funding and began funding the establishment of religion and religious studies departments around the country.

In July of 1965 the University of Alabama submitted a proposal to the Danforth Foundation for a grant to assist in the establishment of a department of religion—the department within which I work. I do not know the total of the grant request because the budget page is missing from the copy of the proposal in our files. In the application to Danforth, the University of Alabama argued that "the State of Alabama and the region in which it is located are experiencing sociological and economic changes which are perhaps more profound than any other state or region...Developments at the university are especially important and promise to have extraordinary influence as social, economic, and cultural forces" (University of Alabama 1965: 3). A religious studies department would help Alabama navigate the rough cultural waters of Vietnam, the Cold War, and Civil Rights Movement. With help from the Danforth Foundation the Department of Religious Studies was founded in 1967 with two faculty members, Joe Bettis and Leon Weinberger. A third faculty member, Patrick Green, joined the department in 1969. All three jumped into the anti-Vietnam and Civil Rights protests swirling on campus. Bettis even had a Doberman follow him everywhere out of fear of reprisals from the KKK (Green 2019).

As Sarah Imhoff has argued, this cultural and social turbulence of the 1960s was one of the motivations for founding religious studies departments around the country. "Perhaps the most explicit example of the Cold War rationale—or at least the Cold War as an opportunity to convince Americans of the value of the academic study of religion," she writes "came from the Danforth Foundation" (Imhoff 2016: 488). Merrimon Cuninggim, a former professor and dean of theology at Southern Methodist University, directed the Danforth Foundation during the 1960s and led the charge as Danforth began funding religious studies departments around the country. As Imhoff has concluded, "Merrimon Cuninggim and the Danforth Foundation, which helped fund the creation or early development of dozens of religious studies departments—more than any other foundation—used language of democracy, morality, and religion in its support of the creation of religious studies departments" (ibid.: 490). The academic study of religion would produce good moral citizens for difficult political and moral times.

Again, insofar as the Danforth Foundation's wealth came from the success of Ralston Purina, and insofar as the Foundation is responsible for the founding of not just my department but numerous departments at both public and private universities, then we can argue, for better or worse, that the expansion of our field relied on dog chow.

Finally, dharma. Here the story is not a success story. In February of 2016 the University of California at Irvine announced that it was returning $3 million in gifts that were going to fund two endowed chairs in Hindu studies (Redden 2016). The gifts came from the Dharma Civilization Foundation (DCF), a California non-profit whose mission is "To promote philanthropic giving for creating academic and intellectual infrastructure for the systematic study of 'Dharma'," its interpretation and application in modern contexts, in formal academic settings" (Dharma Civilization Foundation 2019a). Rather than the gift of a single successful family like Danforth or Lilly, the DCF has a number of prosperous trustees and members that fund its projects. The DCF promotes an alternative academic approach to the study of so-called "dharmic religions" of South Asia through funding academic chairs, departments, and centers and is critical of current academic studies of these "dharmic religions." Its gift was returned after faculty and graduate students at UCI protested and argued that the DCF was a "right-wing Hindu group" with ties to the Hindu nationalist RSS (Dharma Civilization Foundation 2019b). Despite its failure at Irvine, the DCF has successfully funded faculty positions at the University of Southern California and the Graduate Theological Union.

So, let me close with a few conclusions about these three examples and what they may tell us about private funding in the study of religion. First, religious studies has always relied on private funding. Second, as we see with Danforth and Lilly, that private money has come largely from liberal Protestants who saw the study of religion in general as a good thing for the American church and American society. Third, the model of old money endowments from a single rich family is giving way to the "new money" of groups like the DCF that link together prosperous first and second-generation immigrant donors to fund one academic position at a time. The anonymous funding of a chair of Mormon Studies at the University of Virginia is another example of the religious studies nouveau riche. Lastly, studies of religion, even the kind of critical work many of us seek to do, aligns nicely with liberal Protestantism in ways that it does not align with, say, Hindutva. The Lilly Endowment funds programs that study religion because they think that it will strengthen the American church but when the DCF funds chairs that will strengthen American Hinduism faculty protest. Where are the letters protesting the pernicious influences of liberal Protestantism on religious studies? The problem the DCF ran into is that it made its goals too plain. It openly names scholars it finds objectionable on its website and it takes a belligerent posture toward the academic study of religion. It also tried to control who would fill the chairs it funded in order to ensure they were the right kind of scholar. The DCF made the mistake of saying the subtext out loud. "We would like our chair of Hindu studies to be a good Hindu." To put it simply, liberal Protestants reach their goals by funding chairs for the study of religion, while Hindus have to fund chairs of Hindu studies.

As scholars of religion, not university administrators or funders, I think the takeaway from these three examples is that funders have a variety of interests and we have a variety of goals for our scholarship. There will not be a funder whose goals perfectly align with ours and we will have to approach each funding opportunity strategically. For example, my own department was just awarded a grant from the Henry Luce Foundation to fund a program for early career scholars of religion (Altman 2020). Luce wants to fund programs that further the public understanding of religion, and our program does that, but it also has a research and teaching component. So insofar as Luce made his money in publishing, the future of our department, at least in part, depends on *Time Magazine*.

Michael J. Altman is the author of *Heathen, Hindoo, Hindu: American Representations of India, 1721-1893* (Oxford, 2017) and *Hinduism in America: An Introduction* (Routledge, forthcoming). He is also director of American Examples, a workshop for early career scholars of religion, and editor of the series of American Examples anthologies. His research interests include Asian religions in America, evangelicalism, and professional wrestling.

References

Altman, Michael J. 2020. "The Report: American Examples, or, How I Stopped Being an Americanist and Learned to Study Religion in America All Over Again." *Bulletin for the Study of Religion* 49(1–2): 32–34.

Dharma Civilization Foundation. 2019a. "Mission Statement." Retrieved from www.dcfusa.org/about-us/mission-statement (accessed November 19, 2019).

Dharma Civilization Foundation. 2019b. "FAQ." Retrieved from www.dcfusa.org/about-us/faq (accessed November 19, 2019).

Green, Patrick. 2019. "The Department of Religious Studies—Early Times, Part 1." Retrieved from https://religion.ua.edu/blog/2019/11/19/the-department-of-religious-studies-early-times.

Imhoff, Sarah. 2016. "The Creation Story, or How We Learned to Stop Worrying and Love Schempp." *Journal of the American Academy of Religion* 84(2): 466–497.

Lilly Endowment. 2018. *Lilly Endowment Annual Report 2018*. Indianapolis, IN: Lilly Endowment. Retrieved from http://lillyendowment.org/wp-content/uploads/2019/06/annual-report-2018.pdf.

Redden, Elizabeth. 2016. "Uc Irvine Moves to Reject Endowed Chair Gifts from Donor with Strong Opinions About the Study of Hinduism." *Inside Higher Ed*, February 22. Retrieved from www.insidehighered.com/news/2016/02/22/uc-irvine-moves-reject-endowed-chair-gifts-donor-strong-opinions-about-study.

Tweed, Thomas A. 2010. "Expanding the Study of US Religion: Reflections on the State of a Subfield." *Religion* 40(4): 250–258.

University of Alabama. 1965. "A Proposal by the University of Alabama to the Danforth Foundation for a Grant to Assist in the Establishment of a Department of Religion." July 12. Records of the Department of Religious Studies at the University of Alabama.

Chapter 12

Between Wittgenstein and Zuckerberg
Selling the Academic Study of Religion in a Buyer's Market

John W. McCormack

In a time of constricting higher education appropriations and increased anxieties around student loan debt, the academic study of religion faces an acute funding problem for which private foundation dollars might seem an attractive answer. However, as Gregory Alles notes in his essay (Chapter 10, this volume), this threatens to skew quite drastically the questions that scholars are willing and able to pursue. Those working at non-elite, teaching-focused, and tuition-dependent institutions are particularly vulnerable to such pressures—especially those working without the traditional protections of tenure. When budget-conscious administrators, market-conscious students, and mission-conscious philanthropists are driving the financial realities of academic work, the freedom of scholars of religions to pursue their work is constrained by the definitions and expectations of these stakeholders. What these stakeholders "know" about religion is shaped by a range of political and confessional commitments extraneous to the redescriptive and explanatory work pursued by the academic study of religion.

Our efforts to teach and pursue research that pushes back against an essentialized notion of "religion" can run aground on a public discourse shaped by the contest of political liberalism and Christian conservatism and disseminated to our students via social media platforms. Students enter our classroom knowing what religion is or is not, and administrators trained in other fields evaluate our work, because we all labor in a linguistic field in which, as Ludwig Wittgenstein suggested, the meaning of a word is its use in the language. Scholars of religion have always fought to unmask the social and political practices driving attempts to codify such binaries as "religious/secular" and "sacred/profane," but this work only advances insofar as it is legible as religious studies. Thus our arguments against the "specialness" of "religion" particularly imperil the academic study of religion at this moment in academic history.

Alles poses a question in the title of Chapter 10 that bluntly situates academic labor in a context of contingency and vulnerability: "Can Private Money Save the Study of Religions?" He identifies a Scylla and Charybdis hemming in the work pursued by scholars of religion dedicated to what Bruce Lincoln has defined as "critical inquiry" (Lincoln 1996). On the one hand, funding agencies such as the Museum of the Bible support research that Alles terms "corrupted knowledge goods" (Chapter 10, this volume), directing money toward a project "only to the extent that it confirms rather than threatens the funders' own ideological agendas and commitments" (ibid.). Though Alles grants to "people with money … the right to seek 'greater effectiveness in the achievement of' whatever outcomes they seek" (ibid.), the resulting work surely runs the risk of contributing to what McCutcheon calls "a normative and uncritical notion of religion as a beneficial (i.e., peaceful, beautiful, and civil) force in human affairs," or more broadly, "pre-critical notions of religion as a socio-politically autonomous force" (Chapter 6, this volume). On the other, universities continue to cut funding for the humanities in general and religious studies in particular, which frequently means the elimination of both programs and faculty positions. Though his chapter focuses on the funding of scholarly activity rather than teaching, Alles notes that "the major cost involved in research in the study of religion is generally an indirect labor cost: the ability to earn a living in a manner that allows enough time to read, think, and write … For most scholars of religions, this indirect cost is met in some way, shape, or form by teaching" (Chapter 10, this volume). Alles muses briefly on the possibility of a privately funded academic study of religion untethered from its institutional home in the university, before rejecting that as "removed from the give and take" of academia as we currently know it (ibid.). He does not unequivocally answer his own question, but I take his answer roughly to be: *no, it cannot save us, but it may be our only hope.*

My own answer to the question is perhaps even less sanguine, because I understand the availability of private funding and shrinking university support (public or private) for religious studies to be two sides of the same coin: the problem of rendering our work legible to publics that already understand what "religion" means. Though scholars of religion within, around, and outside of NAASR have been working diligently to explain defining, classifying, and boundary-policing of "religion" as so much "religioning" (see Smith, Chapter 1, this volume), public understanding of religion remains informed by essentialized notions still rooted in Christianity and masquerading as common sense (Smith 1990). In such a climate, I am not convinced that a critical study of religion as proposed by McCutcheon in this volume and elsewhere can survive on its own in the marketplace of ideas apart from the institutional support of the modern university. Moreover, with public support for higher education in the United States waning—both in financial and moral terms—increasingly *all* of our funding is "private" in the form of tuition dollars, even when those dollars are backed by federally subsidized loans. Indeed, scholars of religion might be uniquely well placed to note that, in neoliberal political economy, the private/public distinction with regard to funding is shown to be as much a contingent, motivated construction as it is in the field of religion (on neoliberalism and religion research, see Alles 2019; on public/private in religion, see Casanova 1994; Cavanaugh 2009; Fitzgerald 2011; Gregory 2012; Hurd 2015). This leaves the scholar of religion trapped, I would suggest, between "Wittgenstein" and "Zuckerberg." By the former, I mean Ludwig Wittgenstein's oft-quoted insight in *Philosophical Investigations* that "for a large class of cases—though not for all—in which we employ the word 'meaning' it can be defined thus:

the meaning of a word is its use in the language" (Wittgenstein 1953: §43). By the latter, I mean the field of contemporary public discourses as shaped and shared on social media. College teaching is not merely essential because academic "give and take" sustains scholars of religion in their critical enterprise, but also because it is the primary way in which scholars reach the public. Without the opportunity to teach students in the classroom, critical attempts to re-describe religion as a social practice—as a verb—will have little chance to move from "the field" (defined as a jury of our scholarly peers) into the wider field of public conversation.

The headlines for the humanities, and for the study of religion in particular, are grim. Since the Great Recession of 2007–2009, cuts to programs in religious studies have been deep, and these have only accelerated in the COVID-19 era. Alles mentions that his liberal arts college cut the major in religious studies and does not plan to fill his position after his retirement (Chapter 10, this volume). My own institution decided to sunset its religion minor in 2016, followed by the major in 2018, leaving me the sole full-time faculty member in the study of religion, temporarily housed in a Department of General Education. Recently both small liberal arts colleges (Goucher, Guilford, Alma) and larger research universities (Vermont) have announced departmental restructuring or reduction that threaten religion faculty and courses at these institutions. Alumni have pushed back on these cuts with some success at schools including Illinois Wesleyan University and Adrian College, but such reversals should not obscure the long-term picture, shaped primarily by declining numbers of students choosing to major in religion or theology, which Alles documents for both the United States and the United Kingdom. Even institutions with ties to Christian denominations (Wheeling, Gordon, Canisius) have sought to reduce faculty size in religion and theology, in spite of the apparent links between such departments and institutional mission. Clearly it is no longer possible, if it ever was, to presume that either liberal arts colleges or research universities might understand their educational mission to entail a commitment to maintaining a department for the study of religion or staffing that department with faculty sufficient to "cover" a range of courses or topics. To the extent that departments and curricula powerfully shape teaching agendas, research possibilities, and scholarly networks (see King 2019), such cuts are catastrophic for the study of religion, even when individuals are relocated to other units in the same institution.

While alumni resistance, and the private donation dollars it threatens, has not proven successful in most cases, public pushback on cuts to the study of religion has typically centered on the role of religion courses in promoting tolerance and diversity. At many institutions, including my own, courses in religion count toward general education requirements in cultural literacy or intercultural knowledge, variously formulated. One non-profit organization, Interfaith America, vigorously promotes this through funding of institutional initiatives both curricular and extracurricular, with some of the dollars going directly to student life organizations for event planning and to scholars for curriculum development (full disclosure: I have received two small curriculum development grants from IA). The founder of IA, Eboo Patel, has written extensively to promote the centrality of religion in discourses and practices of diversity, on the grounds that religious ideas are self-evident sources of meaning in the lives of individuals and historically central to narratives of American identity (Patel 2018). The AAR's very public proposal of goals and best practices for the teaching of religious literacy in higher education, regardless of its sincerity or effectiveness, surely represents a plea for the relevance of its members in the face budget cuts, the growth of contingent faculty, and the creeping precariousness of being a religion professor, whatever ones ideological, political, or disciplinary commitments (American Academy of Religion undated). This initiative receives substantial attention in this volume from McCutcheon, Smith, and King, each of whom worries that such an initiative coming from the "Big Tent" threatens to further marginalize thinking about religion not as merely given, but as a contingent set of discourses and social practices to be historicized. I do not disagree with McCutcheon's characterization of his approach to the study of religion as still outside the mainstream of the field. Indeed, a presentation at the 2020 NAASR conference by Wesley Wildman and Connor Wood statistically confirms this impression with its data about the sheer quantity of journal articles with an empirical orientation toward religion as a set of given data (practices, beliefs, claimed identities) being published in subfields at the intersection of religion and health, dwarfing publications in the humanities (of which, presumably, only a small set operate with something like the critical orientation advocated by McCutcheon). What this data set suggests, on the other hand, is that in both academia and in the general public, interest in religion and discussion of its multiple roles in society will continue apace, with or without the AAR, NAASR, and the departments of theology and religion in which the members of these organizations have historically done their work. If an insistence on the civic value of "our 'special promise' as teachers" puts limitations on the critical work of the scholar (McCutcheon 2001), our role as teachers is, I would argue, the condition of possibility for making sure religion can be a subject of critical, analytical study *at all*, at least in North America.

I believe the insistence on religious literacy as an integral part of education for inclusive citizenship in a diverse, religiously plural society is a worthy project, and I likewise respect the ideological critiques of this position generated by the other contributors. From my perspective, the problem is not that it represents an undertheorized scholarly position (though that may be true), but rather that it is a shaky foothold on a quite slippery slope for scholars of religion amidst the current budget contractions in higher education. I worry less about a future in which ossified imperatives of diversity education would cast critical inquiry in the study of religion as a threat than one in which the majority of college courses in cultural literacy or diversity that do address religion are taught by specialists in other disciplines at institutions with no regular, full-time faculty in the study of religion. Here the stakes are high regarding the "specialness" of what scholars of religion do and what they do "it" *on*. If the academic study of religion were successful in promoting the view that "religion" is neither a way of knowing, a sort of knowledge, nor a type of experience, but merely a discourse of identification and classification, the field would effectively undercut its data as *raison d'être*. I recognize, of course, this this is far from a winning battle at present. My own experience in the classroom—for example, using chapters from the book *Stereotyping Religion* to push back against students' assumptions that religion is primarily a matter of internal, private belief and that "good" religion is peaceful—suggest that much work remains to be done (Stoddard and Martin 2017; see also Shagan 2019; Smith, Führding, and Hermann 2020).

But if cultural and religious literacy is our curricular foothold, our grip may weaken to the extent that we are successful in relativizing and de-essentializing "religions" (as a plural noun, rather than a verb). More than any other stereotype, it may be the idea that religion not just simply *there*, but potentially a force for *good* in the world (variously through community cohesion, moral conduct, and individual self-affirmation) that gives religion its staying power as an object of study for the humanities and a place on the general education "menu." If religion is not inherently good and somehow worth preserving, or *inherently* (as they say) "even a thing," why then are we requiring, or offering at all, courses in it? Why, too, are specially trained faculty possessing multiple graduate degrees necessary? To the extent that religion is a remnant or (I shudder at the word) an adjunct of cultural diversity, perhaps area studies faculty can "cover" it. Alternatively, if we insist that the academic study of religion is primarily, even exclusively, an exercise in social theory, there are sociology faculty who will, no doubt, have "an app for that." Finally, if neither the content nor the methods of the study of religion are in any sense proprietary, then the imperative of training students may lie primarily at the level of attitude, affect, or mere awareness, things that could be part of a professional studies curriculum (in social work, perhaps) or relegated to co-curricular programming run outside of academic programs altogether. To the extent that the critical perspective McCutcheon and others advocate has not naturalized itself across the field, or throughout North American academia, such scenarios remain unlikely. However, to the extent that our colleagues in sociology, anthropology, languages and literatures, and area studies are in many cases no safer than scholars and departments of religion, the shifting of responsibility for cultural literacy and diversity training onto non-specialists in general education and non-faculty is already at least partly under way.

Scholars of religion not working at wealthy institutions of higher education, in short, do not control their own fiscal and curricular destiny. But their (I should say *our*) foothold is not primarily threatened by the attraction of external funding that may shape research agendas and outcomes, but rather by the tension between the imperatives of critical study and those of the general education curriculum in which the place of religion is somewhat akin to the classic course in art appreciation (see McCutcheon, Chapter 6, this volume). Or, if it does not serve the outcome of cultural literacy, nor one of the rapidly evaporating theology requirements at institutions with an explicitly religious mission, it likely fits into a still more general need to teach skills in critical thinking, which depends even less on our disciplinary expertise and offers no particular job security whatsoever. Teaching effective oral and written communication, along with critical thinking, is certainly something that the academic study of religion can do, but so can other disciplines with more apparently self-evident connections to lines of post-graduation employment. The only thing, we are learning, that keeps the lights on for the department of religion (however conceived and staffed) is students choosing to major in it. And those numbers continue a sharp decline across "theology and religion" and the humanities more generally. Given the costs of higher education, the bevy of options available to students in terms of both majors and schools, and the relative demographic decline in the number of high school graduates nationally in the United States, it is without a doubt a buyer's market.

So it falls to scholars of religion to "sell" their field, both to administrators looking to cut budgets and to students whose tuition dollars represent the primary line of "private funding" available to keep the study of religion anchored in the academy and (to abuse the metaphor) its scholars afloat in teaching positions. Here I will return to my titular invocation of "Wittgenstein" and "Zuckerberg." Because when students tour an institution or seek to choose a major, what "religion" is—and what they would *do* with it, post-graduation—is primarily dictated by "Zuckerberg." If they have religious convictions that they seek to work into their career plans, students' ideas about religion may well have been shaped by participation in Christian churches or other traditional social groups. But if like an increasing number of young Americans, they are religiously unaffiliated—whether cast as "spiritual but not religious," "None," or "Remixed" (Fuller 2001; Drescher 2016; Burton 2020)—their understanding of "religion" has likely been acquired through a smattering of social media platforms through which they exchange memes, quotes from religious scriptures, inspirational photos, and (occasionally) journalism. Not only is "screen time" often their primary form of social engagement with peers, but in the realm of religion, such exchange frequently enables a level of selectivity, creative ownership, curating, and self-fashioning that would not be possible in traditional on-ground communities and institutions (Campbell 2012; Burton 2020). "Zuckerberg" (in all its forms) empowers students as consumers, and even as religious authorities, long before they have entered our classrooms. It enables the kind of essentialized thinking that McCutcheon's critical study of religion works to undercut and perpetuates the many, occasionally conflicting stereotypes analyzed by the contributors to Stoddard and Martin's volume. To the extent that we advertise ourselves as problematizing their notions of what constitutes "religion," they simply may not be interested in buying our product. Many institutions offering majors in religion, including George Washington University and Boston University, have employed the rhetoric of former Secretary of State John Kerry in order to sell the relevance of studying religion for understanding the contemporary world (Kerry 2015). As Richard Newton has already noted, Kerry's approach to religion in international relations "involves engaging religion as an ontological datum to be managed and not a social dynamic to be negotiated" (Newton 2019: 241). If our approach to Religion 101 does not sufficiently cater to their desire for religious tourism (see for example Smith Roberts 2020), they may not wish to major in the field.

Moreover, if the institutional rhetoric of general education stresses cultural literacy as the purpose of a category of courses that includes the study of religion, scholars teaching those courses may not be entirely free to approach the curriculum from the perspective of critical inquiry and social theory. Institutions or accreditors may require assessment of student learning in cultural literacy for a course to count toward the general education requirement, and fulfilling that requirement may be the primary reason for the institution offering, and students taking, the course in the study of religion, whatever its topical content. Here, "Wittgenstein" rears its head again, in two ways. Again, to the extent that we accept that the meaning of "religion" might be primarily a function of its common usage, administrators and students, as well as colleagues across the faculty and staff of the university, may already "know" what "religion" "is." But if scholars nevertheless insist on teaching a critical approach to religion when students have been primed to expect discreet snippets of cultural tourism, students may, having only 10 to 14 weeks of exposure to the scholarly vocabulary and methods, take the meaning of "critical" in its common usage as well. The assessable artifacts of student learning (that is, the papers and projects) and the ubiquitous, indirect indicators of learning (which rather directly measure student satisfaction, as well as implicit and explicit bias) may not indicate the "success" of the instructor who was supposed to teach an appreciative sense of diversity and instead is shown to have taught students to be "critical" of religion. Such findings may threaten the place of religion courses in the general education curriculum if instructors are not able to balance the imperatives of cultural literacy and critical inquiry. Even if they are rather more successful at teaching students the apt meaning of the word "critical," for example, through a case study-orientated approach that foregrounds methods of critical inquiry (as envisioned by J. Z. Smith 2013), students may not leave the course with their "Wittgenstein"-ian intuitions about religion sufficiently unsettled to render those critical and methodological insights portable to other courses they take, in the study of religion (if more are even offered) or beyond.

In the end, I come to praise the academic study of religion, not to bury it. My own introductory courses count toward a cultural literacy requirement, and in each of them I use either historical "Reacting to the Past" pedagogy (Carnes 2014) or a "fictive religion" assignment (Laycock 2015; Zeller 2018) to create liminal space in the classroom for critical insight to come about through play. It is certainly possible to stress both the expected "content" of "religion" and the critical methods that might demonstrate to students not how "religion" "works" but how people "work" with "religion" for particular social and political ends—not all of them nefarious. But the insistence on cultural and religious literacy as the space the study of religion can inhabit in general education ratchets up the tension between my pedagogical goals and "Wittgenstein." For example, I transformed the "world religions" course I inherited into one driven entirely by Reacting "games" focused on the social and political dynamics shaping the development of religious ideas, institutions, and practices (Henderson and Kirkpatrick 2016; Gardner and Carnes 2014; Embree and Carnes 2016), instead of "covering" Christianity, Confucianism, Islam, and Hinduism. One student reported at the end of the semester that, while he enjoyed the games, what he had learned was "politics" and "philosophy," not "religion." Inhabiting the lives of historical actors motivated by religious ideologies for nearly 14 weeks had not, in his estimation, taught him about "world religions" as advertised. This one comment represents only the tip of a somewhat amorphous, "Wittgenstein"-ian iceberg, one on which my religion curriculum and those of many of my colleagues might run aground if we are not careful.

If Gregory Alles has framed the academic study of religion as navigating between a Scylla of private donor agendas and Charybdis of eager budget cutters, then "Wittgenstein" and "Zuckerberg" represent the two interlocked blades of the scissors that do the cutting. The legibility of our pedagogical work—and therefore the survival of our research funding—depends on carefully balancing our critical inquiry with an ability to speak to the assumptions, stereotyped or otherwise, of students and colleagues. Leslie Dorrough Smith puts it most bluntly in Chapter 1 of this volume: "I don't believe I oversimplify the matter when I say that, for many of us, this separation of analysis from data is part of our job security." In the present economic climate, exacerbated greatly by the still-unfolding impacts of COVID-19, neither distribution requirements nor diversity initiatives will ultimately save religious studies. Critical work in religion depends on our ability to walk a fine line as we appeal to students to engage deeply in this study with us. We should never forget, to use the language of Laurie Patton, that the study of religion represents a kind of "scandal" (Patton 2019), in the sense that critical study often unsettles the beliefs of religious practitioners about what they do and simultaneously survives in part *because* the controversial attention it draws underscores the problems on which critical scholars want to focus their attention. The critical study of religion is not yet mainstream, and as an academic discipline it remains the younger cousin of other fields in the social sciences and humanities. If the academic study of religion is to survive long-term in its precarious relationship to the institutions of higher education in North America, it will be, I suspect, *because* it is scandalous, not in spite of it.

John W. McCormack is associate professor of religion and history at Aurora University, Illinois (USA). His research interests include religion and politics in sixteenth- and seventeenth-century France, early modern European encounters with non-Christian peoples, history of emotions, and religion in popular culture.

References

Alles, Gregory D. 2019. "Research: Religious Studies Research in an Era of Neoliberalization." In Leslie Dorrough Smith (ed.), *Constructing Data in Religious Studies: Examining the Architecture of the Academy*. Sheffield: Equinox.

American Academy of Religion. Undated. "AAR Religious Literacy Guidelines: What US College Graduates Need to Understand about Religion." Retrieved from www.aarweb.org/AARMBR/Publications-and-News-/Guides-and-Best-Practices-/Teaching-and-Learning-/AAR-Religious-Literacy-Guidelines.aspx

Burton, Tara Isabella. 2020. *Strange Rites: New Religions for a Godless World*. New York: PublicAffairs.

Campbell, Heidi A. 2012. "Understanding the Relationship between Religion Online and Offline in a Networked Society." *Journal of the American Academy of Religion* 80: 64–93.

Carnes, Mark C. 2014. *Minds on Fire: How Role-Immersion Games Transform College.* Cambridge, MA: Harvard University Press.

Casanova, José. 1994. *Public Religions in the Modern World.* Chicago, IL: University of Chicago Press.

Cavanaugh, William T. 2009. *The Myth of Religious Violence.* New York: Oxford University Press.

Drescher, Elizabeth. 2016. *Choosing Our Religion: The Spiritual Lives of America's Nones.* New York: Oxford University Press.

Embree, Ainslie T., and Mark C. Carnes. 2016. *Defining a Nation: India on the Eve of Independence, 1945.* New York: W. W. Norton.

Fitzgerald, Timothy. 2011. *Religion and Politics in International Relations: The Modern Myth.* New York: Continuum.

Fuller, Robert C. 2001. *Spiritual, but not Religious: Understanding Unchurched America.* New York: Oxford University Press.

Gardner, Daniel K., and Mark C. Carnes. 2014. *Confucianism and the Succession Crisis of the Wanli Emperor, 1587.* New York: W. W. Norton.

Gregory, Brad S. 2012. *The Unintended Reformation: How a Religious Revolution Secularized Society.* Cambridge, MA: Belknap.

Henderson, David E., and Frank Kirkpatrick. 2016. *Constantine and the Council of Nicaea: Defining Orthodoxy and Heresy in Christianity, 325 CE.* Chapel Hill, NC: University of North Carolina Press.

Hurd, Elizabeth Shakman. 2015. *Beyond Religious Freedom: The New Global Politics of Religion.* Princeton, NJ: Princeton University Press.

Kerry, John. 2015. "John Kerry: 'We Ignore the Global Impact of Religion at Our Peril.'" *America Magazine*, September 14.

King, Rebekka. 2019. "Departments: Competencies and Curricula: The Role of Academic Departments in Shaping the Study of Religion." In Leslie Dorrough Smith (ed.), *Constructing Data in Religious Studies: Examining the Architecture of the Academy.* Sheffield: Equinox.

Laycock, Joseph. 2015. "Create Your Own Religion (Out of Someone Else's): A Class Exercise." Retrieved from https://bulletin.equinoxpub.com/2015/03/create-your-own-religion-out-of-someone-elses-a-class-exercise.

Lincoln, Bruce. 1996. "Theses on Method." *Method and Theory in the Study of Religion* 8: 225–227.

McCutcheon, Russell. 2001. *Critics Not Caretakers: Redescribing the Public Study of Religion.* Albany, NY: State University of New York Press.

Newton, Jr., Richard W. 2019. "Teaching: Teaching in the Ideological State of Religious Studies: Notes Towards a Pedagogical Future." In Leslie Dorrough Smith (ed.), *Constructing Data in Religious Studies: Examining the Architecture of the Academy.* Sheffield: Equinox.

Patel, Eboo. 2018. *Out of Many Faiths: Religious Diversity and the American Promise.* Princeton, NJ: Princeton University Press.

Patton, Laurie L. 2019. *Who Owns Religion? Scholars and Their Publics in the Late Twentieth Century.* Chicago, IL: University of Chicago Press.

Shagan, Ethan H. 2019 *The Birth of Modern Belief: Faith and Judgment from the Middle Ages to the Enlightenment.* Princeton, NJ: Princeton University Press.

Smith Roberts, Martha. 2020. "The Strange and Familiar Spiritual Journey of Reza Aslan." In Leslie Dorrough Smith, Steffen Führding, and Adrian Hermann (eds), *Hijacked: A Critical Treatment of the Public Rhetoric of Good and Bad Religion*. Sheffield: Equinox.
Smith, Jonathan. Z. 1990. *Drudgery Divine: On the Comparison of Early Christianities and the Religions of Late Antiquity*. Chicago, IL: University of Chicago Press.
Smith, Jonathan Z. 2013. *On Teaching Religion: Essays by Jonathan Z. Smith*, ed. Christopher I. Lehrich. New York: Oxford University Press.
Smith, Leslie Dorrough, Steffen Führding, and Adrian Hermann (eds). 2020. *Hijacked: A Critical Treatment of the Public Rhetoric of Good and Bad Religion*. Sheffield: Equinox.
Stoddard, Brad, and Craig Martin, eds. 2017. *Stereotyping Religion: Critiquing Clichés*. New York: Bloomsbury Academic.
Wittgenstein, Ludwig. 1953. *Philosophical Investigations*. Trans. G. E. M. Anscombe. London: Macmillan.
Zeller, Benjamin E. 2018. "'Make Your Own Religion': The Fictive Religion Assignment as Educational Game." *Teaching Theology and Religion* 21: 321–335.

Chapter 13

Religious Studies: A Pawn in the Culture Wars

Natalie Avalos

Although Greg Alles's essay (Chapter 10, this volume) focuses on private money for the study of religion, public funding is shaped by political ideologies that are primarily influenced by private interests. Public funding for higher education has steeply declined in recent years. In California, it has been dwindling for decades, making a sharp about face from its 1960 Master Plan that created a framework for a tuition-free higher education system for all eligible high school students. We have to ask, what happened? What kinds of social struggles were taking place that might turn us away from such fortuitous initiatives? The positive structural shifts that began in the 1960s and 70s coincided with what have been described as the culture wars, such as the rise of the moral majority and fiscal conservatism in response to the civil rights movement and the radical possibilities of social equity. Alles notes that private interests invested in research on science, technology, defense, even agriculture. However, both state and private interests funded the social sciences, which served their often overlapping and contingent form of what anthropologist David Nugent calls "commercial empire" (Nugent 2010: 7). The US and other European powers used knowledge production as a complement to imperialist projects in order to understand how to manage its colonies and the peoples within them (see Smith 2002). Religious studies contributed to these ends through its own deeply racialized assumptions about the nature of religious traditions, producing stratifications that we still live with today (see Masuzawa 2005). While the reflexive turn in the social sciences and the postmodern turn in the humanities challenged the universalist discourses that served imperial goals, these strides have been stigmatized by political factions in the last several decades as radical leftist thought. I contend that the field has gotten caught in the crosshairs of these culture wars and it does not know it because it has failed to explore the structural mechanisms of our present social conditions, such as white supremacy, settler colonialism, and racialization in more critical ways that other disciplines in the Social Sciences and Humanities have. In fact, it may unwittingly act as a pawn in these culture wars.

I will begin by discussing *why* public funding for higher education has steeply declined in recent years. Most of us here are privy to the ways higher education was impacted by the 2008 recession. State funding for higher ed in the last ten years has not recovered from this financial crisis. According to a 2017 report from the Center on Budget and Policy Priorities:

> A decade since the Great Recession hit, state spending on public colleges and universities remains well below historic levels, despite recent increases. Overall state funding for public two- and four-year colleges in the 2017 school year (that is, the school year ending in 2017) was nearly $9 billion below its 2008 level, after adjusting for inflation ... The funding decline has contributed to higher tuition and reduced quality on campuses as colleges have had to balance budgets by reducing faculty, limiting course offerings, and in some cases closing campuses.
> (Mitchell, Leachman, and Masterson 2017: 1)

But this story is much more complex. In California, where I grew up, funding for higher education had been dwindling for decades. Many in the state blame Proposition 13, enacted in 1978 (Rancaño 2018). Under Prop 13, real estate tax was limited to 1 percent of its assessment value and subsequently, could only increase by a maximum of 2 percent per year. While the central reason why Californians agitated for such a law was likely financial, such as rising housing prices, it is popularly understood as a response to a 1971 and 1976 ruling that redistributed property taxes from wealthy to poor school districts. Again, while there was major public support for these initiatives, there was simultaneously a sense that local property taxes were not necessarily directly supporting local schools.

I was a product of what many believed was the California dream, its higher education system. I attended community college in Oakland and Berkeley, then transferred to UC Berkeley where I would complete my undergraduate degree in 2006. I began graduate work in religious studies at UC Santa Barbara in 2007. Tuition and fees at the UC's would nearly double during my graduate tenure. According to Evolve California a non-profit based in San Francisco dedicated to improving California education, the state's higher education system was initially enviable:

> In 1960, the California Master Plan for Higher Education established a framework for a tuition-free, three tiered higher education system to educate all eligible high school graduates and make California grow as a leader in education. The Master Plan committed to providing access to quality education for young Californians without taking their family's financial status into account. Today, the University of California, California State University, and California Community Colleges are among the largest higher education institutions in the nation.[1]

They go on to note:

> In 1976, higher education accounted for 18% of the state budget. In 2016, it accounted for just 12%. State funding per student at the UC fell from more than $23,000 to $13,650 over the same period. 66% of Californians believe that the cost of college keeps students from enrolling. Today, California spends roughly as much on corrections as it does on funding higher education. Since 1980, California has built one new UC campus and 21 prisons.

---

1. Accessed at www.evolve-ca.org/higher-education-in-california in November 2020 (the link is no longer accessible).

We have to ask, what happened? What kinds of social struggles were taking place that might turn us away from such fortuitous initiatives? The positive structural shifts that began in the 1960s and 70s coincided with what have been described as the culture wars, such as the rise of the moral majority and fiscal conservatism in response to the civil rights movement and the radical possibilities of social equity (Balmer 2014).

While this conversation is about private funding, my brief research demonstrates that public funding is shaped by political ideologies that are primarily influenced by private interests. However, this should come as no surprise. Alles notes (Chapter 10, this volume) that private interests invested in research on science, technology, defense, even agriculture. However, both state and private interests funded the social sciences, which served their often overlapping and contingent form of what anthropologist David Nugent calls "commercial empire" (Nugent 2010: 7).

The US and other European powers used knowledge production as a complement to imperialist projects in order to understand how to manage its colonies and the peoples within them (see Smith 2002). Nugent writes:

> Western and non-Western scholars alike were involved in an historically based analysis of the role of North Atlantic industrial capitalism and European imperialism and colonialism in shaping regional and local arenas around the globe, in undermining indigenous economic and socio-political forms, in precipitating enormous population movements, and in stimulating novel cultural configurations and new forms of political affiliation.
>
> (Nugent 2010: 7)

Anthropology was the central purveyor of scholarship on Indigenous peoples, while area or Oriental studies focused on the polities and peoples to the east who were also targets for imperial exploitation. Religious Studies contributed to these ends through its own deeply racialized assumptions about the nature of religious traditions, producing stratifications (i.e., more or less "civilized" and complex) that we still live with today (see Masuzawa 2005). While the reflexive turn in the social sciences and the postmodern turn in the humanities challenged the universalist discourses that served imperial goals, these strides have been stigmatized by political factions in the last several decades as radical leftist thought.

This discrediting discourse is not incidental; it has been carefully crafted over time to serve powerful interests, in essence, those of "commercial empire." American Studies scholar, Christopher Newfield, argues in his book *Unmaking the Public University: The Forty-Year Assault on the Middle Class* that these powerful interests worked diligently to undermine "the public importance and economic claims of the American university and its graduates" (Newfield 2008: 6). He notes that these "culture wars" were actually economic wars that sought to obfuscate the real mechanisms of economic decline that everyday Americans began to experience in the 1970s. Conservative elites sought to maintain political and economic hegemony through what he calls a culture war strategy that operated like "a kind of intellectual neutron bomb, eroding the social and cultural foundations of a growing, politically powerful, economically entitled, and racially diversifying middle-class, while leaving its technical capacities intact" (ibid.). Nugent's work explains that while the social sciences produced data that benefitted commercial empire, it also produced work that began to critique it. Newfield positions this very outcome as the primary reason that conservative elites sought to both discredit but also reconfigure the university into a neoliberal commodity, saying:

> Social movements were demanding egalitarian forms of human development, which if enacted would transform economic, race, and gender relations. Social movements were also getting unusual support from academic experts, whose research showed that the problems were real and that the progressive solutions would work. Not only were universities producing new and potentially disrupting knowledge; by 1980 they were also producing nearly a million graduates a year. These graduates would bring their new technological *and* cultural learning to insider positions in the American economy. For conservative leaders, a quiet, continuous, unrelenting, and internal revolution was a clear and present danger.
> (Newfield 2008: 30)

The humanities were a particular point of ire for conservative forces who critiqued them as producing no useful knowledge, in essence, knowledge that could not be directly operationalized for the sake of capital. Even worse, they were linked to what the right calls identity politics as well as such unproductive aims as "job satisfaction, personal freedom, self-actualization, and plenty of mind-expanding leisure" (ibid.: 25).

Universities began to internalize these neoliberal logics, adopting its language but also its emphasis on economic versus cultural capital. For instance, in the early 2000s the University of California's website provided a list of "UC contributions to the California economy," emphasizing that scientific research produced new inventions, patents, products, and new industries, which, naturally, led to the creation of more jobs (Newfield 2008: 209). In a subsequent 2003 UC generated report on UC related research titled "California's Future: It Starts Here," again, the economic value of STEM research was the central point of discussion; "the social sciences and humanities were all but nonexistent in it" (ibid.). In essence, the idea that the exploration and analysis of culture and social systems did not "produce knowledge" of any real value, particularly economic value, had become tacitly accepted as true by university's themselves, despite having no data to support this assumption. In the last few years, the common assumption that humanities degrees were worthless was challenged, ironically, by some tech industry leaders and social scientists, who argued that the industry was best aided by employees who could solve human problems, versus those with specialized technical expertise (Olejarz 2017; Johnson 2018).

So, what does the gaslighting of the university at large have to do with religious studies? I contend that the field has gotten caught in the crosshairs of these culture wars and it does not know it because it has failed to explore the mechanisms of our present social conditions in more critical ways that other disciplines in the social science and humanities have. In fact, it unwittingly acts as a pawn in these culture wars. As a Chicana scholar of Apache descent trained in religious studies and now housed in an ethnic studies department, I have experienced this academic myopia first-hand. While on the job market, I received critiques that my work is "more ethnic studies than religious studies." The assumption being that research on contemporary Indigenous religious responses to settler colonialism is somehow just about race or ethnicity as opposed to religion *and* that these two realms are and should be mutually exclusive. In addition, scholars of color that research and teach about non-Christian/non-Western religious traditions and do not center Western materialist methodologies and theorists are also often critiqued as being either "insiders," and thus lacking in objectivity, and/or as doing theological work, meaning that we are taking the beliefs of the religious communities we work with at face value. Some scholars have even asserted that Native American or Indigenous scholars in the field that seek to take an Indigenist approach to research cannot possibly be doing legitimate scholarship, since it is primarily a "Western" enterprise, intimating that Indigenous theoretical frameworks cannot possibly be identified or explored in any legitimate way (see Gill 1994, 1997; Jocks 1997). While these issues were a point of debate twenty years ago, they persist because the field has failed to interrogate how these racist assumptions might express themselves materially much less how they may be rooted in its own structural history.

Recent attempts to explore what it means to decolonize the field have highlighted why its reluctance to understand the impacts of racialization persist. Mallory Nye reminds us that the field was inspired by and built upon colonizing aims and discourses:

> the text-focused orientalist scholarship associated with philology, the thematic (and speculative) approaches of Edward Tylor, the functionalism of sociology, the ethnographic and particularist approaches of anthropology, or the contemporary phenomenology that was popularized by Ninian Smart in the 1960s and 70s.
>
> (Nye 2019: 4)

Maori scholar Linda Tuhiwai Smith argues that the racist characterizations of Indigenous peoples as less intelligent and irrational, permeating this modern body of knowledge is so thoroughly naturalized, they continue to shape the way Native peoples and their knowledges are perceived even today (see Smith 2002). Nye argues that decolonizing the field necessitates interrogating its historical preoccupation with "so called primitive religion" as a social evolutionary project, but also white scholars understanding the "privilege of not having to experience the low key and/or life threatening forces of structural racism that are premised on the exclusion of people of colour from the centres of power and academic life" (Nye 2019: 6). However, the problem is not *just* primitivism. It also a Christian bias that colors how many in the field evaluate the work of others reflective of a naturalized white supremacy. Travis Warren Cooper argues that the field's struggle over objectivity is rooted in what he calls the Protestant secular, or the ways in which Protestantism divides the world into two domains, the public (secular) and private (religious) (Cooper 2019: 9–10). In essence, a Christian worldview permeates not only our social world but also the field, structuring how it operates. This naturalized view creates a neutral public sphere that appears to serve the collective good, concealing not only liberal Christian norms embedded in knowledge production but also power, specifically the white Christian operations of the state. This Western Christian bias continues to operate in religious studies departments across the United States. Along with the common assumption that the raced underclass is structurally dispossessed due to their own dysfunctional culture, this discursive structure masks the material dimensions of our increasingly collective dispossession.

Alles makes the case that private funding institutions are interested in funding what could be described as theological explorations of religion in the classroom. He is resistant to this option, mostly because even as an insider he can distinguish the difference between taking religious ideas seriously and doing theology. However, this differentiation may not be obvious to private funding institutions mostly because very few people understand the difference, particularly since the boundaries here generally shift within the field according to power and positionality. He notes that it was private funding that drove the initial study of theology and religion, in addition to the creation of now familiar pillars of higher education like Dartmouth and Colombia. How might this discussion shift, if we understood these institutions as structural expressions of settler colonialism, intended to either civilize Americans Indians on the one hand and/or strengthen the internal discourse of European-decent superiority on the other? In other words, if we understand these institutions and those funding sources as doing the ideological work of white supremacy, as deeply steeped in the goals of the rich and powerful among us, we may rethink the pursuit of such funding.

Alles observes that in the nineteenth century, the creation of research universities began to shift the overall aims of higher educations as not only disseminating but also creating knowledge. This century coincides with the massive expansion of settler colonialism in North America and Oceania. Universities began to play an important role in what Aboriginal scholar Aileen Moreton-Robinson would call the white possessive, or the monopolization of knowledge production that sought to concretize settler appropriations of Native land through ideological and institutional means see (Moreton-Robinson 2015). In his brief discussion of these first such research universities in the US, many of which were initiated with private funds, Cornell was noted as a land-grant university. The 1862 Morrill Act annexed 11 million acres of Native American land "from nearly 250 tribes, bands, and communities through over 160 violence-backed land cessions" for the sole purpose of funding colleges across the US (Lee and Ahtone 2020). These land grabs raised endowment funds for 52 US institutions that amounted to "$17.7 million for university endowments, with unsold lands valued at an additional 5.1 million" by the early twentieth century (ibid.). This amounts to approximately half a billion dollars today. While these "grants" were viewed as generous federal donations, we must understand them as violent acts of Native dispossession, really operations of settler colonial power. When Alles raises the issue of how to make teaching religion viable to private foundations, it begs the question where are these monies coming from, "public" or private? Maybe appealing to philanthropists is not the solution. One strategy for survival may be rethinking the boundaries of the field itself, so we can begin to interrogate larger structural solutions to institutionalized white supremacy.

In my experience teaching, religious studies as a discipline is not as readily legible to students as it once was, particularly compared to growing fields like American studies, which I have heard described informally as "ethnic studies for white students" because it dares to center discussions on genocide, slavery, and other expressions of structural violence in their storying of the United States. When I taught in a religious studies department, the students who took my classes appeared to be interested in purpose and existential meaning, but also the intersections of colonialism and religion, and the ways in which religion is interpellated by race, gender, and power. These were often the themes of queries as well as responses I received from students when I asked them what drew them to my classroom. I, too, was interested in all these issues as a young person and continue to be as a scholar. I invite religious studies scholars to reconsider the ways structural violences are not only relevant to the field, but constitutive of it. In the process, how might we tether these structural violences to the access or foreclosure of religious meaning and/or self-actualization?

As we begin to turn away from the traditions-based approaches that have shaped the field, I ask that you join other scholars and communities in the labor of unpacking the very relations of power in these realms that would dispossess us all. When scholars misattribute the waning support for the field, as an issue of funding as opposed to ideology then we are collectively missing an opportunity to see the ties that bind us not only to the humanities at large, but also implicate us in our own racist legacy. When we as a field refuse to recognize the material outcomes of racism and the stratified goals of settler colonialism within our ranks, we are less likely to recognize the workings of white supremacy as neoliberal thoughts and structures. In particular, how it is willing to destroy higher education to tighten its grip on the social landscape. Neoliberalism has been described as the most advanced form of white supremacy. If we understand the loss of funding as an ideological strategy that has shifted and morphed for decades but remained focused on the singular goal of concentrating power among the rich and white, we are also better able to understand that poor *and* well-meaning middle class "white liberals" have been manipulated towards these ends. While whiteness has shielded many in the academy from neoliberal deprivations, you are no longer immune to its aims. This ugly truth has been laid even more bare during our current COVID-19 pandemic. It is in this moment of horror that scholars in the field could organize with the most marginalized among us to fight not only for higher education but the equity, dignity of life, and wellness that we collectively deserve.

Natalie Avalos is an assistant professor of Native American and Indigenous studies in the Ethnic Studies Department at University of Colorado, Boulder, which sits within Ute, Cheyenne, and Arapaho territories. Her work explores urban Native and Tibetan refugee religious life as decolonial praxis. She takes an endogenous approach to Indigenous life to write about land-based logics, the embodiment of colonialism as historical trauma, and the liberatory and healing possibilities of engaging intersubjective realities. She is a Chicana of Apache descent, born and raised in the Bay Area.

References

Balmer, Randall. 2014. "The Real Origins of the Religious Right." Retrieved from www.politico.com/magazine/story/2014/05/religious-right-real-origins-107133 (accessed November 19, 2019).

Cooper, Travis Warren. 2019. "Objectivity Discourse, the Protestant Secular, and the Decolonization of Religious Studies." *Method and Theory in the Study of Religion* 31(4–5): 376–415.

Gill, Sam. 1994. "The Academic Study of Religion." *Journal of the American Academy of Religion* 62(4): 965–975.

Gill, Sam. 1997. "Rejoinder to Christopher Jocks." *Journal of the American Academy of Religion* 65(1): 177–182.

Jocks Christopher. 1997. "American Indian Religious Traditions and the Academic Study of Religion: A Response to Sam Gill." *Journal of the American Academy of Religion* 65(1): 169–176.

Johnson, Sydney. 2018. "As Tech Companies Hire More Liberal Arts Majors, More Students Are Choosing STEM Degrees." Retrieved from www.edsurge.com/news/2018-11-13-as-tech-companies-hire-more-liberal-arts-majors-more-students-are-choosing-stem-degrees (accessed November 19, 2019).

Lee, Robert, and Tristan Ahtone. 2020. "Land-Grab Universities." Retrieved from www.hcn.org/issues/52.4/indigenous-affairs-education-land-grab-universities (accessed November 19, 2019).

Masuzawa, Tomoko. 2005. *The Invention of World Religions: Or, How European Universalism Was Preserved in the Language of Pluralism*. Chicago, IL: University of Chicago Press.

Mitchell, Michael, Michael Leachman, and Kathleen Masterson. 2017. "A Lost Decade in Higher Education Funding: State Cuts Have Driven Up Tuition and Reduced Quality." Retrieved from www.cbpp.org/research/state-budget-and-tax/a-lost-decade-in-higher-education-funding (accessed November 19, 2019).

Moreton-Robinson, Aileen. 2015. *The White Possessive: Property, Power, and Indigenous Sovereignty*. Minneapolis, MN: University of Minnesota.

Newfield, Christopher. 2008. *Unmaking the Public University: The Forty-Year Assault on the Middle Class*. Cambridge, MA: Harvard University Press.

Nugent, David. 2010. "Knowledge and Empire: The Social Sciences and United States Imperial Expansion." *Identities* 17(1): 2–44.

Nye, Mallory. 2019. "Decolonizing the Study of Religion." *Open Library of Humanities* 5(1): 43.

Olejarz, J. M. 2017. "Liberal Arts in the Data Age." Retrieved from https://hbr.org/2017/07/liberal-arts-in-the-data-age.

Rancaño, Vanessa. 2018. "How Proposition 13 Transformed Neighborhood Public Schools Throughout California." Retrieved from www.kqed.org/news/11701044/how-proposition-13-transformed-neighborhood-public-schools-throughout-california (accessed November 19, 2019).

Smith, Linda Tuhiwai. 2002. *Decolonizing Methodologies: Research and Indigenous Peoples*. London: Zed Books.

Part IV

International Perspectives on the Field

Chapter 14

International Perspectives on/in the Field

Rosalind I. J. Hackett

As the Igbo of Nigeria say, you do not stand in one place to watch a masquerade. Likewise, there are manifold ways to explore international perspectives both *on* and *in* the field of religious studies. Plus, it goes without saying that any treatment of such a vast topic is partial and context-driven. That said, I am both motivated and probably well positioned to offer some reflections on this timely question. I studied in British universities, conducted graduate research and taught in Nigeria over several years, have been employed in US universities since 1986, have served on the International Connections Committee (2001–2004) at the American Academy of Religion (AAR), and have been active in the leadership of the International Association for the History of Religions (IAHR) from 1995 to 2015. I currently serve as an IAHR Honorary Life Member and as Vice President of the International Council of Philosophy and the Human Sciences [CIPSH] (related to UNESCO). Over the last two decades in particular, I have attended and/or helped organize conferences and meetings in various parts of the world, whether Africa, Asia, South America, or Europe. Together with my ongoing research and networking with colleagues in Africa, particularly Nigeria, Uganda, Zimbabwe, and South Africa, I get a lot of exposure to developments and challenges in the field, particularly in terms of its professional and structural dynamics. It is why I can offer some "thick description" of these dynamics and address some consequential questions. I acknowledge the invaluable help of numerous colleagues who have kindly shared information and reflections on internationalizing trends in the study of religion in their respective constituencies.[1]

At the heart of this essay is a question that I often get asked: to what extent can we claim that the non-normative, historical, critical, and comparative study of religion exists as an international field?[2] Behind this question lie anxieties about how well religious studies travels outside of Western academe into national and

---

1. My thanks go to Joseph Allen, Greg Alles, Amy Allocco, Bolaji Bateye, Jenny Berglund, Elias Bongmba, Megan Bryson, Manuela Ceballos, Edward Curtis IV, Satoko Fujiwara, Armin Geertz, Adrian Herman, Cynthia Hoehler-Fatton, Elizabeth Shakman Hurd, Morny Joy, Chongsuh Kim, Amarjiva Lochan, Phillip Lucas, Marco Pasi, Robert Puckett, Lee-Shae Scharnick-Udemans, Johan Strijdom, Bron Taylor, Abdulkader Tayob, and Cathy Wessinger.
2. Given the scope of this chapter, it is hard for me to avoid what Russell McCutcheon terms the "big tent" approach, but not at the expense of the "family resemblances" listed in my descriptors above (McCutcheon, Chapter 6, this volume).

institutional contexts where theological and/or utilitarian agendas may predominate.[3] It is not as if those agendas do not exist in or have not existed in Europe or North America, but there is a sense in which religion scholars in the global South (or marginalized areas of Europe, for that matter) are perceived as facing more challenges to function academically, given political, social, economic, and religious constraints, limited or out-of-date resources, relative lack of access to fellowships, international (and even national or regional) conferences, and publishing opportunities, and possible communication and language issues.

In what follows, using a range of sources, I make the case, that, despite the ongoing domination of global North academic institutions, there is sufficient evidence of, in the words of Armin Geertz, "scholars around the world slowly transforming the study of religion in relation to critical issues and coming out with significant and respectable research" (personal communication, June 5, 2020). My methodological considerations are threefold.

First, while I could have centered my remarks on the IAHR as the "preeminent international forum for the critical, analytical and cross-cultural study of religion, past and present," I have chosen to focus on certain aspects of its work, such as its regional and affiliate associations, that tie into the particular angles I wish to explore in this venue.[4] I am cognizant of the fact that there may be limited awareness of the work of the IAHR, beyond NAASR, and maybe even within NAASR itself.[5] However, information on the various IAHR national and regional member (now up to 40) and affiliate (6) associations is readily available through its website, reports, publications, and social media.[6] Moreover, a recent 60th anniversary issue of the IAHR's flagship journal, *NVMEN* (Jensen and Geertz 2016), constitutes a valuable resource, containing over four hundred pages of historical documents and addresses, retrospectives, and current reflections on the achievements of both the journal and the association.[7] From its formative period in the 1950s to the present day, one reads how the IAHR has struggled with its Eurocentric origins, despite significant international outreach and affirmative action from the 1990s onwards to develop a more global character.[8] For example, in my contribution to the issue, I reflect on IAHR growth from 1995 to 2015, and the challenges and benefits of conference planning in various parts of the world, particularly the global South (Hackett

---

3. See Chitando (2008). But institutional association does not necessarily entail compromise of core academic values, as in the case of University of Zambia's Department of Religious Studies, housed in the School of Education www.unza.zm/department-of-religious-studies (accessed June 15, 2020).
4. See www.iahrweb.org/about.php (accessed November 2, 2019).
5. See https://naasr.com. NAASR was founded in 1985 and adopted as an IAHR member association in 1990.
6. See www.iahrweb.org/members.php (accessed November 2, 2019).
7. See https://brill.com/view/title/32420 (accessed November 2, 2019).
8. See, e.g., the IAHR Book Series, launched in 2013 and published by Equinox, "The Study of Religion in a Global Context" (www.iahrweb.org/bookseries.php, accessed June 12, 2020). See also Pye (2016a, 2016b) and Jensen and Geertz (2016).

1988).⁹ However, those with foundationalist leanings (namely, the argument that the study of religion should be strictly "scientific," take issue with tendencies toward less analytical and more applied religious studies that they perceive as endemic in non-Western locations (Wiebe 2016). In fact, following complaints about the Tokyo Congress program in 2015, the IAHR Executive Committee moved to tighten up its academic profile with a new policy statement and addition to the Constitution, stating that the IAHR is "not a forum for confessional, apologetic or other similar concerns" (Jensen and Geertz 2016: 204).

Second, another entry point for learning about the international status of the field would be via country or regional reports, from either a scholarly association (such as an IAHR member association) or publications that track the development of the study of religion in a particular region (see, for example, Adogame et al., 2013, 2012). To some extent the IAHR incorporates such data in its reports, however this does not offer the more holistic and historical view that Greg Alles aimed for in his ambitious publication, *Religious Studies: A Global View* (Alles 2008). This important book explores the trends of the past sixty years from a global perspective, with chapters from scholars in ten different regions of the world. Alles concludes that while it would be premature to claim a global vision of the comparative study of religion, there is ample evidence that religious studies is not the sole preserve of the Western academy. Here, I seek to echo and amplify those findings.

This brings me to my third consideration, my preference for a multi-perspectival approach that reveals the centrifugal and centripetal forces at work in our academic enterprise in this globalizing, technology-driven world. This dynamic view also tallies better with the broader, more polythetic concept of religious studies as a "field" (happily chosen by NAASR for this series of Working Papers) rather than the narrower idea of a "discipline." By examining a range of IAHR regional and affiliated associations, along with communities of scholars, learned societies, book series, journals, publications, working groups, and collaborative research initiatives, we can better appreciate the diverse range of responses and strategies in relation to internationalization processes in our field, whether internally or externally generated (or both). By using what I term a "nodal" and "interstitial" approach, one can better discern how the "international" trope is variously defined and deployed, whether as best practice, value addition, recalibration, legitimacy, elitism, or redemption. As in other academic fields, the aspirations and anxieties that are attendant upon greater inclusion, outreach, and diversity in our academic work are inseparable from the broader forces of globalization, neoliberalism, and marketization (see Alles 2019: 256–266; Scott 2019: 79.¹⁰ Similarly,

---

9. See, especially, the chapters by Michael Pye (2016a, 2016b), who has been one of the most effective advocates for the importance of non-Western perspectives, leadership, and conference locations in the IAHR.
10. See also a recent initiative by Kenyan scholars of religion to counter these trends, "Reimagining the African Academy: Towards a Humanities-Science Nexus," www.a-asr.org/call-for-anthology-contributions-reimagining-the-african-academy (accessed November 12, 2019).

as Malory Nye (2019: 43) reminds us, internationalist discourses invoke, just as much as they may deny, the imperatives of decolonization and postcoloniality.

Internationalizing the Field

Scholarly Associations: National and Regional

It makes sense to begin with the American Academy of Religion, given that NAASR's meetings take place at the annual AAR conference. On the AAR webpage designed for international participants, we read that "the AAR has long been interested in how it can best serve the needs of its international members and facilitate critical conversations about the diverse ways that religion is studied in different geographical settings and institutional contexts."[11] The AAR does not have any formal policy on internationalization, although the charge of the International Connections Committee (ICC) is a good indication of its priorities:

> The International Connections Committee fosters attention to the worldwide scope of scholarship in religion and the international composition of the Academy's membership. To fulfill its charge, the committee sponsors special programs, communicates with scholars abroad, and extends hospitality to international attendees at the annual meeting. The ICC's signature program is the Collaborative International Grant competition, for which ICC members evaluate proposals and serve as the grants jury.[12]

The AAR joined the IAHR in 2010 after years of delicate deliberations (in which I participated) (see Pye 2016a: 237–238). It claims that IAHR membership "has enabled us to foster cross-national scholarship and collaboration and to establish new relationships with others among the IAHR member organizations." According to Amy Allocco, who helped steer the Collaborative International Research Grants (CIRG) program into existence, this hallmark program, which is jointly administered with the IAHR Executive, has generated some important scholarship and provided access to international research opportunities.[13] For example, Adrian Herman, an active AAR, EASR, and SSEASR (the South and South East Asian Association for the Study of Culture and Religion) member from the University of Bonn, submitted a project proposal in 2018, "The Philippines as a Site of Religion: Regional Connections and Global Entanglements," that was successfully funded. The seeds for the project were sown at the SSEASR (an IAHR regional association) biennial conference in Manila in 2013. The grant allowed the three project leaders (based in Germany, the US, and the Philippines respectively) to organize a small

---

11. See www.aarweb.org/AARMBR/AARMBR/Membership-/International-Members.aspx (accessed June 12, 2020).
12. The current chair of the ICC is Professor Olga Kazmina of Moscow State University.
13. See www.aarweb.org/AARMBR/AARMBR/About-AAR-/Grant-Programs-/Research-Grants-/Collaborative-International-Research-Grants.aspx (accessed June 12, 2020).

conference and develop a book-length publication. Many other examples of this type of productive international networking with seed money could be adduced.[14]

In contrast to the above-mentioned multi-sited projects, we should also note the ongoing efforts by the AAR to attract international members and participants.[15] The data on international attendees for the 2019 AAR were as follows: 619 international out of 4176 registered.[16] Thirty travel grants were awarded, 11 of those to international members (Robert Puckett, AAR chief scholarly engagement officer, personal communication, November 4, 2019. The country breakdown reflects the domination of the global North, with a few individuals coming from global South countries such as South Africa and Nigeria.[17]

Given the costs of attending the AAR, or the quinquennial IAHR World Congress for that matter,[18] it is not surprising that the IAHR regional and special conferences have grown in popularity over the years (Pye 2016a: 238). We can now turn to the three most active IAHR regional associations (in addition to NAASR), namely the European Association for the Study of Religions (EASR), the African Association for the Study of Religions (AASR), and the South and South East Asian Association for the Study of Culture and Religion (SSEASR).[19] I will not dwell on statistics but rather on how these various associations have developed multiple strategies to serve their members and promote their scholarly work more widely.

The European Association was founded at the IAHR Special Conference in Cracow, Poland in 2000.[20] It became affiliated with the IAHR at the XVIIIth congress in the same year.[21] It describes its goals as follows on its home page:

> The European Association for the Study of Religions promotes the academic study of religions through the international collaboration of scholars in Europe whose research has a bearing on the subject. The objective of the EASR is pursued by the usual means of scholarly activity such as the arrangement of conferences, symposia or colloquia, the encouragement of scholarly publications, the exchange of information through electronic or other means, and other activities.[22]

---

14. I submitted a successful proposal in 2019 to develop an edited book on Rastafari in Africa with two Zimbabwean colleagues, Fortune Sibanda and Ezra Chitando.
15. It should be noted that international scholars can join the AAR for an annual fee of $15.
16. An average of just over 600 attend each year (since 2013).
17. Canada (176), United Kingdom (120), Germany (46), Australia (35), Norway (33), Sweden (23), Netherlands (20), Japan (17), Denmark (13), South Africa (12), Switzerland (10).
18. That notwithstanding, the quinquennial world congress is *the* primary international gathering for religion scholars and for advancing the work of the IAHR. The 22nd World Congress was scheduled to take place from August 23 to 29, 2020 in Dunedin, New Zealand with a theme of "Centres and Peripheries" (www.iahr2020.kiwi), but it had to be cancelled due to the COVID-19 pandemic.
19. There is also the Latin American regional association: ALER (Asociación Latino Americana para el Estudio de las Religiones/ Latin American Association for the Study of Religions).
20. See www.easr.eu. On the founding of the EASR, see Pye (2016a: 238–242).
21. On the relationship between the EASR and the IAHR, see Jensen (2016).
22. See www.easr.eu.

As the number of member associations has grown to 24, notably from Central and Eastern Europe, so, too, has the size of the conferences. As an indication of the vibrant scholarly hub that the EASR has become, the recent 17th Annual EASR conference that took place in Tartu, Estonia, attracted nearly 700 participants.[23] Given that the European region is composed of many countries and languages, an interesting feature of the EASR is the emphasis it places on the networks it supports: (1) a network of electronic discussion groups for various language regions, and (2) a network of general links for its member associations. As noted on the EASR website, the main reason for having more than one electronic discussion list is to avoid domination by any one language.[24] The discussion groups are as follows: Candide (French); Dolmen (English); Most (East European languages); Synkron (Nordic languages plus English); Tonantzin (Spanish, Portuguese, Italian); Yggdrasill (German).

The African Association for the Study of Religions (AASR) website boasts a detailed history of the association.[25] It attributes its genesis to broader internationalizing initiatives in the IAHR "to explore the institutional and ideological constraints on the study of religion to be met with in various parts of the world" (Pye 2016b: 117). It underscores its intimate connection with the IAHR, having been founded at an IAHR Regional Conference at the University of Zimbabwe at Harare, Zimbabwe, in September 1992.[26] It was formally admitted as an IAHR affiliate in the XVIIth IAHR World Congress in Mexico City in 1995. In addition, it reveals how multilateral the drive was to create an African association, and still to sustain it. As the African saying goes, it takes a village to raise a child. Spearheaded by Jan Platvoet in the Netherlands, the initiative involved Africa-based scholars, Africans based in Europe or North America, as well as Western scholars working in Europe, North America, or Africa.[27] To build a membership structure in such a vast continent (at least in its sub-Saharan region), the AASR developed a system of regional representatives, including for Europe and the US. The biennial conferences rotate around Africa and are usually lively, productive, and well-attended, including by enthusiastic religious studies students.[28] The ongoing challenge is the engagement of francophone (and lusophone) African scholars, given language issues and the institutional reality that the study of religion does not exist as an autonomous discipline in those regions. The association's

---

23. See https://easr2019.org.
24. Michael Pye, who has held office in both the IAHR and EASR, has long worked to foreground the language issue in IAHR developmental goals (Pye 2016a: 116). He pioneered the electronic discussion groups and the journal, *Science of Religion Abstracts and Index of Recent Articles (SOR)*, that summarizes articles in the field from journals published in English and other languages.
25. See www.a-asr.org/about.
26. See Ezra Chitando's important account of the study of religions/religious studies in Zimbabwe and other sub-Saharan African countries (Chitando 2008).
27. The Zimbabwe conference was hosted by Dr. James Cox, then teaching at the University of Zimbabwe.
28. This was very much the case for the 2018 conference in Lusaka, Zambia www.a-asr.org/aasr-zambia-conference-highlights (accessed June 15, 2020).

diasporic connections are strong, thanks to the sessions organized annually at the AAR as a related scholarly organization and to the migrations and peregrinations of individual African scholars, such as Elias Bongmba, Jacob Olupona, Afe Adogame, Ezra Chitando, Damaris Parsitau, Simeon Ilesanmi, Musa Dube, and Asonzeh Ukah, to name but a few. The AASR publishes an open-access e-journal, the *Journal of the Religions of Africa and its Diaspora,* with an internationally diverse editorial board.[29] The profile of the association is also enhanced by its links to two published journals, the *Journal of Religion in Africa*[30] and the *Journal of Africana Religions*[31] (see below for more on the latter). The well-maintained AASR website constitutes a useful resource for researchers on African religions.[32] We should note also that the first IAHR World Congress ever held in Africa took place in Durban, South Africa in 2000 (see Hackett and Pye 2009). With funds left over from the congress, an African Trust Fund was created. This proved valuable in supporting the research of a younger generation of Africa-based scholars of religion for a few years.[33]

Apart from the Nigerian Association for the Study of Religions (NASR) that was founded in 1976 and admitted as an IAHR member association in 1980,[34] and still organizes rotating annual conferences and publishes a local journal, national African associations would appear to be relatively unviable. The sub-regional Association for the Study of Religions in Southern Africa (ASRSA) is more of a success story. Founded in 1979 and admitted to the IAHR in 1980, it was initially isolated academically due to apartheid. In its post-apartheid phase, it organizes conferences that focus mainly on local and regional issues. Its journal, the *Journal for the Study of Religion,* launched in 1980, is an accredited and peer-reviewed journal whose main interest is the phenomenological and comparative study of the diversity of religions, religious traditions, and the religious movements and formations of Southern Africa.[35] Of particular note is the special issue of the journal (2018), ably edited by Johan Strijdom and Lee-Schae Scharnick-Udemans, honoring the work of its former editor and recently retired University of Cape Town professor of religious studies, internationally renowned scholar of religion David Chidester.[36] Eight of the thirteen articles were written by South African or

---

29. See www.a-asr.org/journal. This journal has the potential to play an important intermediary role between the international journals headquartered in the West and the older nationally-linked journals, such as *Religions: A Journal of the Nigerian Association for the Study of Religions* or newer department-linked journals that have proliferated at the local level, such as the *Ilorin Journal of Religious Studies* or *Orita: Ibadan Journal of Religious Studies.*
30. See https://brill.com/view/journals/jra/jra-overview.xml.
31. See www.psupress.org/Journals/jnls_JAR.html.
32. See www.a-asr.org.
33. See www.a-asr.org/iahr-african-trust-fund-research-publication-grant-applications-for-2014.
34. Membership lapsed due to non-payment of fees.
35. See www.scielo.org.za/scielo.php?script=sci_serial&pid=1011-7601&lng=en&nrm=iso
36. See www.scielo.org.za/scielo.php?script=sci_issuetoc&pid=1011-760120180002&lng=en&nrm=iso.

South Africa-based scholars. One notes the themes of materiality, mediality, sensoriality, decoloniality, indigeneity, race, and frontier zones coursing through the contributions, as in the case of Abdulkader Tayob's notable piece, "Decolonizing the Study of Religions: Muslim Intellectuals and the Enlightenment Project of Religious Studies" (2018).

Another regional association that has faced many local challenges, but borne fruit, is the South and Southeast Asian Association for the Study of Culture and Religion (SSEASR). The SSEASR was established in 2005 during its inaugural conference in New Delhi, India, which was also designated as an IAHR Regional Conference.[37] Some of the hurdles and harassment faced (and eventually transcended) by the SSEASR President, Amarjiva Lochan, in organizing the conference, are even noted in the annals of the IAHR.[38] The association's webpage states that the Delhi meeting was the first opportunity for scholars from the whole region to join together in a common academic endeavor.[39] The SSEASR became formally affiliated with the IAHR in Tokyo, 2005. Members and institutions hail from Afghanistan, Bangladesh, Bhutan, Cambodia, Hong Kong, India, Indonesia, Laos, Macao, Malaysia, Maldives, Mongolia, Myanmar (Burma), Nepal, Pakistan, the Philippines, Sri Lanka, Singapore, Thailand, Timore Leste, and Vietnam. Its biennial conferences are lively affairs that succeed despite logistical challenges, whether it is negotiating with governments (such as India [see above], Bhutan, Bangladesh, and Vietnam) to allow academic conferences on religion to take place on their turf, or simply coordinating the participation of such a diverse range of conference attendees and national representatives. The imprimatur of international logos, whether of the IAHR, or the International Council on Philosophy and the Human Sciences (CIPSH), that the IAHR belongs to and which has ties to UNESCO, clearly help the SSEASR cause. Additionally, protocol issues loom large at these conferences as government officials are often present at opening and closing ceremonies.

The SSEASR Constitution notes that it is open to researchers in various disciplines (e.g., history, linguistics, political science, anthropology, sociology, literature, cultural studies, law, folklore, etc.). This is not surprising as religion is generally studied in this region under the auspices of other disciplines. For example, the recent SSEASR conference in Bangladesh (June 2019) was populated by several archaeologists who study ancient cities, temples, and mosques in Bangladesh.[40] In some instances, the framing and publicizing of the conferences may play up cultural heritage at the expense of the religion trope, as was the case with the 2017 SSEASR conference in Vietnam. In fact, there was a decision to add "culture" to the title of the 2nd SSEASR conference in Bangkok conference in 2007

---

37. See http://sseasr.org The SSEASR publishes a peer-reviewed journal, bi-annual newsletter and books related to South and Southeast Asian culture and religion.
38. See page 36 of www.iahrweb.org/bulletins/Bull38-mar05.pdf.
39. See the excellent report on the inaugural conference in New Delhi in 2005 at https://elinepa.org/en/the-2005-sseasr-regional-conference-new-delhi (accessed November 17, 2019).
40. See http://sseasr.org/images/pdf/8th_SSEASR_Conference_FINAL_ANNOUNCEMENT.pdf.

as none of the Thai universities in those days had any departments of religious studies. Religion was studied under the auspices of Buddhist Studies, Buddhist Culture, and the Centre for Asian Culture Studies. The addition of the term "culture" proved helpful and it was eventually added to the association title (without changing the acronym).[41] That notwithstanding, there appears to be a genuine commitment to developing the critical, historical, and comparative study of religion in the region, as evidenced by the launch of the Bangladesh Association for the Study of Culture and Religion in June 2019. Several international scholars attend the SSEASR conferences for their research and networking affordances, let alone the popular pre- and post-conference field trips to key religious heritage sites such as Borobudur or Angkor Wat, in the company of local experts and learned colleagues.[42]

Affiliate Associations and Societies

In addition to the work done by national and regional associations, we should also note the rise of international scholarly associations that focus on particular manifestations or methodologies of religion, usually from a multi- or interdisciplinary perspective. Some of these IAHR- and/or EASR affiliated associations are longstanding, while others are newer creations, reflecting emergent research areas. These research communities serve as crucibles for promoting and developing their respective (sub-) fields whether with publications series, journals, meetings, or social media. Some are internationally or cross-nationally constituted from the outset, while others are working to encourage more international participation.

The European Society for the Study of Western Esotericism (ESSWE) began in 2005 to "advance the academic study of the various manifestations of Western esotericism from late antiquity to the present."[43] While it has a more narrowly defined portfolio, ESSWE holds an international conference every two years, and publishes the journal *Aries* and the associated Aries book series (both published by Brill). In addition to awarding a thesis prize, the association targets its bursaries to junior scholars and scholars from the former Eastern bloc, and has a resource-rich website. The International Study of Religion in Eastern and Central Europe Association (ISORECEA) also has a specific geographic focus, describing itself as an international scientific association that "focuses on the exchange of academic knowledge on the situation of religion in the Central-Eastern European area."[44] It was established in December 1995 after a series of conferences. Its nearly 80 members represent various disciplines, e.g., sociology, anthropology, history, philosophy, and come from diverse countries, Belarus, Belgium, Bulgaria, Croatia, the Czech Republic, Denmark, Finland, France, Great Britain, Hungary,

---

41. Both the Greek (Greek Society for the Study of Culture and Religion) and the Philippine (Philippine Association for the Study of Culture, History, and Religion) associations also rely on the inclusion of "culture" to provide legitimacy.
42. The 2021 SSEASR conference will take place in Myanmar.
43. See www.esswe.org.
44. See www.isorecea.net.

Lithuania, Poland, Russia, Slovakia, Slovenia, Ukraine, and the USA. The association has a book series, information on the status of religion in the region, and an open-access peer-reviewed annual academic journal, *Religion and Society in Central and Eastern Europe* (RASCEE), "reflecting critical scholarship in the study of religion in the region."[45]

The International Association for the Cognitive Science of Religion (IACSR) was founded in 2006, as "an association open to scholars from the humanities, social and natural sciences interested in explaining religious cognition and cultures as natural phenomena."[46] This multidisciplinary association aims to promote excellence in the cognitive science of religion through international collaboration with scholars whose research has a bearing on the empirical investigation of religious cognition. They currently advance their work through biennial conferences and interim local meetings; the encouragement of research projects; the facilitation of scholarly publications; the exchange of information through electronic media; and by other means. The IACSR also wants to "develop vehicles to promote excellence in teaching, to support recent graduates in their respective fields, and to enhance promising research activities across disciplines." According to Armin W. Geertz, past president of the association, and current senior editor of their official journal, *Journal for the Cognitive Science of Religion*,[47] the cognitive science of religion was originally initiated by founding members of NAASR around 1990, but was quickly taken up by research teams in Europe and Canada and spread into a variety of social, psychological and historical disciplines (see Geertz 2016). Although American religious studies scholars have been reluctant to use cognitive approaches, the first chair in the Cognitive Science of Religion was established in the Religious Studies Department at California State University, Northridge, and is currently held by Claire White who is also co-chair of the Cognitive Science of Religion Group, at the American Academy of Religion.[48] Cognitive scientists of religion have developed theories and hypotheses which are international in scope and provide an important supplement to the psychology of religion by gathering data and testing their hypotheses in non-Western, as well as Western, contexts (see for instance Cohen 2007; Martin and Wiebe 2017).

The International Society for the Study of Religion, Nature and Culture (ISSRNC) was in the making from the 1990s but eventually took off in 2005 when faculty and students in the Graduate Program in Religion and Nature at the University of Florida, spearheaded by Professor Bron Taylor,[49] sent out an open invitation to scholars interested in forming an interdisciplinary society.[50] The process led to the formation of the ISSRNC at the first conference of the association in 2006.

---

45. See www.rascee.net/index.php/rascee.
46. See www.iacsr.com/iacsr/Home.html.
47. See https://journals.equinoxpub.com/index.php/JCSR. The journal was founded in 2013. There is also a supplement book series, Advances in the Cognitive Science of Religion.
48. See www.csun.edu/humanities/religious-studies/claire-kravette.
49. See https://religion.ufl.edu/graduate-studies/fields-of-study/religion-nature.
50. See www.issrnc.org/about/history.

From the outset, the ISSRNC's objective was to create an international association, a "community of scholars engaged in critical inquiry into the relationships among human beings and their diverse cultures, environments, religious beliefs and practices," through conferences, publications, and outreach.[51] Despite initial fears of overreach, they have made significant efforts to realize their objectives, hosting or co-hosting conferences in many countries, so far including Mexico, the Netherlands, South Africa, Italy, Australia, the Netherlands, Sweden, and the United States. A conference is currently being planned in Turkey. They seek to build scholarly capacity in their field around the world, despite meagre funds and still only about 200 members; they have managed to fund a dozen scholars at their major conferences from less affluent regions. They have three working groups, including one on Gender and Ecology that is "interested to learn from those using a gender critique to approach the nature-culture nexus, both in the global south and north."[52] The ISSRNC's bylaws envisioned regional bodies, but these have not emerged in the global South, although more one-off gatherings are reportedly occurring. Hot on the heels of the *Encyclopedia of Religion and Nature* (2005) of which Bron Taylor was the editor-in-chief,[53] and which includes 1,000 entries from 520 international contributors, the first issue of the affiliated *Journal for the Study of Religion, Nature, and Culture* appeared in 2007.[54] This publication has also attracted an international array of authors, including several anthropologists.

Another area of academic inquiry with international ramifications is that of new religious movements and new kinds of religious consciousness. The most internationally active scholarly association in this regard is the Center for Studies on New Religions (CESNUR), founded in 1988 and directed by Massimo Introvigne out of Torino, Italy.[55] It is an affiliate of the European Association for the Study of Religions (EASR). The annual conferences that began in the early 1990s have been held in a range of universities in Europe and North America, as well as South Korea, Jerusalem, and, more recently, Taiwan. They feature both research presentations and outreach to public officials and the media, owing to the controversies surrounding new religions, as well as field trips for conference participants to significant sites of new religious movements.[56] After more than thirty years of activity, the CESNUR website notes that more than 1,000 scholarly papers have been presented at the Center's international conferences and seminars. Many have been posted on CESNUR's website (in English, Italian, Spanish, and French), while others have been published in international journals. In 2017, the organization launched its own journal, the *Journal of CESNUR*, opting for an *online open access* journal, given the trends in international scholarly publishing.[57] The

---

51. See www.issrnc.org.
52. See www.issrnc.org/working-groups/ecology-and-gender-working-group.
53. See www.religionandnature.com/ern.
54. See www.issrnc.org/journal/about-jsrnc.
55. See www.easr.eu/cesnur.
56. On this and other activities of CESNUR (library, network of experts, conference cyber-proceedings), see www.cesnur.org/about.htm.
57. See https://cesnur.net.

International Society for the Study of New Religions (ISSNR), which is an international membership association originally formed in Sweden in 2009 for scholars of new religions, normally meets in conjunction with CESNUR conferences every two years.[58]

The Society of Biblical Literature (SBL) describes itself as "the oldest and largest learned society devoted to the critical investigation of the Bible from a variety of academic disciplines."[59] It is potentially the newest addition to the list of IAHR affiliates, having been recently recommended by the IAHR Executive Committee, pending the vote by the IAHR International Committee and admission by the next IAHR General Assembly.[60] Perhaps less widely known is that the SBL has been holding annual international meetings in many parts of the world since 1983. The majority of these gatherings are held in European locations, with occasional meetings in Australia, New Zealand, South Africa, Israel, Argentina and South Korea. The international meeting is billed as "a unique forum for international scholars who are unable to attend the North American meeting and for all who wish to engage more directly SBL's growing international membership and scholarship."[61] There are materials on the website (such as the substantive calls for papers) and the *Review of Biblical Literature* blog that are accessible to non-members. Finally on the list of affiliated associations is the Society for Ancient Mediterranean Religions (SAMR) which was founded to foster the interdisciplinary study of the religions of the ancient Mediterranean basin, and especially the interaction of the multiple polytheistic religions with each other and with the emerging monotheistic religions of the region.[62] The SAMR organized a colloquy, "Religion on the Ground," at the IAHR World Congress in Erfurt in 2015.[63]

Networks and Working Groups

Less formal than, or preliminary versions of, associations are networks and working groups. For example, the IAHR Women Scholars Network (IAHR-WSN) is an IAHR initiative that was launched at the EASR conference in Bremen in 2007 to support the work of women scholars of religion around the world.[64] Morny Joy and I had become increasingly aware of the particular challenges facing women in their respective academic institutions and associations, whether in the form of discrimination, harassment, or lack of resources on or resistance to research on gender issues (see Joy 2016).[65] Thanks to the work of Canadian colleagues and graduate students, a listserv was created to supply information on grants, conferences, and publications, as well as a forum for discussion of pertinent issues.

---

58. See www.issnr.org/about.
59. See www.sbl-site.org.
60. See www.iahrweb.org/affiliates.php.
61. See www.sbl-site.org/meetings/Internationalmeeting.aspx.
62. See https://samreligions.org.
63. See https://samreligions.org/2016/02/01/erfurt-2015-final-program.
64. See www.iahrweb.org/wsn.
65. Jenny Berglund and Jay Johnston took over the leadership in 2015.

This was linked to membership in the network (no cost). The Facebook page regularly lists job and fellowship opportunities, as well as publications and media items of interest to the group.[66] Arguably, the IAHR-WSN's greatest success lies in the meetings it has held at numerous IAHR regional (SSEASR, AASR, and EASR) conferences and world congresses over the years. These have proved popular and productive, in terms of emphasizing our academic mission, providing a safe space for professional concerns, and connecting local and international scholars for research collaboration. We also take time to celebrate our achievements and the pioneering work of senior colleagues, as at the well-attended (over 70 participants) meeting and reception held at the 2015 Erfurt Congress.[67] There were plans for a multi-media academic symposium at the Otago Congress in August 2020 (since cancelled), entitled: "Founding Mothers and Women of Influence in the Study of Religion(s)—Past, Present, and Future." We are now exploring other ways of getting the academic and professional contributions of women religion scholars around the world better publicized and on the record.[68]

While not an official network, one might consider the activities of scholars in the field of the study of religious or religion education as another example of a loose concatenation of scholars with shared intellectual and professional interests who are working to build their research area and expand international participation. They navigate among different associations, conferences, working groups, and publications. They have a working group in the EASR, for example, on "Religion in Public Education," which aims to "to critically study European ways of having or not having education about religion/s and to help promote a study-of-religions (SOR)/religious-studies (RS) approach to education about religion/s."[69] They note that this includes individual research, networking, conferences within and outside the EASR annual framework and related publications. Their work within the EASR is now enhanced by greater participation of scholars from Eastern Europe in the biennial conference. There is also an international (Europe-based) seminar on religious education and values that some members of the working group participate in.[70] However, while there is some improvement in the internationalization of their area of study, it is still heavily dominated by Europeans and North Americans, with the participation of a few South African, Australian, and Japanese scholars. To extend their international connections, they have to work with the reality that, in many parts of the world, the study of religious education may be dominated by theological scholars, as with scholars from Muslim majority countries, for example. This is reflected in recent publications such as *European*

---

66. See www.facebook.com/groups/iahrwomenscholarsnetwork.
67. For pictures of the event, see www.iahrweb.org/wsn.
68. For example, some women members of the Australian Association for the Study of Religion created a video at the annual conference in December 2019 honoring their senior women mentors in the field.
69. See http://easr.info/easr-working-groups/public-education.
70. See www.yorksj.ac.uk/isrev.

Perspectives on Islamic Education[71] and the new Brill Series on Research Perspectives on Religion and Education, both in terms of the content and the editorial board.[72]

Journals and Projects

In addition to the journals discussed above in relation to various scholarly associations,[73] I wish to highlight two more journals for their exemplary roles as agents of internationalization in the contemporary study of religion. One is *Nova Religio*, a journal that "presents scholarly interpretations and examinations of emergent and alternative religious movements."[74] While it originated (in 1997) in the work of the New Religious Movements Group (now Unit) in the American Academy of Religion, and the founding editor and co-general editors and reviews editors have been North American, *Nova Religio*'s editors insist it is international in both its scope and authors (Phillip Lucas, personal communication, October 25, 2019; Cathy Wessinger, personal communication, October 25–27, 2019, June 7, 2020). The journal's ambit was always international, but the special issues (on new religious movements in Africa, China, Oceania, Brazil, Israel, India, and other regions and countries), as well as individually submitted papers relating to new religious movements in Korea, Haiti, Russia, Japan, India, the Philippines, as well as countries in Africa, the Middle East, Eastern Europe, and South America, have brought many young scholars from around the world into new religions studies. In addition to the journal's leadership in broadening NRM scholarship across cultures and historical periods, we should note the role of international conferences, such as CESNUR, INFORM,[75] the AAR, and the Society for the Scientific Study of Religion (SSSR),[76] in stimulating transdisciplinary scholarship on NRMs and encouraging submissions from younger scholars, along with the growing interest in religious freedom issues, minority religious movements, religious persecution, and global terrorism. The focus in NRM studies on the "cult wars" in the US has long been a thing of the past, and the field has expanded far beyond those groups and issues, now intersecting with a number of other areas of focus in religious studies.

Coming onto the scene in 2011, the *Journal of Africana Studies* has made some strategic moves to position itself at the intersection of the study of religion within African American studies and African studies, with a mission of internationalizing the journal and increasing the participation of African readers, writers, and board members. The editors and their board are keen to address the challenge of getting scholars in Africa, the Americas, and Europe reading and talking to one another. The hallmark of their effort in this respect is through their recent partnering

---

71. See www.equinoxpub.com/home/european-perspectives-on-islamic-education-and-public-schooling.
72. See https://brill.com/view/journals/rpre/1/1/article-p1_1.xml.
73. See, for example, the impressive list of national and cross-national journals associated with the EASR at www.easr.info/publications/599-2.
74. See nr.ucpress.edu.
75. See https://inform.ac.
76. See https://sssreligion.org.

with the African Association of the Study of Religions (AASR).⁷⁷ The journal has many African academics, including several Africa-based scholars, on their board.⁷⁸ It is also sponsored by the Association for the Study of the Worldwide African Diaspora.⁷⁹ Africa-based scholars receive a free e-subscription to the journal. The editorial team reaches out to Africa-based scholars via Facebook and Twitter, through the AASR, and by sending delegations to AASR conferences in Africa. The new partnership's most ambitious component is the creation of pan-Atlantic research teams that will unite scholars from Africa, the Americas, and Europe for mentoring and collaborative research and writing.⁸⁰ The hope is that some of these jointly authored book manuscripts will find their way into the book series on Africana religions, also created by the founding journal editors, Edward Curtis IV and Sylvester Johnson.⁸¹

We should mention, in closing, the efforts of the Korean Association for Religious Studies (KARS), established in 1970, to publish its journal, *Chonggyo Yeongu* (Journal of Religious Studies), in English, from 2010 onwards.⁸² Chongsuh Kim, who served as president of the association from 2006-08 wrote a position piece, "The Concept of 'Korean Religion' and Religious Studies in Korea," that was published in the inaugural English issue. Both religious studies scholars and theologians belong to the association, whose regular meetings are organized primarily by the former. The launch of the original Korean-language journal was linked to moves in the 1990s to invite more foreign scholars to its meetings and to encourage more Korean scholars to participate in AAR or IAHR meetings. The KARS receives support from the Korean Research Foundation.

Balancing Centripetal and Centrifugal Forces

Using what I termed a nodal and interstitial approach, I set out to explore in this essay some of the translocal, transregional, and transnational initiatives seeking to instantiate a more internationally active and equitably diverse study of religion. These do not necessarily translate into what Greg Alles calls a "global vision of religious studies" (2008: 9), but they seem to represent a more complex dynamic in terms of centrifugal and centripetal flows. These efforts need to be assessed in relation to the historical trajectory of the field, as in the case of the IAHR which has sought to balance its goal of developing "a more widely ranged intercultural base for the study of religion" while "retaining its coherence" (Pye 2016b: 117). Whether these forms of international engagement, be they networks,

---

77. See www.a-asr.org/partnership-with-joar.
78. See http://africanareligions.org/editorial-board.
79. See http://aswadiaspora.org. The journal's founders attended the ASWAD international conference in the Dominican Republic in 2013.
80. See http://africanareligions.org/pan-atlantic-scholarship-initiative.
81. See www.psupress.org/books/series/book_SeriesAfRel.html.
82. See www.Koars.org. It had been published since the beginning of the association in Korean (Chongsuh Kim, personal communication, November 4, 2019).

journals, scholarships, conferences, or associations, are deemed to matter or succeed will depend on current benchmarks, positionality, and ideology. Broader institutional and scholarly trends can also account for divergent perspectives on the internationalization of the field.

For example, the trend of higher education institutions around the world to "internationalize" in response to globalization may be viewed negatively in an era of increasingly scant resources, particularly for the humanities and social sciences. For minority subjects like religious studies, the survival stakes are currently high in the face of broader shifts away from the liberal arts to an emphasis on professional education. Thus, the antidote to "field insecurity" for some Western scholars of religion is to resist internationalizing trends and return centripetally to the roots of the field, reemphasizing its non-confessional, comparative, historical, and "scientific" orientation (hence the preferred use of *Religionswissenschaft* or the "science of religion" (Martin and Wiebe 2016). Others opt for a revitalized method-and-theory approach that emphasizes deconstructive and reconstructive analytical skills as the hallmark of the twenty-first-century critical study of religion, challenging *sui generis* interpretations of religion and unmasking overt or covert theological assumptions.[83]

For scholars who are more empirically and/or historically inclined, the growing interdisciplinarity of contemporary studies of religion lends itself to more diverse international participation on an array of topics such as secularism, law, religious freedom, new religious movements, religious education, conflict and violence, indigeneity, migration, diaspora, tourism and heritage, ecology, health and healing, spatiality, media, materiality, and race, gender, and sexuality.[84] Moreover, as evidenced by the 2016 publication, *Contemporary Views on Comparative Religion*, these topics can be generative of fresh thinking on core conceptual and methodological frameworks in the field, such as comparison.

Furthermore, it is important to consider to what extent the postcolonial and decolonial turns in the humanities and social sciences, and in the study of religion more specifically, have provided a theoretical and methodological platform to connect scholars internationally and generate a more international footprint for the field. For example, we could look to the topics of gender and women's studies (Joy 2001; Dube 2012), sexuality (Klinken 2019), and indigeneity for evidence of this type of scholarship (Johnson and Kraft 2017). Along these lines, it is noteworthy that in a special issue of the journal *Religion* on the future of the study of religion, several authors called for a broader "remapping" of the field.

In the latter publication, Birgit Meyer's appositely titled piece, "Remapping our Mindset: Towards a Transregional and Pluralistic Outlook" (Meyer 2020),

---

83. See, for example, McCutcheon (2018a, 2018b) and Cotter and Robertson (2016).
84. See, for example, Sullivan et al. (2015). These diverse topics are also grist for the mill of global South researchers trained in the sociology of religion (see, e.g., Echtler and Ukah 2016; Ukah and Wilks 2017), whose work may approximate the type of problematizing, contextualized, and analytical scholarship on religion (minus the "critical self-consciousness") that McCutcheon advocates for so unequivocally (Chapter 6, this volume).

makes this very point by capturing both the spirit and the exigency of the shifting academic terrain.[85] In wanting to rethink and reconfigure the study of religion/s against a global horizon, she calls for a liberation from the "religious studies–theology binary" in order to develop concepts and methods that are more in keeping with the projected future of religion on a global scale.[86] This future, according to the Pew Foundation 2015 report, will entail the decline of Christianity in Europe and the United States as it continues to expand in Africa, Asia, and South America, along with religious pluralization more generally.[87] Furthermore, she observes that religious studies now finds itself in "some kind of limbo" in the aftermath of the deconstructions of religion as a post-Enlightenment Protestant category and secularization as "imbued with a Western teleology" (Meyer 2020: 114). She stresses the importance of working within the transdisciplinary humanities and social sciences for developing a "broader mindset" to discern the changing interrelationships between religion, culture, and secularism (ibid.: 115).

Perhaps more importantly for our purposes, Meyer, as an Africanist scholar like myself, argues that there is more to be gained from studying religion not just *in* but also *from* Africa. She recognizes the significance of David Chidester's work on how the conceptual vocabulary of "comparative religion" derived from the colonial encounters of southern Africa (Chidester 1996, 2014). Tracing the trajectory of religion as a term and concept that was initially foreign to Africa, through colonization and missionization, "helps us recognize the longstanding transregional connections, through which what we call 'religion in Africa' and Western notions of 'religion' have become entangled with each other" (Meyer 2020: 117). Like Meyer, I would argue that such vantage points, coupled with their location in the global South with its religious vitality and plurality, have more potential for theory formation in religious studies from a decolonial angle.[88]

Others attest to how ramping up international scholarly collaboration can bring new attention to marginalized voices,[89] as well as overlooked theories, in the academy.[90] It can trigger much-needed processes of decentering and recentering in terms of where we think *from*, and what and who we think *with*, in our

---

85. This is well evidenced by her website at the University of Utrecht: https://religiousmatters.nl/author/birgit-meyer (accessed June 12, 2020).
86. Cf. Abdulkader Tayob's observation that this "theological shadow runs quite deep and may even be lurking in the critical scholarship that regularly announces its opposition to it" (Tayob 2018: 12).
87. www.pewforum.org/2015/04/02/religious-projections-2010-2050/ (accessed June 12, 2020).
88. Related articles include Klinken (2020) and Day (2020).
89. This has become integral to the various projects on religion and global politics that Elizabeth Shakman Hurd has (co-)directed in recent years at Northwestern University. She claims that her international visits and work with local scholars in various countries informed her efforts to decenter the American experience and recenter the rest of the world vis-à-vis the law and politics of religious difference and diversity (Elizabeth Shakman Hurd, personal communication, October 25, 2019).
90. Satoko Fujiwara (2020) makes a strong case for theoretical and methodological pluralism because of the failure of Western scholars to understand the theoretical orientation of Japanese scholars in their interpretation of contemporary religion and culture in Japan.

disciplinary areas. It can also bring greater awareness of the inter- and transdisciplinary moves that particular dispensations compel, as argued by Satoko Fujiwara in the case of Japan.[91] Additionally, international work brings to our attention new academic hubs and funding sources in the study of religion/s, beyond the powerful ambits of the IAHR and the AAR,[92] that may reshape the contours of particular sub-fields.[93]

In sum, while it may be too bold to claim that the academic study of religion exists on a global scale as an integrated and coherent field, there is clear evidence of multifaceted and multilateral efforts to continue developing the field internationally.[94] These efforts deserve our attention for the insights they afford into possible futures, rather than failures, of the field.

Rosalind I. J. Hackett is chancellor's professor emerita, and professor of religious studies emerita at the University of Tennessee. She is also extraordinary professor, Desmond Tutu Centre for Religion and Social Justice, University of the Western Cape, South Africa. She publishes in the areas of indigenous religion, new religious movements, gender, art, human rights, and conflict in Africa. Recent (co-edited) books are *New Media and Religious Transformations in Africa* (2015) and *The Anthropology of Global Pentecostalism and Evangelicalism* (2015). She is past president and honorary life member of the International Association for the History of Religions (IAHR).

References

Adogame, Afe, Ezra Chitando, and Bolaji Bateye (eds). 2012. *African Traditions in the Study of Religion in Africa: Emerging Trends, Indigenous Spirituality and the Interface with other World Religions*. Farnham: Ashgate.
Adogame, Afe, Ezra Chitando, and Bolaji Bateye (eds). 2013. *African Traditions in the Study of Religion, Diaspora, and Gendered Societies*. Farnham: Ashgate.
Alles, Greg. 2008. *Religious Studies: A Global View*. New York: Routledge.

---

91. See Fujiwara (2016) on the rethinking of the interdisciplinarity and relevance of research in Japan.
92. The AAR is described as "the largest scholarly society dedicated to the academic study of religion, with more than 8,000 members around the world." See www.aarweb.org/AARMBR/About-AAR/AARMBR/About-AAR.aspx?hkey=32443cfe-2a95-439d-a625-25831c44b085 (accessed June 15, 2020). The IAHR has fewer members, but greater international presence.
93. For example, the Canadian research project on Buddhism and East Asian Religions known as FROGBEAR, where Chinese scholars operate independently, reconstituting China as a center for research on Chinese religions (https://frogbear.org). Moreover, most Chinese conferences on Chinese religions invite at least a couple of international scholars (often from Korea, Japan, Europe, or North America, but sometimes from South or Southeast Asia), but mainly feature scholars from China (Megan Bryson, personal communication, October 28, 2019).
94. The increasing availability of open access electronic resources and academic social networking sites, such as Academia and ResearchGate, may also be a factor in strengthening and reshaping international participation.

Alles, Greg. 2019. "Research: Religious Studies Research in an Era of Neoliberalization." In Leslie Dorrough Smith (ed.), *Constructing Data in Religious Studies: Examining the Architecture of the Academy* (pp. 256–266). Sheffield: Equinox.

Chidester, David. 1996. *Savage Systems: Colonialism and Comparative Religion in Southern Africa.* Charlottesville, VA: University of Virginia Press.

Chidester, David. 2014. *Empire of Religion: Imperialism and Comparative Religion.* Chicago: University of Chicago Press.

Chitando, Ezra. 2008. "Sub-Saharan Africa." In Greg Alles (ed.), *Religious Studies: A Global View* (pp. 102–125). Abingdon: Routledge.

Cohen, Emma. 2007. *The Mind Possessed: The Cognition of Spirit Possession in an Afro-Brazilian Religious Tradition.* Oxford: Oxford University Press.

Cotter, Christopher R., and David G. Robertson (eds). 2016. *After World Religions: Reconstructing Religious Studies.* New York: Routledge.

Day, Abby. 2020. "Towards Increasing Diversity in the Study of Religion." *Religion* 50(1): 46–52.

Dube, Musa W. 2012. "Postcolonial Feminist Perspectives on African Religions." In Elias Bongmba (ed.), *The Wiley-Blackwell Companion to African Religions* (pp. 127–139). New York: Wiley.

Echtler, Magnus, and Asonzeh Ukah. 2016. *Bourdieu in Africa: Exploring the Dynamics of Religious Fields.* Leiden: Brill.

Fujiwara, Satoko. 2016. ""An Analysis of Sixty Years of NVMEN: How Much Diversity Have We Achieved?" In Tim Jensen and Armin W. Geertz (eds), *NVMEN, the Academic Study of Religion, and the IAHR: Past, Present and Prospects* (pp. 391-414). Boston, MA: Brill.

Fujiwara, Satoko. 2020. "The Current Conflict of the Faculties and the Future of the Study of Religion/s." *Religion* 50(1): 53–59.

Geertz, Armin W. 2016. "Cognitive Science." In: Michael Stausberg and Steven Engler (eds), *Oxford Handbook of the Study of Religion* (pp. 97–111). Oxford: Oxford University Press.

Hackett, Rosalind I. J. 1988. "The Academic Study of Religion in Nigeria." *Religion* 18: 37–46.

Hackett, Rosalind I. J. 2016. "Reflections on Twenty Years of IAHR Service—Mexico City 1995 to Erfurt 2015." In Tim Jensen and Armin W. Geertz (eds), *NVMEN, the Academic Study of Religion, and the IAHR: Past, Present and Prospects* (pp. 245–251). Boston, MA: Brill.

Hackett, Rosalind I. J., and Michael Pye (eds). 2009. *History of Religions: Origins and Visions. Proceedings of the 18th IAHR World Congress, Durban August 5-12, 2000.* Cambridge: Roots and Branches.

Jensen, Tim. 2016. "The EASR within (the World Scenario of) the IAHR: Observations and Reflections." In Tim Jensen and Armin W. Geertz (eds), *NVMEN, the Academic Study of Religion, and the IAHR: Past, Present and Prospects* (pp. 163–220). Boston, MA: Brill.

Jensen, Tim, and Armin W. Geertz (eds). 2016. *NVMEN, the Academic Study of Religion, and the IAHR: Past, Present and Prospects.* Boston, MA: Brill.

Johnson, Greg, and Siv Ellen Kraft (eds). 2017. *Handbook of Indigenous Religion(s).* New York: Brill.

Joy, Morny. 2016. "Reflecting on Women and the Study of Religion in NVMEN." In Tim Jensen and Armin W. Geertz (eds), *NVMEN, the Academic Study of Religion, and the IAHR: Past, Present and Prospects* (pp. 349–376). Boston, MA: Brill.

Joy, Morny. 2001. "Postcolonial Reflections: Challenges for Religious Studies." *Method & Theory in the Study of Religion* 13(2): 177–195.

Klinken, Adriaan van. 2019. *Kenyan, Christian, Queer: Religion, LGBT Activism, and Arts of Resistance in Africa*. University Park, PA: Penn State University Press

Klinken, Adriaan van. 2020. "Studying Religion in the Pluriversity: Decolonial Perspectives." *Religion* 50(1): 148–155.

Martin, Luther, and Donald Wiebe (eds). 2016. *Conversations and Controversies in the Scientific Study of Religion: Collaborative and Co-authored Essays by Luther H. Martin and Donald Wiebe*. New York: Brill.

Martin, Luther H. and Donald Wiebe (eds.). 2017. *Religion Explained? The Cognitive Science of Religion after Twenty-five Years*. London: Bloomsbury Academic.

McCutcheon, Russell T. 2018a. *Fabricating Religion: Fanfare for the Common e.g.* New York: de Gruyter.

McCutcheon, Russell T. 2018b. *Studying Religion: An Introduction*. New York: Routledge.

Meyer, Birgit. 2020. "Remapping our Mindset: Towards a Transregional and Pluralistic Outlook." *Religion* 50(1): 113–121.

Nye, Malory. 2019. Decolonizing the Study of Religion. *Open Library of Humanities* 5(1): 43.

Pye, Michael. 2016a. "IAHR Landmarks and Connections." In Tim Jensen and Armin W. Geertz (eds), *NVMEN, the Academic Study of Religion, and the IAHR: Past, Present and Prospects* (pp. 221–244). Boston, MA: Brill.

Pye, Michael. 2016b. "Cultural and Organisational Perspectives in the Study of Religion." In Tim Jensen and Armin W. Geertz (eds), *NVMEN, the Academic Study of Religion, and the IAHR: Past, Present and Prospects* (pp. 111–117). Boston, MA: Brill.

Scharnick-Udemans, Lee-Schae, and Rosalind I. J. Hackett (eds). 2019. "Introduction: Religion and Gender in the Media Marketplace." *African Journal of Gender and Religion* 25(2): 1–13.

Scott, Joan Wallach. 2019. *Knowledge, Power, and Academic Freedom*. New York: Columbia University Press.

Sullivan, Winnifred Fallers, Elizabeth Shakman Hurd, Saba Mahmood, and Peter Danchin (eds). 2015. *Politics of Religious Freedom*. Chicago, IL: University of Chicago Press.

Tayob, Abdulkader. 2018. "Decolonizing the Study of Religions: Muslim Intellectuals and the Enlightenment Project of Religious Studies." *Journal for the Study of Religion* 31(2): 7–35.

Ukah, Asonzeh, and Tammy Wilks. 2017. "Peter Berger and The Sacred Canopy and Theorizing the African Religious context." *Journal of the American Academy of Religion* 84(4): 1147–1154.

Wiebe, Donald. 2016. "Memory, Text, and Interpretation: A Critical Appreciation of IAHR International Congresses—1975–2010." In Tim Jensen and Armin W. Geertz (eds), *NVMEN, the Academic Study of Religion, and the IAHR: Past, Present and Prospects* (pp. 253–282). Boston, MA: Brill.

Chapter 15

Field of Dreams
What do NAASR Scholars Really Want?

F. LeRon Shults and Wesley J. Wildman

Introduction

In her chapter on "International Perspectives on/in the Field" (Chapter 14, this volume), Rosalind Hackett has helpfully mapped the activities and emphases of some of the most significant scholarly organizations and initiatives outside of North America, highlighting the dynamism and value of international collaboration, and encouraging solidarity and the "much-needed processes of decentering and recentering in terms of where we think *from*, and what and who we think *with*, in our disciplinary areas." Here we attempt to complement her contribution by mapping some of the methodological and motivational values of scholarly organizations within North America, drawing from the findings of a recently completed multi-year survey of scholars of religion in a wide variety of disciplines. We describe some of the newly discovered features of this axiological map of the field, focusing on the distinctive values of members of the North American Association for the Study of Religion (NAASR), and explore some of the challenges and opportunities that those who think *from* this location face when trying to think *with* those in the Global South.

Following Professor Hackett's lead, we'll begin with some brief autobiographical remarks. LeRon is currently a professor at the Institute for Global Development and Social Planning at the University of Agder in Kristiansand, Norway, where he's been since 2006. However, he was born and educated in the US and taught theology and philosophy of religion at American institutions for many years before moving to Norway. Wesley is currently a professor at the School of Theology at Boston University, where he has been since 1993. However, he was born and began his education in Australia, whose status in relationship to the "Global South" (like the phrase itself) is ambiguous and contentious. We are white, cisgender, hyper-educated white males in tenured positions at financially healthy Universities. We want our scholarship (or at least some of it) to be "public," that is, to have an impact on broader discussions about the way in which "religion" plays a role in human lives, including those in less existentially secure locations. We recognize the dangers of paternalism, but we also want our scholarly constructions and depictions of religion to "help." We dream of justice, but are we just dreaming? What do we really want? We'll return to these questions at the end of the chapter.

Our title is an allusion to the 1989 movie of the same name, in which Kevin Costner played the role of a sentimental farmer and baseball enthusiast Ray Kinsella, who hallucinates the disembodied spirits of dead baseball players whose ingroup reinforcing sporting rituals are played out in his crop fields. While pondering the call for papers to which this chapter emerged as a response, this movie popped into the head of the first author—why? Like the protagonists in *Field of Dreams*, many scholars of religion in North America, especially within schools of theology, colleges promoting confessional philosophy of religion, and even some AAR-oriented religious studies departments, are all too often uncritical toward or even actively participate in and promote rituals allegedly engaging supernatural agents whose thoughts and intentions are considered existentially relevant for the success of its ingroup members. What people do in their private lives is one thing, and also worth discussing in another venue, but is presupposing and embracing supernaturalism the optimal way to conduct research in the academic study of religion? We'll return to the potential theoretical and practical ramifications of this tendency within some circles in scholarship on religion at the end of the chapter.

As we will see below, NAASR members stand out in the field for their (relatively) strong concern about the potentially deleterious effects of participating in imaginative supernatural worldviews in the context of serious scholarship about religion. This means that they may be able to play a uniquely critical and creative role in ongoing public discourse about the way in which American dreams are impacting the construction and practice of religion in developing nations in the Global South, which we will take up as a case study in the fourth and longest section below. The second and third sections provide a brief analysis of some of the distinctive features of the methodological and motivational dreams of NAASR members, compared to others within the academic fields of religion. First, however, we provide some background about the multi-year research project whose findings made these insights possible.

The "Values in Scholarship on Religion" Project

Scholars who study religion often disagree strongly over the values that ought to guide their academic work. Researchers within and across disciplines debate which methods to use, which audiences to address, how to define their object of study, and the extent to which an individual's own religious faith (or lack of faith) should influence his or her scholarship. Most scholars of religion seem to be aware of the variety of values alive within the field, but there is no general agreement about what to do about those differences or the conflicts they sometimes provoke. The environment within which these conversations typically play out is somewhat like that of an extended family gathering at a reunion: some want to avoid discussing these disciplinary tensions, while others won't stop talking about it. Do most members of this "extended family" of academics share common scholarly values such as commitment to critical self-reflection, openness to correction, and a desire to avoid conflict of interest? What do American (and other) scholars of religion really want? What dreams and values inspire their academic efforts?

Answering these questions was the goal of the multi-year "Values in Scholarship on Religion" (VISOR) project, which developed several new measures and surveyed scholars from a wide variety of disciplines and academic associations that foster research and teaching in the academic study of religion. VISOR was a collaboration between Ann Taves, Ray Paloutzian, and the two authors of this chapter. We gathered and analyzed data on the similarities and differences in values within and across the relevant disciplines and associations, so that the broader community of scholars who study religion might make progress toward a shared and stable understanding of the types of values that shape the field. By providing information about actual scholarly values across a wide variety of sub-disciplines and associations, the VISOR project aimed to help foster a more transparent and informed conversation around the academic table about the fundamental assumptions and worldviews that divide (and unite) us as scholars of religion.

Some of our initial findings were published in the *Journal of the Scientific Study of Religion*, where we focused on distinctive features of the Society for the Scientific Study of Religion, most of whose members take a primarily sociological approach to the subject (Shults et al. 2020). The VISOR project was primarily focused on North America although we did get a good sample of European participants and good representation from the International Association for the History of Religion (IAHR). However, this phase of the VISOR project did not target the other international associations identified by Professor Hackett in her chapter.

In this context, we focus primarily on some of the insights into NAASR compared to other associations, and then examine some of the implications of these American academic dreams for our understanding of the role of religion (and scholarship on religion) in the Global South.

Methodological Dreams in the Academic Field of Religion

One of the new measures created by the VISOR team was the Methodological Naturalism and Methodological Secularism (MNMS) scale, which was designed to capture the differences among scholars of religion in their attitudes related to the appropriateness of appealing to supernatural agency or supernatural authority in scholarly activity *per se*. Other demographic questions in the survey asked participants about their own personal levels of religious belief and practice, but the purpose of this scale was to assess the extent to which they value naturalistic and secular approaches when doing academic work. The terms "naturalism" and "secularism" are almost as contentious in other disciplines as "religion" is in ours. We operationalized our constructs in the following way:

- *Methodological naturalism* (MN): Preference for academic arguments that optimize the use of theories, hypotheses, methods, evidence, and interpretations that do not appeal to supernatural agents or forces or authorities.

- *Methodological secularism* (MS): Preference for academic practices that optimize the use of scholarly strategies that are not tied to the idiosyncratic interests of a religious coalition.

Affirming naturalism typically signals one's resistance to including disembodied intentional forces in one's inventory of ontological items in the world. However, even scholars who do not strongly defend this metaphysical position are often or even usually *methodologically* naturalistic (qua scholars) in the sense that they exclude appeals to supernatural agency from their causal explanations of the phenomena they study. Analogously, a "metaphysical" secularist will deny the existence of transcendent divine revelations about social norms. However, many scholars who do not go this far are likely to argue that at least in secular university settings, research and organizational processes should not be guided by supernatural authorities tied to a particular religious ingroup. That is, they tend toward what we are calling *methodological* secularism (Shults 2015). The MNMS Scale was administered online along with the other VISOR surveys (www.visorproject.org) in order to find out more about the diversity of methodological dreams in the field. Answers to all items were measured on a 6-point Likert scale from strongly disagree to strongly agree. A higher score indicates a stronger preference in favor of academic strategies conforming to the MN or MS constructs. A lower score indicates a stronger preference against academic strategies conforming to the MN or MS constructs. The scale also included two reliability-item pairs, which are opposite-pole versions of the same item; and two "catch and calibration" items, which force respondents to use extreme ends of the scale. These were used to exclude answers from unreliable or insincere respondents. Scale reliability coefficients, assessed by Cronbach's alpha, were 0.91 for the MN subscale and 0.86 for the MS subscale. Exploratory factor analysis isolated three factors with eigenvalues above 1.0, cumulatively explaining 57 percent of the variance. Factor 1 encompassed the entire scale, indicating that the MNMS as a whole is a coherent measure, even though findings for the two subscales are reported. Factor 2 suggests that the MN and MS subscales make sense individually. Factor 3 separates the positively and negatively valenced items within each subscale reasonably clearly. Rotating this factor solution yielded no further insight. In short, it is a very well-behaved measure.

The MNMS scale was pre-tested and validated prior to launch, and this aspect of the VISOR survey was able to garner enough respondents across professional association affiliations to allow insightful statistical analysis.

Figure 15.1 portrays the differences in reported MN and MS levels of scholars with different primary professional association affiliations. For details behind this and the next section, see the supplemental materials at https://github.com/IBCSR/VISOR-JSSR (Shults et al. 2020).

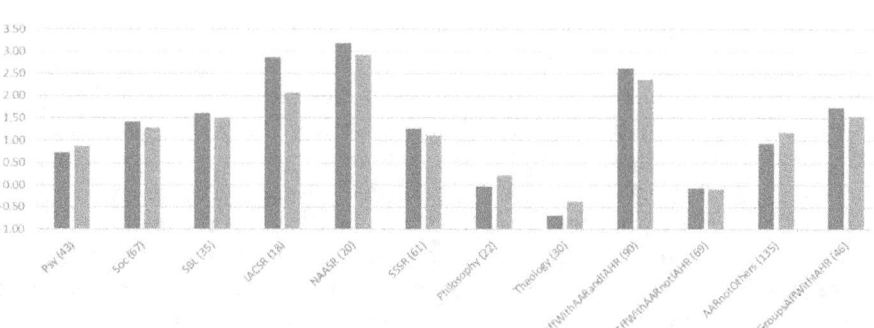

Figure 15.1 Methodological naturalism (MN) and methodological secularism (MS) by scholarly association. Higher scores indicate higher levels of MN and MS.

Psy = associations promoting the psychology of religion; Soc = associations promoting the sociology of religion; SBL = Society for Biblical Literature; IACSR = International Association for the Cognitive Science of Religion; NAASR = North American Association for the Study of Religion; SSSR = Society for the Scientific Study of Religion; Philosophy = associations promoting philosophy of religion; Theology = associations promoting theological approaches; GroupsAffWithAARandIAHR = groups affiliated with the AAR and the IAHR; GroupsAffWithAARnotIAHR = groups affiliated with the AAR but not the IAHR; AARnotOthers = the group of people affiliated with the AAR but not any other groups; SBLnotGroupsAffWithIAHR = the group of people affiliated with the SBL but not with groups affiliated with the IAHR.

What do NAASR scholars really want? For our purposes here, the important point is that in comparison to other scholars of religion, NAASR members clearly stand out when it comes to their tendency toward methodological naturalism and methodological secularism in their scholarly work. They are more likely than others in the field to believe that scholars of religion should pursue the same sort of intellectual and coalitional impartiality as scholars in other disciplines in the secular academy. And they are less likely to argue that critically reflective scholarship of religion in the academy should be pursued for the purpose of promoting or sustaining religious communities. These tendencies are hardly surprising given the historical founding documents and mission statement of NAASR (https://naasr.com/about-2).

Motivational Dreams in the Academic Field of Religion

What are the values that *motivate* scholars of religion in North America and Europe, whatever their methodological proclivities may be? To find out, VISOR also gathered data using a "Scholarly Values Questionnaire" (SVQ). This part of the survey was composed of three parts. The first two parts are the well-known

Schwartz values scale (Schwartz 2012), modified slightly to fit the values of scholars in the academic study of religion. Respondents were asked to rate how important a value is "as a guiding principle" in their "academic and scholarly life." They received the following instructions. "What you think others should value is not relevant here. What matters are the values that you personally express in your actions. Try to distinguish as much as possible between the values by using all the numbers. Before you begin, read the values [and] choose the one that is most important to you and rate its importance. Next, choose the value that is most opposed to your values and rate it –1. If there is no such value, choose the value least important to you and rate it 0 or 1, according to its importance."

The third part of the SVQ was constructed based on review and analysis of university and academic websites. Respondents were invited to apply the Schwartz-style numbering scheme to a list of values that included items such as: intellectual freedom, avoiding conflict of interest, synthetic theory building, shared governance, respect for senior scholars, capacity to communicate to a popular audience, collegial networks, and gender and cultural diversity.

The SVQ suggests that NAASR member respondents valued four values more highly than their peers: academic fairness, intellectual capacity, knowledge style depth, and multi-disciplinary approaches. It is important to note that this does not mean that they *are* more academically fair, have greater intellectual capacity, etc., but that they rank these *values* as more important guides in their scholarly work than others. "Fairness" is a moral foundation common among folks who are less religious and more politically liberal (Haidt 2007), which many NAASR members tend to be. The prizing of intellectual capacity speaks for itself. Moreover, NAASR members strongly value both in-depth knowledge style (valuing a focus on the details of a specific context or sub-discipline) and multi-disciplinary approaches to research (which could be taken to imply a broader focus). This suggests that NAASR attracts scholars who both enjoy diving into the details in their area of expertise and enjoy collaborating with other deep-diving scholars who have other areas of expertise.

NAASR respondents also rated the value of writing for a popular audience lower than their colleagues who identify primarily with other scholarly associations. This might be taken to imply that they are less interested in "public" scholarship of the type thematized at the 2019 conference in San Diego. However, "popular" is not quite the same as "public;" it could be that they want to engage the public through rigorous intellectual analysis that might not be accessible to a popular lay audience. NAASR members also ranked "social concern" relatively low as a value that motivated their academic work. We found this surprising, given the extent to which the association has a reputation for attracting scholars who are interested in addressing discrimination and injustice related to gender, class, and race, but the SVQ result reflects a comparison not an absolute judgment.

The VISOR project was meant to provide data that could be used to hold up a mirror to scholars of religion in a way that could serve as a basis for informed conversations about the values we share—and the values that separate us. Do we like what we see? Does any of this worry us? In the remainder of this chapter we identify some of the challenges and opportunities that face NAASR members as they reflect on this brief glance in the mirror, and take up Professor Hackett's encouragement to consider more carefully where we think *from* and *with* whom we think as we expand our international perspectives.

American Dreams and the Global South

Many Americans like to think that the American dream is for everyone, but in reality the path to prosperity is quite narrow and, unfortunately, typically requires the ability to manipulate the capitalist machine in a way that knocks others off that path. Like many scholars in our field, we want to resist the economic and social injustices driven by excessive consumerism and nationalist politics—not only personally, but also as public intellectuals. But insights from post-colonial analysis convince us of the need to avoid paternalism by being careful not to "care" for "others" in a way that inadvertently reinforces problematic divisions between us and them, North and South, rich and poor, etc. On the one hand, we do not want to West-splain to the Rest what is good for them, invading their cultures and forcefully implanting our own values. On the other hand, we do not want to throw up our arms and say "OK, go right ahead mutilating your daughters' genitals and praying to water spirits to fix your famine, we don't want to judge you as you continue psychological and physical torture while starving and dying from preventable diseases." Is there a middle path between these extremes? Where do we go from here, with which partners and stakeholders, and with what understanding of ourselves and others? Colonialism in all its forms, including especially Western colonialism during the modern period, might have brought some benefits but it has largely been socially coercive, economically exploitative, and ignorantly dismissive of the wisdom of the colonized. When we risk engaging with other cultures, especially when we aim to "help," we have to be ourselves, with our natural moral reactions; but we have to be a less ignorant version of ourselves and we also have to be honest about the wisdom and freedom and rights of others.

The SVQ analysis suggests that NAASR scholars are interested in what we can learn from multi-disciplinary approaches and engaging the work of scholars in other fields with areas of expertise other than our own. So, what happens when we take these values "on the road?" Here we briefly explore a potential case study: how might scholars operating *from* these non-supernaturalist NAASR values work *with* scholars in global development studies with a special interest in the role of religion in the Global South?

In his comprehensive analysis of data from multiple disciplines in *Religion and Development in the Global South*, Rumy Hasan (2017) argues that the evidence compels us to accept two "unmistakable" facts. First, as countries develop, the importance of religion to the population-at-large declines—to the point that a significant percentage self-proclaim to be non-believers and, for a rising majority, religion is a declining or unimportant part of their life. Second, in all the socio-economic indicators, developed countries occupy the highest rank; by contrast, the least developed countries invariably reside at the bottom. This is the case for the Human Development Index, political freedom, corruption, gender equality, life expectancy, infant mortality rate, child welfare, healthcare, economic competitiveness, and environmental protection.

Hasan argues that in the Global South religion, while being manifestly important to developing populations, also plays a key role in reducing openness to scientific solutions to sustainable development. "Adherence to religious doctrines is necessarily in tension with cognitive thinking for the simple reason that faith obviates the need for evidence and to a significant extent for rational thinking; hence, cognitive faculties are diminished. Criticism, curiosity, critiquing, hypothesizing, theorizing, experimentation and the search for evidence all appear to be suppressed or discouraged" (Hasan 2017: 198). Naturalistic education about the actual (non-supernatural) causal mechanisms at work in the world is necessary for developing the capabilities and skill formation of a population. Hasan concludes that high levels of religious belief in the Global South suppress all this. He suggests there is a "pressing need to move towards a reduction in the role of religion and a decisive move towards the secularization of society... minds not secularized are infused with supernatural and irrational thinking, and these powerfully militate against the dynamic of growth, development and the uplifting of people" (ibid.: 211).

Moreover, according to Hasan, religion is "a major driving force for conflict and wars... particularly so in the modern world between countries where the level of religiosity is high. Despite the confluence of other factors... it is religious differences that is the primary motivating force" (Hasan 2017: 195). While many scholars in our field would wince at such a narrow definition of "religion," Hasan is here following the standard approach in global studies and related disciplines, in which religion—operationalized as belief in gods and spirits or exclusive commitment to norms authorized by supernatural authorities—is consistently shown to be a predictor of societal dysfunction, conflict, and inequality (Paul 2009; Zuckerman 2010; Barber 2011; Bormann et al. 2017). If countries in the Global South are to develop and "catch up" with the developed world, insists Hasan, they "must downplay the role of religion in people's lives and institutions writ large, and move towards secularizing culture and society. This is not only essential for the cognitive development of children but is also a rational approach to the tasks necessary for economic development and modernization" (ibid.: 210).

Karl Marx was a compassionate man who, like Hasan, pondered the role of religion in exacerbating social problems. He would have agreed with Hasan's analysis, in the main, but his prescription for handling the malady of needless under-development started with economic revolution rather than with directly challenging religious beliefs and behaviors. Marx regarded the deliberate suppression of religion as a form of brutality, cruelly harming a population that needs religion to handle the suffering of life. Suffering, for Marx, is the power source of delusional supernatural worldviews, the nourishment that keeps religion alive. Deal with the root problem of suffering through perpetual revolution of the means of economic production and the social structures that control access to those resources, and supernatural religion will wither on the vine, like grapes drying up in the boiling summer sun.

Marx would have objected to the suppression of religion and superstition in the USSR, China, and other Communist nations, seeing it as further exacerbating suffering. It is better to leave it be, he believed, and focus on the causes of the suffering that sustain the human need for supernatural delusions. And while we wait, we can be grateful that religion does succeed in helping some people cultivate prized virtues such as selflessness, even as it intensifies dangerous ingroup identification among others. It seems that Hasan might urge us to work more quickly and directly to disrupt the steely grip of religiously reinforced delusion in order to put development on a faster track, thereby ameliorating suffering as quickly as possible. Even if Marx is right about the cruelty of suppressing supernatural religion, it is crueler, Hasan might argue, to let its oppressive consequences reign unchecked while we work on alleviating underlying sources of injustice in the economic and social order.

From a postcolonial perspective, how are we to find a balance? We want to alleviate suffering but who are we to decide about people's sacred values and to impose upon them replacement values that we deem more conducive to healthy socio-economic and cultural development? If the postcolonial aftermath of interference in the affairs of other nations has taught us anything, it is that we should be cautious about academic parachuting into developing nations in the Global South and telling them "the truth" about supernatural agents and authorities.

We need to connect this back to NAASR. Returning to Kevin Costner will help us do that. What does his character Ray Kinsella's shared imaginative engagement with axiologically relevant spirits in "Field of Dreams" have to do with the scholarly construction and analysis of "religion" in NAASR and other scholarly organizations supporting the academic study of religion? The category of "religion" is often used in religious studies, philosophy of religion, and related disciplines, to depict a broad range of features that capture a certain "family resemblance" in the phenomena they study (Wildman 2011). This approach is quite common among NAASR scholars. In disciplines such as Hasan's, which fit broadly into what can be referred to as the "scientific" study of religion, it is more common to operationalize "religion" in such a way that specific variables can be measured in a population and statistically analyzed. When Hasan uses the term, he has in mind variables such as level of belief in supernatural agents and level of participation in ingroup rituals that reinforce commitment to supernatural authorities.

When "religion" is constructed in this way, scholars consistently find that these variables exacerbate superstition and segregation (for a review of the literature, see Shults 2018). In turn, superstitious thinking complicates responses to pandemics and climate change insofar as it blocks people's openness to scientific analyses and solutions to such challenges and promotes logical errors and conspiracy thinking. And segregative behaviors complicate reconciliation and peacemaking insofar as they intensify prejudice, antagonism, and support for violence toward outgroup members.

What can we as scholars do about this? Is there a way to act that doesn't replicate the disasters of paternalistic and exploitative colonial pretensions to wisdom? Figure 15.1 suggests that NAASR members are more methodologically naturalist and methodologically secularist than their colleagues who identify primarily with other professional associations that promote the study of religion. This means that NAASR members are more like scholars in other academic disciplines that do not study religion, in the sense that they are less likely to tolerate appeals to supernatural entities as causal explanations and more likely to challenge scholarship driven by an apologetic concern to defend the supernatural authorities of a particular religious coalition. Every other academic discipline promotes attempts to seek the correction of idiosyncratic superstitious beliefs and to avoid conflict of interest by challenging motivational reasoning fueled by the protection of in-group segregative behaviors. As Figure 15.1 indicates, some scholars in the field of religious studies do not, which may help to explain why it is so often marginalized in the contemporary academy.

It follows from this that NAASR scholars are uniquely positioned to step up to the plate (another baseball metaphor) and deliver clear and public assessments of the deleterious psychological and political consequences that religion (in the sense used in the scientific disciplines that study the relevant phenomena) can have in human populations, especially those with fewer resources and higher levels of existential insecurity. Scholars in gender studies are critical of *sexism*. Scholars in liberation studies are critical of *classism*. Scholars in African-American studies are critical of *racism*. Why can't scholars in religious studies be critical of *supernaturalism*? Like the other problematic positions just mentioned, supernatural religion is the result of evolved cognitive and coalitional biases that probably helped our progenitors survive in early ancestral environments but have arguably become maladaptive in many contemporary global contexts (Cliquet and Avramov 2018).

Today we have an opportunity to work *from* our current position within the NAASR academic community *with* scholars such as Hasan and others in the scientific study of religion to highlight the negative effects of the religious factors mentioned above on the well-being of human individuals and the peaceful functioning of human societies, especially in the Global South. No doubt, such efforts could easily become paternalistic if we were intervening directly, which could easily make things worse, further activating worldview defense mechanisms and reinforcing ingroup anxiety. But there is less of a problem honestly describing what we see. After all, we are sharply self-critical of injustice in our home cultures, including the exacerbation of hardship due to supernatural worldviews and coalitions; we should be respectfully and cautiously critical of what we see in other cultures as well. The transition to action within developing nations would be a very different proposition, crucially involving local stakeholders. And it is far from obvious that all such stakeholders would find NAASR members suitable partners for implementing action plans! But that needn't stop NAASR members from diagnosing the role of supernatural worldviews and coalitions in exacerbating suffering, especially given that scholars of religion affiliated with other associations seem less likely to do so.

Conclusion

What do we really want? Speaking for ourselves (as NAASR scholars), one of the things we want is for our multi-disciplinary and intellectually rigorous academic efforts to support practical and positive effects on public discussions and policy decisions about how to facilitate psychological well-being and political transparency as we all struggle to address concerns about climate change, pandemics, income inequality, and other societal challenges related to the UN Sustainability Development Goals. There are many ways to do this, but one way that we commend is computational modeling and simulation. This methodology is unfamiliar to most humanities scholars, including those in religious studies, but it is growing rapidly in popularity as some of the latter are joining multi-disciplinary teams to construct "artificial societies" in which they can test their hypotheses about the role of religious beliefs and rituals in human life (Diallo et al. 2019; Gore et al. 2018; Shults et al. 2018a, 2018b).

We conclude by illustrating one of the ways in which computer modeling can shed light on the kind of question we were discussing in our case study above. Our "Future of Religious and Secular Transitions" (FOReST) systems-dynamics model is based on the conceptual integration of the most empirically validated aspects of six leading theories of secularization (Wildman et al. 2020). It was designed to identify and track the factors that contribute to the increase or decrease of the percentage of post-supernaturalist believers in a population. Supernaturalist believers have dominated every civilization we know about throughout human history, and they continue today to outnumber post-supernaturalists. However, the latter are growing rapidly in a variety of areas globally. Under what conditions would they continue to grow?

Or, to put it the other way, what are the variables that drive down supernatural agent beliefs and ritual practices of the sort that promote, for example, resistance to scientific insights about pandemics and prejudice toward outgroup members? FOReST showed that this requires the emergence and ongoing maintenance of four factors: existential security, education, freedom of expression, and pluralism. When one or more of these factors are weakened, supernaturalism can begin to gain ground again in the simulated population. What does this mean for those who share with Marx and Hasan a desire to diminish the influence of supernaturalist and superstitious beliefs and segregative behaviors, but want to avoid paternalistic attitudes and colonializing policies? The results of FOReST suggest that fostering post-supernaturalist cultures is most likely to succeed if one invests energy into making people feel safe, providing them access to scientific and humanist education, protecting their right to express themselves freely, and encouraging them to value cultural differences. That sounds like a pitch at which most NAASR scholars would be willing to take a swing.

F. LeRon Shults is Professor at the Institute for Global Development and Planning, University of Agder, Norway. He has published 19 books and over 160 articles or book chapters on topics including the scientific study of religion, philosophy of religion, and cognitive science of religion.

Wesley J. Wildman is Professor of Philosophy, Theology, and Ethics in the School of Theology and Professor in the Faculty of Computing and Data Sciences at Boston University. He is Executive Director of the Center for Mind and Culture, a research organization seeking solutions to complex and urgent social problems using multidisciplinary methods in conjunction with data sciences and stakeholder engagement. His most recent books are *Spirit Tech: The Brave New World of Consciousness Hacking and Enlightenment Engineering* (St. Martin's, 2021; co-authored with Kate Stockly) and *The Winding Way Home* (Wildhouse, 2021). For more information, see www.wesleywildman.com.

References

Barber, N. 2011. "A Cross-National Test of the Uncertainty Hypothesis of Religious Belief." *Cross-Cultural Research* 45(3): 318–333.

Bormann, Nils-Christian, Lars-Erik Cederman, and Manuel Vogt. 2017. "Language, Religion, and Ethnic Civil War." *Journal of Conflict Resolution* 61(4): 744–771.

Cliquet, Robert L., and Dragana Avramov. 2018. *Evolution Science and Ethics in the Third Millennium: Challenges and Choices for Humankind*. Cham: Springer.

Diallo, Saikou, Wesley J. Wildman, F. LeRon Shults, and Andreas Tolk (eds). 2019. *Human Simulation: Perspectives, Insights, and Applications*. Berlin: Springer.

Gore, Ross, Carlos Lemos, F. LeRon Shults, and Wesley J. Wildman. 2018. "Forecasting Changes in Religiosity and Existential Security with an Agent-Based Model." *Journal of Artificial Societies and Social Simulation* 21: 1–31.

Haidt, Jonathan. 2007. "The New Synthesis in Moral Psychology." *Science* 316(5827): 998–1002.

Hasan, Rumy. 2017. *Religion and Development in the Global South*. New York: Palgrave Macmillan.

Paul, G. 2009. "The Chronic Dependence of Popular Religiosity upon Dysfunctional Psychosociological Conditions." *Evolutionary Psychology* 7(3): 398–441.

Schwartz, Shalom H. 2012. "An Overview of the Schwartz Theory of Basic Values." *Online Readings in Psychology and Culture* 2(1).

Shults, F. LeRon. 2015. "How to Survive the Anthropocene: Adaptive Atheism and the Evolution of Homo Deiparensis." *Religions* 6(2): 1–18.

Shults, F. LeRon. 2018. *Practicing Safe Sects: Religious Reproduction in Scientific and Philosophical Perspective*. Leiden: Brill Academic.

Shults, F. LeRon, Ross Gore, Wesley J. Wildman, Christopher Lynch, Justin E. Lane, and Monica Toft. 2018a. "A Generative Model of the Mutual Escalation of Anxiety Between Religious Groups." *Journal of Artificial Societies and Social Simulation* 21(4).

Shults, F. LeRon, Justin E. Lane, Saikou Diallo, Christopher Lynch, Wesley J. Wildman, and Ross Gore. 2018b. "Modeling Terror Management Theory: Computer Simulations of the Impact of Mortality Salience on Religiosity." *Religion, Brain & Behavior* 8(1): 77–100.

Shults, F. LeRon, Wesley J. Wildman, Ann Taves, and Raymond F. Paloutzian. 2020. "What Do Religion Scholars Really Want? Scholarly Values in the Scientific Study of Religion." *Journal for the Scientific Study of Religion* 59(1): 18–38.

Wildman, Wesley J. 2011. *Religious Philosophy as Multidisciplinary Comparative Inquiry: Envisioning a Future for the Philosophy of Religion*. New York: SUNY Press.

Wildman, Wesley J., F. LeRon Shults, Saikou Y. Diallo, Ross Gore, and Justin E. Lane. 2020. "Post-Supernaturalist Cultures: There and Back Again." *Secularism & Nonreligion* 9(6): 1–15.

Zuckerman, Phil. 2010. *Society without God: What the Least Religious Nations Can Tell Us About Contentment*. New York: NYU Press.

Chapter 16

The Benefit of Comparison

Vaia Touna

Rosalind Hackett's contribution in this volume (Chapter 14) seeks to answer the extent to which, as she writes, "can we claim that the non-normative, historical, critical, and comparative study of religion exists as an international field?" Her various academic positions in many parts of the world, but also her active engagement with various international groups for the study of religion, make her ideal in presenting an overview of, what could be broadly described as, the "field of religious studies." Despite though her attempt to provide, as she writes, "thick description" of the various religious associations across the world, it is unclear to me what exactly unites all these associations other than their obvious affiliation with IAHR. Whether there is such a thing as an "international religious studies field," or not, in response to Hackett, my paper discusses aspects of the study of religion in Greece and North America, and what I find to be the benefits of my exposure to various international settings and the gains from comparing them. Furthermore, I argue, that such a comparative endeavor can guard against taken-for-granted assumptions, whether it is about that thing we commonly call "religion," or any other concept familiar to *us*(!).

Have you ever found yourself in a conference where you talk to, or hear, someone who is in the field of religious and therefore assume that you "speak the same language" because they, too, are engaged in a non-normative, historical, critical and comparative study of religion but as the discussion progresses you realize that what you thought united you couldn't be further from the truth? Leaving you more perplexed and confused? I think this is how I could describe my early exposure to "the field" as an undergraduate student and well, maybe, to this day.

For those who don't know me: I'm from Greece, where I also did my undergrad and master's studies at the School of Theology, at Aristotle University of Thessaloniki. I continued my PhD studies at the program of religious studies, at the University of Alberta in Edmonton, Canada, and now I'm working at the Religious Studies Department at the University of Alabama in the US. My chapter will therefore mostly discuss my experiences both as a student in Greece and Canada as well as a professor at a US public university, addressing the similarities and differences in all three countries in relation to the study of religion.

I obviously have a rather good picture of the situation in Greece, though possibly somewhat dated given that I left in order to pursue a PhD in Canada ten years ago, and I have to say that the situation in Greece is very different from North

America and I think, to some extent it is more similar to other European countries when it comes to the study of religion. As Hackett rightly observes in relation to religious studies scholars, who in order "[t]o extend their international connections, they have to work with the reality that, in many parts of the world, the study of religious education may be dominated by theological scholars, as with scholars from Muslim majority countries, for example." One of the reasons is that many religious studies programs or departments operate within Theological Schools, as was the case at Aristotle University of Thessaloniki.

In Greece there are 24 public universities all of which are state-funded and therefore regulated by the Ministry of Education. They all are self-governed; the professors are considered public servants; and, like all higher education there, they all are tuition-free, at least at the undergraduate level. Entrance to the various schools and departments of those universities happens after written exams in the last year of high school, a process that is again regulated by the Ministry of Education. There are no majors and minors in the universities, once a student has successfully been admitted to a degree program their four undergraduate years (eight semesters) will all be spent in their one school/department; so, in Greece, higher education is very specialized—at least more specialized than undergraduate degrees in North America in which only as little as one quarter of a degree is done in the student's specialty (due to, among other things, the requirements of what in the US is often called the core or general education curriculum). As far as the study of religion in Greece is concerned, although it is understood to some extent as different from theology, there are no Religious Studies departments (in the way that they exist in North America); instead, they are subsectors within Theological Faculties. There are two theological faculties in Greece, one at the Aristotle University of Thessaloniki and the other at the National and Kapodistrian University of Athens.[1] More specifically, at Aristotle University the Theological Faculty is divided into two schools: (a) The Theological School and (b) The School of Pastoral and Social Theology (a similar division exists in the Athenian Theological Faculty, too). Since 2018 there has also been a separate program of Muslim studies in the Theological School of Thessaloniki —which was in many ways a response to the current situation in Greece (i.e., with many refugees coming from Syria and Middle Eastern countries).

I attended, for both my BA and MA, the Theological School of the Faculty of Theology at Aristotle University, which is divided into five departments:[2] (a) Department of Biblical Studies and the Study of Religion(s), (b) Department of Church History, Christian Literature, Archaeology and Art, (c) Department of

---

1. There are also four Higher Ecclesiastical Academies, which are under the aegis of the State and the Orthodox Church, though the requirement for attending those academies is that one is Orthodox Christian. Their degrees are equal to those of the two Theological schools—though their graduates can't teach in the public-school system.
2. Though sector might be a more accurate description and thus the inescapable problem of trying to translate one culture to another by assuming there's a correspondence of words and meanings.

Dogmatic Theology, (d) Department of Worship, Christian Education and Church Administration, and (e) Department of Ethics and Sociology. In order for an undergrad to complete their degree they need to take 44 compulsory courses (one of which is a modern language), which are divided equally between all five departments/sectors, plus 14 electives, which can be a further specialization in any of the above five departments/sectors. Perhaps, it is needless to say that the focus of most of these courses are on the study of Orthodox Christianity; in fact, every course during my undergraduate years focused on such topics as: Orthodox Christian interpretations of the Bible, dogmatic history of the Orthodox theology and spirituality, canon and church law, history and literature of the Greek church, history of the Slavic Orthodox churches, Byzantine art and history, Christian sociology (with an emphasis on Orthodox Christianity), inter-religious dialogue, etc. Topics related to studying Roman Catholicism or Protestantism were very much on the periphery of our focus and if studied they were, for the most part, understood as a way to better understand the Orthodox faith—though, if I want to be more specific, I should perhaps say the specifically *Greek* Orthodox faith (a distinction that became apparent to me only when I moved to Canada, by the way, where the presence of different strains of Orthodoxy—e.g., Russian, Ukrainian, etc.—is far more evident than in Greece, where it is reported that well over 90% of the population considers itself to be Orthodox[3]). Here is how the official site of Aristotle University's School of Theology describes the aim of its undergraduate study program:

> [T]o provide high quality education in the academic field of theology as well as the study of religion and culture. The main objective is to prepare theologians, teachers of religion for secondary education, theologically trained clergy for the Church, staff who can offer social work and work for cultural or religious organizations, researchers capable of studying both the Christian (and especially Orthodox) theology and, more generally, the diversity of the religious phenomenon.
> (MODIP 2018)

Throughout my undergrad studies and mostly during my MA I developed an interest in the field of Θρησκειολογία (the Greek term for religious studies, which is closer to the German term *Religionswissenschaft*), and I would often refer to myself not as a theologian but rather as a historian of religion (Θρησκειολόγο). During my studies apart from fulfilling the requirements towards my degree with the compulsory courses from all the five sectors that I described previously almost all of my elective ones (a total of 14) would be in courses offered by the Department of Biblical Studies and the Study of Religion(s). At the time, there were two professors in the Study of Religions section that were offering courses on world religions, and ancient Greek and Roman religions. Gregorios Ziakas (now emeritus professor) with studies in Greece, Austria and Germany, a prolific scholar of eastern religions who would regularly teach courses on Islam, Buddhism, Hinduism, religions of Tibet, but also interreligious dialogue—being

---

3. According to the 2015 census.

himself member of INTRA (Interreligiöse Arbeitsstelle) and Wissenschaftliche Gesellschaft fur Theologie EV actively participating in conferences of interreligious (or interfaith) dialogue. His approach can nicely be summarized in the following passage from one of his books:

> This is why religion has two dimensions one "empirical," which can be studied historically and phenomenologically, and one "transcendental," product of divine apocalypse, which is basically incomprehensible and therefore only the object of theological study. The historian of religions must engage in the double method, the systematic and the historical. In the end though his work is something more than just history, he must not forget the stable and incorruptible (άφθαρτο) element of religion, that is, its sacred character.[4]
>
> (Ziakas 1996: 33)

The other professor, Panayotis Pachis, with studies in Greece, Germany and Italy, would mainly teach courses on ancient Greco-Roman religions but also on theory and method for the scientific study of religion(s). His approach, at the time I was there, was that of a historian of religion (see, for example, Pachis 1998, 2003), but with an interest in the theories and methods of North American scholars such as Donald Wiebe, Luther Martin, and Russell McCutcheon. Near the end of my master studies with him, he also developed an interest in cognitivist approaches as one of his latest publications at the *Journal of Cognitive Historiography* makes plain.[5]

It is also worth mentioning that as an undergrad I could also take elective courses from the other School of the Faculty of Theology. So, one semester I decided to take a course from the religious studies sector of "The School of

---

4. My translation of the original, which reads as follows: "Γι' αυτό ακριβώς η θρησκεία έχει δυο διαστάσεις μια «εμπειρική», που μπορεί να μελετηθεί ιστορικά και φαινομενολογικά, και μια «υπερβατική», προϊόν θείας αποκάλυψης, που είναι βασικά ακατάληπτη και συνεπώς αποτελεί αντικείμενο θεολογικής μόνο μελέτης. Ο ιστορικός των θρησκειών πρέπει να ασχοληθεί με τη διπλή μέθοδο, τη συστηματική και την ιστορική. Τελικά όμως το έργο του είναι κάτι παραπάνω από απλή ιστορία, πρέπει να μη του διαφύγει το σταθερό και άφθαρτο στοιχείο της θρησκείας, δηλαδή ο ιερός της χαρακτήρας."

5. The abstract of that paper reads as follows: "During the Graeco-Roman Age there were a great many testimonies from sick and physically disabled people who sought healing in the sanctuaries of the Egyptian deities, Isis and Sarapis. The most popular kind of healing which was practised in those sanctuaries was that of incubation (incubatio), during which the adherents—after following certain rules of diet, hygiene and purification—slept in the temple until they received a therapeutic dream or vision from the god(s). The research frame of this paper will be on the one hand the study of specific historical, cultural and social context of the cult of the Egyptian deities, and on the other cognitive structures and abilities. The importance of using the methods of the cognitive sciences to study religiosity in antiquity indicates that these practices are not data coming just from "dead minds" but from human minds generally. They acquire a particular meaning and may encourage us in our effort to propose new research projects. It should not escape us that the student of antiquity acts like a detective while using these methods in examining modes of religious behaviours, which belong to the framework of universals" (Pachis 2014).

Pastoral and Social Theology." The professor Ilias D. Nikolakakis was teaching a course on Euripides, discussing the reason why Euripidean tragedies, in comparison to Aeschylus' and Sophocles' tragedies for example, were more acceptable by early Christian authors. The course's textbook, his book, was entitled *The Idea of God in the Tragedies of Euripides: Contributions in the Study of Ancient Greek Religion* (Nikolakakis 1993). The yellow cover of the book had an image of Euripides from a seventeenth-century fresco of the church of Saint Nikolaos in Tsaritsani, Greece, with his face slightly tilted looking upwards, pointing with his finger at the same direction and on the other hand holding a papyrus; surely his whole attire was similar to that of a saint as found in byzantine paintings (which makes sense given that this was a fresco in a church). I mention the cover of the book because it was telling since the course was implicitly about the Christian logos in the Euripidean tragedies and the continuation of Greek identity from the classics, to the Byzantines, to modern Greeks. It has been a long time since I took that course, obviously, but I do remember vividly that even at the time I thought it didn't feel like a "religious studies" course, although it was certainly understood as such, both by students and his theologian colleagues.[6]

This rather brief description of my exposure as an undergrad (1998–2002) to the "field of religious studies" is actually quite telling, since it captures the various trends, at least at the Faculty of Theology at Aristotle University, by those who were identifying themselves as religious studies scholars or historians of religions. Now, it might seem that some of my professors were more θεολόγοι (theologians) than θρησκειολόγοι (religious studies scholars), but if we follow Hackett's model of a "family resemblance" approach to the field, then they should either all be included (by virtue of "more or less")or the criteria should be more specific, since the non-normative, historical, critical, and comparative approach might not be sufficient, especially if those qualifiers are not explicitly defined—for in my understanding the professors I mentioned definitely would understood their work as historical, critical and comparative. So, the international aspect of the field might be more complex than we might think. For example, it is of interest when Hackett describes a 2017 SSEASR conference in Vietnam writing that "the framing and publicizing of the conferences may play up cultural heritage at the expense of the religion trope" or that "there was a decision to add 'culture' to the title of the 2nd SSEASR conference in Bangkok conference in 2007 as none of the Thai universities in those days had any department of religious studies. Religion was studied under the auspices of Buddhist studies, Buddhist culture, and the Centre of Asian Culture Studies." What I find interesting here is, one the hand, the lament that "cultural heritage" was used at the expense of "religion" and the fact that up to 2007 Thai universities didn't have a department of religious studies. Given my background and my experience in Greece neither one of those

---

6. Given that his object of study was not purely theological or Christian, his courses would be considered outside of the domain of "actual theology," in some ways similar to the way Christian philosophers would distinguish between ἔξωθεν φιλοσοφία (outside philosophy) referring to Greek philosophers and ὄντως φιλοσοφία (actual philosophy) referring to their philosophy.

surprise me but it does make me wonder the extent to which North American and European understandings of "religion" are still imposed, in one way or another, on other parts of the world.

To continue, though, with my "international" experience, once I completed my BA studies, I carried on by pursuing a Masters in the Department of Biblical Studies and the Study of Religion(s) at the Faculty of Theology at Aristotle University, with a focus on ancient Greek religion. It was only halfway through my Master's degree that I became even more familiar with North American Scholars such as Luther Martin, Don Wiebe, Willi Braun, and Russell McCutcheon; in fact Pachis would assign in his courses a 2003 Greek translation of Braun and McCutcheon's *The Guide to the Study of Religion* (2000) and McCutcheon's *Manufacturing Religion* (1997). Moreover, in 2006 an international conference in Thessaloniki (organized by Pachis—for the inauguration of the Greek Association to the Study of Religion in joining the IAHR the previous year), brought us (those enrolled in the Master's program) even closer to those North American scholars and some Europeans, mainly from the University of Aarhus in Denmark. That was my first actual exposure to the heated debates regarding the concept of "religion" and various issues of definition and classification—though, as I type these words, I know very well that only in retrospect, and because of my current position, I can describe those debates in these terms. Because, admittedly, at the time I wasn't really sure what the issue was all about, for these weren't necessarily the debates within the Theological School of Thessaloniki or even the scholars I would normally read (mainly historians and classicists writing about religion in the Ancient Greco-Roman world).

When I moved to Canada to pursue a PhD in religious studies the difference between religious studies and theological studies became even more clear. I will not discuss in any detail the state of affairs of the study of religion in North America for I assume most readers would be very much familiar with it—a familiarity that as I will discuss later, we should be constantly aware of. So, when I came at the University of Alberta in Canada, one major difference soon became evident to me: in class discussions about religion we would often talk about how various definitions of religion have been influenced, for the most part, by a dominant religion, that is, "Christianity," but it was certainly *not* the Christianity that I had in mind, coming as I did from Greece—and it should not escape our attention what such generalizations create, normalizing a particular type of Christianity in this instance. My professors and my fellow peers in Canada were instead mainly talking about a very particular Christian discourse, one that dominated North America, and that was certainly *not* Orthodox Christianity (that I intuitively had in mind every time I would hear Christianity), and, if I want to be more specific, I should now say Greek Orthodox Christianity. It was therefore interesting how, moving from one continent to the other, "Christianity" *was not* Orthodox Christianity and thus the dominant discourse and, in many situations, not even on the periphery of our discussions. To be honest, conversation on "Christianity," once I arrived in Canada, usually referenced only issues of relevance to the interactions between Roman Catholicism and various strains of Protestantism, as if the so-called East–West schism in the church had not taken place—I'm not suggesting, obviously, that my peers, professors, or colleagues are not aware of it but it is of minor significance. It was certainly an "aha" moment that forced me to re-evaluate the way that I was reading my sources—as well as how I was reading my peers; for I soon learned that even among those in North America who understood their work to be rigorously non-theological (an intellectual tradition far better established and institutionalized there than in Greece, to be sure) a very particular type of Christianity, and thus specific Christian theological issues, were (uncritically, perhaps) understood as self-evident norms,[7] a critique nicely exemplified by my colleague, Steven Ramey, concerning the manner in which non-theological scholars might, unintentionally perhaps, play theological favorites in their work by adopting terms which "implicitly supports a position within a contested landscape, a position that those scholars have not necessarily analyzed and may not intend to support" (Ramey 2015: 224). For example every time I hear or when I say Catholicism I'm reminded of a professor I had in Greece who would constantly correct us that the proper terminology to refer to the Roman Church is not just Catholics but Roman Catholics, because the former implies that they represent the Whole of Christianity (from the Greek words Καθ'όλη), which of course after the schism was not the case—though I never heard him making the same move about Orthodoxy, a move that was certainly been made by scholars, perhaps unintentionally, in North America;[8] either way, to return to Ramey's point, I became a little more self-conscious in my use of terminologies, in order to avoid "playing favorites." A point that is very nicely made by Bruce Lincoln in one of his Theses on Method:

> Those who sustain this idealized image of culture [that is, as if they were stable and discrete groups of people defined by the stable and discrete values, symbols, and practices they share] do so, inter alia, by mistaking the dominant fraction (sex, age group, class, and/or caste) of a given group for the group or "culture" itself. At the same time, they mistake the ideological positions favoured and propagated by the dominant fraction for those of the group as a whole (e.g. when texts authored by Brahmins define "Hinduism", or when the statements of male elders constitute "Nuer religion"). Scholarly misrecognitions of this sort replicate the misrecognitions and misrepresentations of those the scholars privilege as their informants.
> (Lincoln 1996: 9)

In conclusion, moving from Greece to Canada and now to the United States where I work at the Department of Religious Studies at the University of Alabama, afforded me with the benefit of acquiring new insights, and for sure new knowledge produced by comparison and de-familiarization. My previous exposure to

---

7. Brent Nongbri in his book *Before Religion: A History of a Modern Concept* (2015: 18), does point out in the introduction that "religion" in the western world is defined in accordance to modern Protestant Christianity; so, I would argue that the debates as per its proper definition, or even its use or not enter into a specific ideological/theological debate within that particular world.
8. For example, every time they distinguish between Eastern Orthodox Church, or Greek Orthodox Church vs Russian Orthodox Church.

Greece and Canada certainly helped me with my students, not so much in trying to help them appreciate a different culture/religion (as I'm sure some of my theologian professors in Greece would have hoped) but, instead, my experiences became teachable moments when, for example, I would talk about "religion" or "Christianity" not as universal phenomena, as we often think about them, since, as already indicated, what I understand *as* religion or *as* Christianity (coming from Greece) and what they understood *as* both (given their position in the southern US) was very different. For me, the goal is not to try to set aside those differences, and thereby to focus on the similarities (so that we can essentialize "religion" or "Christianity") but, rather, to focus on the discourses themselves so as to look at *which* differences and *which* similarities are brought to our attention when, by whom and for what purpose.⁹

While working in the Department of Religious Studies at the University of Alabama I have also been part of one of the College of Art & Sciences' international initiatives, known as the "Alabama/Greece initiative," a collaborative project between the University of Alabama and Aristotle University of Thessaloniki that brings scholars together from the two universities in order to work in some collaborative project. Both of my Greek collaborators are not as, one would expect, from the School of Theology, however, but rather are from the School of Philosophy (one is an archeologist and the other is a historian of ancient Greece). Our collaboration has involved teaching undergraduate students at both universities. What I find liberating in these collaborations is that what makes us converse is not religion but, rather, a particular approach to the ancient Greek past and how the discourse on "religion" is one among many anachronistic concepts that are regularly used to talk about the ancient world. In other words, when I think of who my conversation partner shall be, whether on a national or international level, is not necessarily someone who studies religion but someone who is looking more broadly at how culture works.¹⁰

---

9. A comparative approach influenced by the works of, for example, Jonathan Z. Smith (1982, 1994) and Aaron W. Hughes (2017).
10. A similar approach informs the very successful "American Examples" initiative at the Department of Religious Studies at the University of Alabama, which is funded by Henry Luce Foundation (see https://americanexamples.ua.edu). The initiative is led by my colleague Mike Altman but it also involves most of my colleagues in the department, who act as mentors, including myself though I would not self-identify as an Americanist. Most of us are using our areas of specialization to encourage all of us in the workshop to consider the "so what?" question more broadly and make connections between our works even though our research specialization may differ. For example, my field of expertise is ancient and modern Greece, with an interest in discourses of religion and the past in general and my colleague's, Steven Ramey, field of expertise is South Asia with an interest in the formation of religious identities through contestations. These connections are not superficial comparisons, such as architectural styles or parenting attitudes in India, Greece, and the United States. Our objective is to identify questions that the scholars who participate in the workshop raise, perhaps implicitly, in their research that also have relevance in other geographical contexts.

Vaia Touna is associate professor in the Department of Religious Studies at the University of Alabama, Tuscaloosa. She is author of *Fabrications of the Greek Past: Religion, Tradition, and the Making of Modern Identities* (Brill, 2017) and editor of *Strategic Acts in the Study of Identity: Towards a Dynamic Theory of People and Place* (Equinox, 2019). Her research focuses on the sociology of religion, acts of identification and social formation, as well as methodological issues concerning the study of religion in the ancient Greco-Roman world and of the past in general.

References

Braun, Willi, and Russell T. McCutcheon (eds). 2000. *Guide to the Study of Religion*. London: Cassell.

Hughes, Aaron W. 2017. *Comparison: A Critical Primer*. Sheffield: Equinox.

Lincoln, Bruce. 1996. "Theses on Method." *Method & Theory in the Study of Religion* 8: 225–227.

McCutcheon, Russell T. 1997. *Manufacturing Religion: The Discourse on Sui Generis Religion and the Politics of Nostalgia*. New York: Oxford University Press.

MODIP. 2018. "Study Guide." Retrieved from https://qa.auth.gr/en/studyguide/60000024/2018/info (accessed May 16, 2022).

Nikolakakis, Ilias D. 1993. *Η Ιδέα του Θεού στις Τραγωδίες του Ευριπίδη: Συμβολή στη Μελέτη της Αρχαίας Ελληνικής Θρησκείας* [*The Idea of God in the Tragedies of Euripides: Contributions in the Study of Ancient Greek Religion*]. Θεσσαλονίκη: Κυρομάνος.

Nongbri, Brent. 2013. *Before Religion: A History of a Modern Concept*. New Haven, CT: Yale University.

Pachis, Panayotis. 1998. *Δήμητρα Καρποφόρος. Θρησκεία και αγροτική οικονομία του αρχαιοελληνικού κόσμου* [*Demeter Bearer of Seeds: Religion and Agricultural Economy of the Ancient Greek World*]. Αθήνα: Ελληνικά Γράμματα.

Pachis, Panayotis. 2003. *Ἶσις Καρποτόκος, vol. I: Οικουμένη. Προλεγόμενα στον συγκρητισμό των ελληνιστικών χρόνων* [*Isis Bearer of Seeds, Vol. I: Ecumene. Prolegomena in the Syncretism of the Hellenistic Period*]. Θεσσαλονίκη: Vanias Editions.

Pachis, Panayotis. 2014. "Data from Dead Minds? Dream and Healing in the Isis/Sarapis Cult During the Graeco-Roman Age." *Journal of Cognitive Historiography*, 1(1), 52-71.

Ramey, Steven. 2015. "Accidental Favorites: The Implicit in the Study of Religion." In Monica Miller (ed.), *Claiming Identity in the Study of Religion: Social and Rhetorical Techniques Examined* (pp. 223–238). Sheffield: Equinox.

Smith, Jonathan Z. 1982. *Imagining Religion: From Babylon to Jonestown*. Chicago, IL: University of Chicago Press.

Smith, Jonathan Z. 1994. *Drudgery Divine: On the Comparison of Early Christianities and the Religions of Late Antiquity*. Chicago, IL: University of Chicago Press.

Ziakas, Gregorios. 1996. *Θρησκειολογία: Η Θρησκεία των Προϊστορικών Κοινωνιών και των Αρχαίων λαών* [*Threskeiologia: The Religion of Prehistoric Societies and Ancient People*]. Θεσσαλονίκη: Αριστοτέλειο Πανεπιστήμιο Θεσσαλονίκης.

Chapter 17

"Developing" the Field

Yasmina Burezah

This chapter will focus on the importance of difference-making as a pivotal tool in the international field of the study of religion and German international development work. I will try to show how in times of growing international expansion and the illusion of alleged equality between otherwise different participants, religionizing the *Other* serves the Western scholar as an instrument to retain the idea of an implicit superiority of Western scholarship and ideas and therefore maintains the asymmetrical power position.

In her essay "International Perspectives on/in the Field" (Chapter 14, this volume), Dr. Rosalind Hackett provides a very helpful and interesting overview of the international situation of our field. In describing the international field she gives a substantial overview of the various associations and networks affiliated with and collaborating in the International Association for the History of Religions (IAHR), and therefore in the field of the study of religion. The overview entails both the geographical variety from, for example, the African Association for the Study of Religions (AASR), the South and Southeast Asian Association for the Study of Culture and Religion (SSEASR), or the Korean Association for Religious Studies, but also various topical affiliate associations and societies such as the European Society for the Study of Western Esotericism (ESSWE), the International Association for the Cognitive Science of Religion (IACSR), or the IAHR Women Scholars Network (IAHR-WSN). For all these groups Hackett offers a comprehensive overview of their history, research profile, and work derived from her extensive work experience, research and expertise in the international field of the Study of Religion. In her closing remarks she identifies six commonalities:

(a) tokenism is passé;

(b) international collaboration pays off;

(c) hubs and flows are shifting;

(d) international work is labor-intensive and costly;

(e) new opportunities abound for traveling, communicating, networking, and publishing; and

(f) political, economic, environmental, linguistic, and institutional realities loom large.

The present chapter will mainly focus on the first of these points and Hackett's identification of the end of tokenism as an important commonality of the internationalization of the field.

Dr. Hackett concludes her paper with the optimistic words: "Ramping up international collaboration and solidarity can bring new attention to marginalized voices and overlooked theories in the academy. It can trigger much-needed processes of decentering and recentering in terms of where we think from, and what and who we think with, in our disciplinary areas. It can also bring greater awareness of the inter- and transdisciplinary moves that particular dispensations compel. It brings to our attention new knowledge and funding hubs in the study of religion/s. Finally, international work can dispel any complacency about the ever-growing threats to our academic freedom by 'neoliberal rationality.'" (Wallach 2019: 79).

To place collaboration and solidarity at the center of international cooperation in the international field of the study of religion is nothing but worth applauding and should be seen as key qualities in every single researcher's work and effort towards our epistemological interests and Dr. Hackett's work has contributed immensely to creating unity and international solidarity between regional associations for the study of religion around the world.

While I generally agree with her notion of the "diversity" potential of the internationalization of the field, I find myself more skeptical of what seems to resemble a "diversity and inclusion" model which is rampant today throughout organizations, companies, and academic institutions. This model, despite its good intentions, maintains an economic focus on the inclusion of social difference, but hardly ever does "diversity and inclusion" work to de-center normative epistemological centers. As the first of this list of commonalities, Hackett states: "tokenism is passé." From my more skeptical position, I have to say that I disagree. The fact that we still do not focus on the ideas offered by the scholarship of members of these organizations, but instead look at the organizations themselves, demonstrates that tokenism might be a default position.

Hackett stays vague about what she means by tokenism. "Tokenism" might as well just be, as Miller and Driscoll put it, one of many *discursive milieus of universalized vagueness*, a "catchphrase" or strategic rhetorical technique that "unduly smuggles in the categorical Others marking what *it* is *not*" and here, while we cannot be sure, what is meant by tokenism, we are supposed to believe, that whatever tokenism is, it is not part of the international field of the study of religion (Driscoll and Miller 2019: xv).

"Tokenism," for me, signifies the only symbolic participation of a minority group. It is clear from Dr. Hackett's chapter that we have come a long way in working on moving past tokenism, with a blossoming of regional and national organizations worldwide, yet "tokenism" still continues to signify the symbolic participation of minority groups, without reflecting on the asymmetrical dimensions of power. The critical study of religion was crucial in establishing that the "Other" is not just to be seen as the necessary empirical object of research, but the inclusion of non-western epistemes as vital to decenter hegemonic epistemological production. We also find this idea in Hackett's notion of "decentering and recentering in terms of where we think from."

But does minority group inclusion really mean that equal footing has been established for all actors to cooperate on eye level, for example the various scholarly organizations that Hackett describes the histories and present of?

The cooperation of academic associations is political. This is important work, but it does not mean that we already have all the tools or even the fundamental possibility to regard the foreign Other truly as equal, because equality might just go against the fundamental distance-making between the religious adherent and the a-religious scholar—using method as the difference-reinforcing tool.

In this institutionalized nature of the international expansion of the field I recognized a familiar different field, the field of development work (in this case German governmental development work). I was wondering: what would happen if we would draw an analogy between development work to the work of "developing" the academic study of religion globally that the IAHR is engaged in. In full disclosure, the idea to draw this parallel is strongly inspired by Monica Miller and Christopher Driscoll's above-cited book *Method as Identity*. In the text, Miller and Driscoll suggest that distance-making is at the heart of method in the academic study of religion.

I will argue that Dr. Hackett, in her chapter, shows us how far we have come, but still belies a minority-group difference deeply established in the field. In order to illustrate what I mean, I will draw on my own research experience. In an analogy to my research on religion in the field of international development, I'll show several faces of tokenism and the crucial role of method to establish identity and differentiate between White and non-White scholars. That is to say, I explore how critical method might unduly be reduced to a marker of (Western and "progressive") identity instead of the indispensable analytical tool to dismantle structures of power and study religion without being religious.

My skepticism derives from my own research on religion in governmental German development work and the analogies one could draw to the situation we are in as scholars in the study of religion. The most prominent analogy one might draw between academia and development work, is the understanding of the Other. During my research I got to understand *the important role that distance-making* plays in developmental work and the variety of tools people use to reinforce that differentiation. And I wonder, without attention to *both*, the form and content of the work of non-White, non-Western scholars, what sorts of distances are manufactured or maintained in the field?

Since the 1990s, the German word for development work has been *Entwicklungszusammenarbeit*, a term that already encompasses all the paradoxes and contradictions of this work: *Entwicklung* means development, *-zusammenarbeit* means cooperation. It is a term that both entails the ideal of equality but also the necessity of a fundamental hierarchical difference between the *developed* and the *undeveloped*. And trying as it may, it does not escape the mechanisms of difference-making.

In 2017 I did research on a rather recently founded department in the German governmental agency for development work (called the "Deutsche Gesellschaft für Internationale Zusammenarbeit," GIZ for short). This department was founded in 2015 and was a personal initiative of the new minister in the Federal Ministry of Economic Cooperation and Development, Gerd Müller, a politician from the Christian-conservative party Christian Social Union in Bavaria (CSU). The department is called "Werte, Religion und Entwicklung" which translates to "values, religion, and development" and the name already entails one of the core understandings of religion: religion is regarded as something the partner organizations in the Global South are affiliated with, whereas the governmental department is seen as led by values.

The department is supposed to create networks with non-European religious partners and faith-based organizations (FBOs) to cooperate with. It was regarded as revolutionary for the GIZ to approach religious actors directly, since as a governmental agency they identify as strictly non-religious. The Federal Ministry for Economic Cooperation and Development divides its budget between the GIZ for the cooperation with secular partners and Christian organizations such as World Vision for working with religious partners. While the Christian organizations mainly work with other organizations defined as Christian, this new department was supposed to facilitate cooperation with organizations of different religious backgrounds, mainly Muslim (especially because of the political interest in regions, where Muslim organizations would be prominent; and because of the German obsession with "inter religious dialogue" between the three Abrahamitic spectra of Islam, Christianity, and Judaism, where, in the German imagination, the German participant is understood as a neutral facilitator with high ethical "values"—the bringer of peace to the otherwise troubled and conflicted world of the religious).

The argument to move beyond that strict distinction between religious and non-religious cooperation, was and still is a functional and neoliberal one. Non-western religious communities might have far better and established infrastructural advantages than western development workers who often come to a country only for a few years and therefore never establish foundational connections to regional organizations or people. Also, in many instances I would witness discussions on how to get in contact with FBOs in communities, where people would pay Zakat (the obligatory alms-giving for devout Muslims, that is rather treated as taxes to support the community), so the German government could maintain cooperation without using their own funds. On a larger scale the neoliberal argument is the idea of having every country participate in a global economic system. A global system or, if you want, a global economic discourse defining the western countries as superior and therefore holding the discursive power and defining the paradigm of success and development. Defining what is desirable and success.

While observing over the course of a year those German "development" workers interacting with colleagues in the global south I realized, that in this new work a discourse of "religion" emerged, in which "religion" was a vital tool to reinstate the hierarchical positions in the field.

A variety of parallels was established: The "undeveloped" were seen as intrinsically religious and had no chance to present themselves and to be seen as not motivated in their actions by religious, "irrational" ideas. The "developed" were seen as rational and "secular," even though it never was clearly articulated what that means. One example: even though one of those German—and for what it's worth White male—development workers I was observing, was a former Catholic theologian, he was nevertheless allowed to choose when to make a "secular" point, and when to be tapping into his theological know-how to argue "religiously." "Religious" worked as a euphemism for "undeveloped" and as a way to use a racist logic and gaze without explicitly talking about race.

The essential difference-making that allows development work to continue to exist is the premise of a distinction between the developed and the not-developed, and further the premise of an intrinsic imbalance in progress, intelligence, prosperity, and so on. In my research on the German development work, the tool to strengthen and constantly re-constitute this difference was "religion," even as the goal was a continuation and strengthening of cooperation and collaboration, that never escaped this distance-making inherent in it.

What if the incorporation of regional associations in a bigger international association is creating a global discourse, whose conditions, rules, and principles are defined and set by Western academia? A discourse that is driven by an equally fundamental asymmetrical distinction, implying a distribution of power that forecloses any possibility to even stand the chance of a cooperation on equal terms. A discourse constantly reaffirming what we already seem to know about the function of religion, so much so that it never allows us to ever question what we consider to be the right method (and identity).

But more importantly, a discourse in which a method serves as a tool of identity making through distance making not only between the researcher (the scholar of religion) and the object of study (religion), but more importantly between the capable and proper researcher (built on the model of the Western scholar) and the insufficiently scholar (the theologian, and the scholar of religion from the Global South). In what ways does the IAHR petition these satellite/national organizations to join? Or, does development not work that way?

As I quoted in the beginning, Dr. Hackett argues in her paper that "tokenism is passé." But in reading her descriptions of the various associations, I wondered, why for some of these associations it was necessary, as with the South and Southeast Asian Association for the Study of Culture and Religion (SSEASR) to stress that there was "a genuine commitment to developing the critical, historical, and comparative study of religion in the region," while for other associations, this goes without saying. I am not trying to imply that this is not an issue for a variety of associations, but it is interesting to ask which associations (and their methods) are deemed adequately "critical" in the eyes of NAASR or the IAHR.

After sketching this view of a continuing imperial and postcolonial function of Western academia even as the IAHR further globalizes, I'm nevertheless still convinced, there is no alternative to a more and increasingly internationalized study of religion. The IAHR is doing important work in this regard. But more than ever before we need to consider what we can learn from the *academic ideas* of the postcolonial. It is not enough to itemize and historicize a White, Western relationship to the Other. That is White history, and as scholars of religion, we've collectively done far enough of this work to last us quite some time. What is our task, perhaps, is what Hackett fails to do here: read, wrestle with, or otherwise take seriously the academic output—the actual ideas generated and knowledge produced—of the members of these IAHR member organizations. Such tendencies to ignore the bodies of scholarship produced by non-White bodies relentlessly points us to the variety of historical and contemporary ways in which the academic study of religion has effectively always configured the non-White body as a religious body, and therefore as having a methodically inadequate and insufficient potential to be a critical scholar. To add emphasis, by the rules of engagement seemingly still at work in the development work of the academic study of religion, I, as a non-White woman could probably never be seen as "critical" of a scholar the same way a White man would. Of course, that last bit was mere emphasis, for, I am writing this here now.

The other side of Hackett's historical accounting is greater recognition, and more legibility, even if in fits and starts. For developing truly international perspectives on the field, we might have to be ready to accept that our field in its method and therefore identity might just as well be as dynamic as our object of research. And this leads us to and necessitates recognizing narratives on religion and the study of religion emerging outside the geographic and ideological/epistemological West. And more importantly to open to alternative epistemes and potentially other forms of understanding critical scholarship. If we already always know the unchanging critical position from which the proper scholar of religion speaks, we are caught in a similar distinction-making as the development work, which cannot get rid of this idea of the "undeveloped" having to be developed.

And just as development work—Entwicklungszusammenarbeit—necessitates a distance-making between the developed and the undeveloped, our discipline necessitates the distance-making of "the researcher" and "the religious." And just as development work uses religion as a tool to strengthen that distance, we use "method" to distance ourselves from alleged insufficiently developed other scholars of religion.

It seems to be inescapable, but maybe it is not, if we don't take that White and postcolonial heritage of the academic study of religion serious—those structures that run so deep in our disciple and our academic self-understanding; that it might just not be sufficient to trust in the self-propagating force of the gospel of incorporating international associations into the critical method and continue to simply engage in academic development work.

To prevent that we might need more than the ongoing work of institutionalized internationalizing that Dr. Hackett sketches so knowledgably in her paper. Tokenism might not be passé. We might just be creating a new institutionalized setting for it.

Yasmina Burezah is a research associate and PhD candidate at the Forum Internationale Wissenschaft at the University of Bonn, Germany. Her research focuses on the intersection of religion, race, and class in German hip-hop. In 2020 she was a Fulbright Fellow at Lehigh University, working on issues in the study of Whiteness/Germanness, racial capitalism, and post-structuralist theory.

References

Driscoll, Christopher M., and Monica R. Miller. 2019. *Method as Identity: Manufacturing Distance in the Academic Study of Religion*. Lanham, MD: Lexington Books.

Scott, Joan Wallach. 2019. *Knowledge, Power, and Academic Freedom*. New York: Columbia University Press.

Index

AAC&U (America Association of Colleges & Universities), 36–38
AAR (American Academy of Religion), 5, 7, 17n7, 18, 36n18, 41–42, 77n1, 81, 82n14, 83n22, 126n13, 135, 157, 175, 178–179, 181, 188189, 192, 196, 199,
AAR Religious Literacy Guidelines, 17n7, 64, 81, 121–122, 128
AASR (African Association for the Study of Religions), 179–181, 187, 189, 217
Abend, Gabriel, 43–44
Abington School District v. Schempp, 103
Adogame, Afe, 177, 181
Ahn, Juhn Y., 43
Albanese, Catherine L., 66n3
Alles, Gregory D., 6, 33n5, 88, 102, 154–156, 161, 164, 166, 169, 177, 189
Altglas, Veronique, 35
Alterman, Eric, 133, 137
Altman, Michael J., 6, 153, 215n10
Ambasciano, Leonardo, 24
Arnal, William E., 78, 113n5, 114–115, 117n10
Asad, Talal, 35
Avalos, Natalie, 6
Aune, Kristin, 145–146

Baer, Hans A., 104
Baldwin, Matthew, 80, 113
Balagangadhara, S. N., 41
Balmer, Randall, 166
Banerjee, Aditi, 142
Barrett, Amy Coney, 94
Barrett, Jacob, 4
Barthes, Roland, 78, 107
Bateye, Bolaji, 175n1
Bell, Catherine, 21, 23,
Berger, Peter L., 89n34
Black religious studies, 102

as discursively contested, 102
essentialization of, 104
Borges, Jorge Luis, 78
Bourdieu, Pierre, 3
Braun, Willi, 213
Brint, Steven, 140–143
British Academy, 135–136
Bucar, Elizabeth, 33n4, 37n19
Burezah, Yasmina, 7
Butler, Judith, 23–24, 51, 57

Campbell, Heidi, 159
Canonization, 134
capitalism, 117, 124, 166
Carnegie, Andrew, 138–139
Carnes, Mark C., 160
Casanova, José, 155
Cavanagh, Sarah Rose, 47–48
Cavanaugh, William T., 127n15, 155
Chakrabarty, Dipesh, 142
Chidester, David, 123n4, 181, 191
Chitando, Ezra, 176n3, 179n14, 180n26, 181
Clark, Elizabeth A., 108n2
Classification, 5, 13–15, 22, 32–33, 41–42, 44, 46, 52–53, 55, 63–65, 67–71, 77, 80, 95, 98, 102, 117, 124, 127, 154, 157, 213
  as boundary formation, 86, 168, 210
  definitional practice as, 46, 66ff., 80
  as essentialized *see* essentialism; critical study of religion
  as socially constructed, 14, 102, 166, 210–215
  as theoretical practice *see* theory
Civil Rights Movement, 103, 134, 151, 166
civility discourses, 5, 85, 89n34, 100, 122, 127
Cognitive Science of Religion, 41, 184, 199, 211n5, 217
Cohen, Emma, 184

Cold War, 34, 77, 117, 119, 151
colonialism, 32n1, 34, 54, 67, 79, 85, 87, 98, 115, 116–117, 119, 123, 166, 168, 170, 191, 201, 204–205
  as colonial colleges, 137
  as European colonialism, 77, 80, 102
  as settler colonialism, 6, 164, 169
Collingwood, R. G., 107
"commercial empire", 164, 166–167
Commission on Religious Education (UK), 124
comparison, method of, 7, 15, 34–35, 64, 90, 127, 175, 183, 190, 208ff., 221
Comparative Religion, 77, 126, 190
  as colonial project, 191
Cone, James, 103
Cooper, Travis Warren, 168
Cotter, Christopher R., 85, 115–116, 118, 190n83
Coviello, Peter, 35
Cox, James, 116n9, 118, 180n27
Crews, Emily D., 79n8, 80
critical study of religion, 4–5, 11, 12ff., 34n11, 36, 42, 45, 52–53, 55, 61–65, 71–72, 77ff., 96–97, 99, 107ff., 154, 158, 164, 215
Culler, Jonathan, 95
Curtis, Edward, IV, 175n1, 189
Cuthbertson, Ian Alexander, 4, 22–23, 40, 41, 80

Danforth Foundation, 151
Davis, Kathy, 51
Day, Abby, 191n88
definition *see* classification
De Nicolás, Antonio T., 142
Descola, Philippe, 142
Dharma Civilization Foundation (DCF), 152
difference
  as boundary for-mation, 117
  as difference-making, 217
  and distance-making, 7, 219, 221–222
  as measured against Protestant hegemony, 117
  as religious difference, 125
  strategic essentialism of, 221
Dinham, Adam, 123
Discourse, 41, 55, 57, 80n9, 85–87, 99–102, 104, 157, 169, 213, 215, 220
  as critical study, 17n7, 19–20, 22, 24, 32, 53, 55–56, 77ff., 128
  as decolonial, 56
  as liberal Protestant discourses, 117, 154
  as internationalist discourse, 178
  as public, 61–62
  as public discourse on social media, 156
  as universalist, 164, 166
diversity *see* difference; pluralism; religious literacy; tolerance
Dube, Musa W., 181, 190
Dubuisson, Daniel, 79
Durdin, Andrew, 5
Durkheim, Émile, 43

Eaghll, Tenzan, 42, 125n11
EASR (European Association for the Study of Religions), 178ff.
Echtler, Magnus, 190n84
Eck, Diana, 64, 110
Eliade, Mircea, 79, 96, 98, 110, 116
endurance, 107ff.
Enlightenment (European), 34, 99, 191
Ennis, Ariel, 64
essentialism, 4–5
  critiques of *see* critical study of religion
  as family resemblance theory, 68, 175, 203, 212
Evans, Curtis J., 102
experience, 90
  as discursive category, 1, 87, 90, 157
  as "the human experience", 17
  as pre-discursive, 126
  Protestant hegemony of, 113n5
Eyl, Jennifer, 125n11

Ferguson, Stephen C., II, 103
Field of Dreams (film), 196, 203
Fink, L. Dee, 47
Fitzgerald, Timothy, 22n9, 41, 85–86, 124n7, 155
Foucault, Michel, 13n3, 32
Francis, Matthew, 123
Frazier, E. Franklin, 103
Frye, Marilyn, 24
Führding, Steffan, 158
Fujiwara, Satoko, 175n1, 191n90, 192
Fuller, Robert, 159

funding, private, 133ff., 150ff., 154ff., 164ff.
    impacts on scholarship, 154
    in the study of religion, 116, 133ff.
funding, public, 6, 164ff.,
    as shaped by political ideologies, 166

Gallagher, Eugene, 65, 81n13, 144–145
Gardner, Daniel K., 160
Geertz, Armin W., 175n1, 176–177, 184
Geiger, Leinie C., 4–5
Geiger, Roger, 137–139
Gandhi, Mahatma, 28
Gill, Anthony, 99
Gill, Sam D., 96, 104, 168
GIZ (Deutsche Gesellschaft für Internationale Zusammenarbeit), 220
Global South, 7, 176, 179, 185, 190n84, 191, 195ff. 217, 220–221
    religion in the Global South, 201–202
Globalism, 98–102, 177, 190
Goldenberg, Naomi R., 20, 26, 32n2, 41, 55–56, 80, 87n31, 113, 124
Governance
    as colonial *see* colonialism
    as tactical method of nation-states for managing religious difference, 26, 88
    as self-discipline, 112n4
Graeber, David, 112
Gray-Hildenbrand, Jenna, 65, 68n4, 100
Great Recession of 2007–2009, 156, 165
Greece, 208ff.
    Greek Orthodoxy, 208ff.
Green, Patrick, 151
Gregory, Brad S., 155
Grimes, D. Jamil, 5

Hackett, Rosalind I. J., 6–7, 176, 181, 195, 197, 201, 208–209, 212, 217ff.
Haidt, Jonathan, 200
Haraway, Donna, 51, 54, 56
Hasan, Rumy, 201–204
Hart, Patrick, 43
Hatch, Nathan O., 150
Hebrew Bible, 133, 135
Henry Luce Foundation, 143, 153, 215n10
Herskovits, Merville J., 103
Hermann, Adrian, 51n1, 158
Higher Education Statistics Agency (HESA), 136

Hinduism, 28–29
    as authentic or real, 29
history of the field, 77ff., 96, 107ff., 177
    historicization of the field, 108
    and the persistent influence of phenomenology, 109
historiography, 2–3, 107, 111, 151
    as narrative construction, 107, 111
Hucks, Tracey E., 103, 104n2
Hughes, Aaron W., 11n1, 77, 78n3, 79n5, 89n34, 91, 126n14, 215n9
Hurd, Elizabeth Shakman, 155, 175n1, 191n89

IAHR (International Association for the History of Religions), 142, 175ff., 197, 199, 208, 213, 217, 219, 221–222
    Eurocentric origins of, 176
IDEA, 4, 32n1, 34–35
IFYC (Interfaith Youth Core), 36–37
Imhoff, Sarah, 126n13, 151
imperialism, 34, 164, 166, 221
    see also colonialism
Indigenous religions, 85n27, 102, 116n9, 166, 168, 182, 190
    in American religions pedagogy, 66
    as primitive, 168
Infinity Foundation, 142
interfaith studies, 33, 36–37, 81n12, 135, 144, 211
    as "interfaith skills", 36
Interfaith America, 156
    contributions to curriculum development, 156
International Connections Committee (ICC), 178
internationalization of the field, 178ff.
    affiliate associations, 183–186
    as collaborative, international funding, 178–179
    as multi-lingual discussion groups, 180
    national and regional associations, 178–183
    as open-access scholarship, 181
interpretation, process of, 13, 15, 22, 29, 32, 34, 43, 57, 63
Islam, 67–68
Islamophobia, 64, 141

Jacobsen, Douglas, 144
Jacobsen, Rhonda Hustedt, 64, 144
Jaggar, Alison M., 47
Jensen, Tim, 176, 177, 179n21
Jocks, Christopher, 168
Johnson, Greg, 190
Johnson, Sydney, 167
Johnson, Sylvester, 189
Josephson-Storm, Jason Ānanda, 35, 79n7, 116n9
Journal of Africana Studies, 188
Journal of the American Academy of Religion, 89n34
Joy, Morny, 175n1, 186, 190
Judaism, 134n3, 135
  as Orthodox, 26

Kant, Immanuel, 33n4
Kendi, Ibram X., 36n18
King, Rebekka, 6, 17, 65, 100, 122n3, 156–157
Klinken, Adria, 190, 191n88
Knibbe, Kim, 57
knowledge production, 3, 13n3, 17–18, 140–141
  as contextual, 146
  as "corrupted knowledge goods", 142
  as imperial enterprise, 164
  as naturalized, 168
Knott, Kim, 123, 124n6
Kraft, Siv Ellen, 190

LaCapra, Dominick, 107
Latour, Bruno, 79
Laycock, Joseph, 32, 36, 160
Leachman, Michael, 165
Lee, Robert, 169
Lester, Rita, 4
Lilly Endowment, 1433
Lincoln, Bruce, 19, 25, 94
lived religion, 87
Lofton, Kathryn, 33, 35
Long, Charles H., 103
LoRusso, James Dennis, 125n11
Loy, David, 43
Lykke, N., 57, 68

Maguire, Joanne, 65
Mahmood, Saba, 33n4

Malhotra, Rajib, 141–142
market, 7, 17, 43, 99, 119, 135, 137, 151, 154ff.
  as marketization, 177
Martin, Craig, 33, 78n2, 81, 91, 113, 114n6, 125n11, 158–159
Martin, Luther, 88, 184, 190, 211, 213
Marx, Karl, 202–203, 205
Masterson, Kathleen, 165
Masuzawa, Tomoko, 85–86, 116–118, 123n4, 164, 166
material religion, 87
Mayrl, Damon, 143
McCormack, John W., 6
McCutcheon, Russell T., 5, 16–17, 20–21, 36n18, 41, 44–45, 64n2, 71, 77, 78, 79n5, 79n7–8, 85, 86n29, 87n30, 88n32, 89n34, 91, 95ff., 107ff., 126n14, 155, 157–159, 175n2, 190n83–84, 211, 213
McDannel, Colleen, 87–88
Mellencamp, John, 112
Meyer, Anne, 47
Meyer, Birgit, 190–191
Mitchell, Michael, 165
MNMS (Methodological Naturalism and Methodological Secularism), 197–198
Moreton-Robinson, Aileen, 169
Moore, Diane L., 64, 81n13, 82n14, 84
Moore, Stephen D., 96
Müller, Friedrich Max, 110
Museum of the Bible, 133
Muslims, 28
  Sufi Muslims, 68
  Turkish Muslims, 51, 57

NAASR (North American Association for the Study of Religion), 7, 11, 12, 32n2, 33n5, 36n18, 52n2, 77, 80, 81, 100, 101, 122n3, 127, 135, 155, 157, 176, 177, 179, 184, 195ff., 221
NABI (North American Bible Institute), 123, 125
narrative construction, 17, 102, 107–112, 141–142, 157, 222
  as myth, 3, 43, 56, 96
Nash, Robert, 144
Neoliberalism, 12, 119, 155, 177, 218, 220
  as academic neoliberalization, 119

as advanced form of white supremacy, 170
as neo-liberal university, 5, 63, 167
New Religious Movements (NRMs), 66, 185, 188, 190
Newfield, Christopher, 166–167
Newton, Richard, 12n2, 17, 20–21, 121n2, 159
Nikolakakis, Ilias D., 212
Noll, Mark, 150
Nugent, David, 164, 166–167
Numen (journal), 176
Nye, Mallory, 4, 21–23, 65, 168, 178

Obergefell v. Hodges, 27
Oeur, Freeden, 143
Olejarz, J. M., 167
Orsi, Robert A., 87, 102
Ortner, Sherry B., 112
Owen, Suzanne, 53, 85–86, 99

Pachis, Panayotis, 211, 213
Paloutzian, Ray, 197
Park, Julie J., 143
past, the, as modern construct, 78–79, 96, 107ff.
Patel, Eboo, 156–157
Patton, Laurie L., 161
pedagogy, 4, 11ff., 32ff., 40ff., 51ff., 57, 61ff., 116, 158, 160–161
    as process-oriented, 52ff.
    as self-reflective, 55ff.
    as student-directed, 47–48
Penner, Hans, 100
Pew Charitable Trust, 33, 69–71, 150, 191
pluralism, 66–67, 82, 121–122, 134, 157, 190–191, 205,
    critiques of, 83, 84n24, 157
    discourses on pluralism, 70, 84n24, 116n8
    as liberal Protestant category, 113n5, 117
    see also religious literacy
postcolonialism, 178, 190, 203, 221–222
postmodernism, 24, 97, 112n4, 114, 144, 164, 166
poststructuralism, 112n4, 114n6, 128
power dynamics, 13, 32, 33n7, 34, 46, 53, 55, 57, 61–63, 66–71, 86, 100, 112, 116–119, 168–171, 217ff.

as coercive violence, 112
as knowledge production, 52, 63
mechanisms of, 112
Proposition 13, 165
Prothero, Steven, 33, 64, 81–82, 110, 145
Proudfoot, Wayne, 86n28
public vs. private, 94–95, 155
    as Protestant hegemony, 168
Pye, Michael, 176n8, 177n9, 178–180, 189

race, politics of, 26, 102–104, 118, 143, 167–168, 170, 182, 190, 221
    racialization, 6, 164, 166, 168
    racism, 54, 102–103,
Ramey, Steven, 33, 89n33, 101, 214, 215n10
Rancaño, Vanessa, 165
Reed, Adolph, Jr., 109
religion
    as Abrahamic religions, 84n4
    as belief, 5, 21, 25, 35, 71, 84, 86–87, 124–125, 127, 155, 158, 168, 185, 202ff.
    as data, 64, 159
    definitions of, 46, 67–71, 78n2, 95
    as discursive category, 2, 12, 13, 53, 55, 61, 66–71, 78–79, 80, 86, 90–91, 109, 113–115, 117n10, 118, 122
    as empirical and transcendental, 211
    as European colonial endeavor *see* colonialism
    as faith, 125
    as identity, 125
    as natural phenomenon, 100
    normative or traditional understandings of, 84–85
    as primary motivating force for war, 202
    as primitive vs. real religion, 168
    as private or personal belief, 87
    as racialized, 164
    as *religioning*, 4, 20ff., 35, 53–54, 63, 65–66, 70–72, 155
    as scholarly creation, 127
    as spiritual but not religious, 159
    as *sui generis* or unique, 41, 55, 62, 110, 114, 116n7, 190
    as system of classification, 13, 88
    as a tactic, 3, 13, 52ff., 88
    as universal, 34, 84, 116
religionization, 20, 22–28, 32, 33, 40, 42, 53–54, 217

religious freedom, 27, 34, 188, 190
religious literacy, 5–6, 11, 17–18, 32–33, 38,
    48, 61ff., 81–88, 91, 98–102, 109–111,
    113n5, 119, 121, 123n5, 125, 145,
    157–158, 160
    discourses on, 84
    as diversity and inclusion model, 218
    in education, 126
    examples of religious literacy initiatives
        in the academy, 82–83
    and pluralism *see* pluralism
    as paradigm, 109
    and tolerance *see* tolerance
Religious Literacy Project (Harvard
    Divinity School), 82–84, 86, 125
religious studies, 1ff., 36, 41, 42ff., 55ff.,
    64ff., 77ff., 87, 96
    ahistoricism of, 115
    as American religious history, 62, 66–67
    analysis of, 109
    as "big tent", 77, 157, 175n2
    crisis of, 135ff.
    as distinct field of study, 1–3, 62
    as "field" vs. "discipline", 3, 177
    as foundationalist or "scientific", 177
    as method and theory approach, 190,
        211
    phenomenological tendencies of, 115
    pre-critical past of, 111
    and the production of good moral
        citizens, 151
    as "religion and ..." model, 78
    as religion vs. secular, 71, 154
    as *Religionswissenschaft* or science of
        religion, 190, 210
    religious studies curricula, 34, 45
    as self-reflective, 51, 54, 57–58, 90, 96,
        197
    theoretical approaches of, 42ff.
    value of, 62, 71, 154, 158, 196–197
    see also pedagogy; theory
rhetoric, 19–20, 159
    as discursive categories, 4, 12, 25–26,
        28–29, 44, 80, 118, 143, 218
    and meaning-making, 156
    see also classification; discourse
Richardson, Laurel, 55, 56n3, 57
ritual, 21, 41, 68, 70–71, 205
    as ritualization, 21, 23

Roberts, Martha Smith, 5, 159
Robertson, David G., 85, 116, 118, 190n83
Rockefeller, John D., 138
Rockenbach, Alyssa Bryant, 143
Rocklin, Alex, 116n9
Rosenhagen, Ulrich, 83–84
Rubenstein, Mary Jane, 90

Said, Edward, 80
Scalia, Antonin, 94–95
science of religion, 77, 95
Scharnick-Udemans, Lee-Schae, 181
Schmeiser, Peggy, 90
Schneider, Wendie, 95n1
Scholarship of Teaching and Learning
    (SoTL), 12
scholarship in religious studies, 1, 13, 94ff.,
    107ff., 153, 195ff.,
    as academic Eurocentrism, 142
    and academic freedom, 154, 167, 200,
        218
    as boundary formation, 4, 103–104,
    as critical scholarship, 143, 77ff., 190n1
    as cross-national *see*
        internationalization of the field
    as essentialist, 80, 34n11, 41
    as normative, 5
    as Orientalist, 168
    as public-facing, 6, 195
    as social/political activism, 95–96
    as scholarly values, 196–197
    white supremacy of, 222
    and writing, 51ff.
Scott, Joan Wallach, 177
secularism, 35, 42, 100, 146, 190–191,
    197–199, 202, 204–205
    methodological secularism, 198–199
    as theories of secularization, 205
Shagan, Ethan H., 158
Sherwood, Yvonne, 96
Shults, F. LeRon, 7, 36n18
"Slave Bible", 134, 147
Smart, Ninian, 118, 168
Smith, Huston, 33n8, 87n30, 117n10, 144
Smith, Jonathan Z., 1, 3, 4, 12, 15, 17, 22,
    32n1, 33n10, 45, 77, 79n8, 88, 90, 96,
    121n2, 127, 155, 160, 215n9
Smith, Leslie Dorrough, 4, 11, 26, 32, 33,
    34n11, 36n18, 40–42, 44, 46, 47, 52ff.,

61ff., 79, 110, 113, 121n2, 155, 157, 158, 161
Smith, Linda Tuhiwai, 164, 166, 168
Smith, Wilfred Cantwell, 118
Society of Biblical Literature (SBL), 126, 186, 199
sovereignty claims, 124
SSEASR (South and South East Asian Association for the Study of Culture and Religion), 178–179, 182, 183, 187, 212, 217, 221
Stack, Trevor, 124n7
Stewart (Diakité), Dianne M., 103
Stevenson, Jacqueline, 145–146
Stoddard, Brad, 33, 125n11, 158–159
Strijdom, Johan, 181
Sullivan, Winnifred Fallers, 190n84
Sun, Anna, 116n9
SVQ (Scholarly Values Questionnaire), 199–201

Taves, Ann, 197
Taylor, Bron, 184–185
Tayob, Abdulkader, 182
theory, 42ff.,
　as critical theory, 112
　as "doing theory", 1–2
　as Indigenous theoretical frameworks in scholarship, 168
　as meaning-making, 43
　as myth-making, 43
　as snowblower, 43ff.,
　theory vs. data, 42, 44, 45,
　as theoretical anarchism, 42
Thomas, Jolyon Baraka, 34, 35
tokenism, 217ff.
　as passé, 217–218
　as symbolic inclusion, 218
tolerance
　as governance tactic, 35–36, 98–99, 102, 124–126, 156
　Protestant hegemony of, 99

as religious tolerance, 5, 61–62, 64, 66–67, 99, 101
see also religious literacy; governance
Tomaselli, Sylvana, 99
Tong, M. Adryael, 88
Touna, Vaia, 7, 79n4, 81
Troeltsch, Ernest, 113n5
Tsing, Anna, 98, 142
Tweed, Thomas A., 150

UDL (Universal Design for Learning), 41, 46–47
Ukah, Asonzeh, 181, 190n84

VISOR (Values in Scholarship on Religion), 7, 197–200
Von Ranke, Leopold, 107

Walvoord, Barbara, 35
White, Hayden, 107, 111
white supremacy, 168–170, 219, 221–222
see also race; racism
Wiebe, Donald, 88, 177, 184, 190, 211, 213
Wiggins, Linda, 103
Wildman, Wesley J., 7
Wilks, Tammy, 190n84
Wilmore, Gayraud, 104
Wittgenstein, Ludwig, 154
Wolfart, Johannes, 81n10
Wood, Connor, 157
World Parliament of Religions, 116n8
world religions paradigm (WRP), 4, 34, 81n13, 89
　as colonial endeavor, 116
　critiques of, 85, 89n33
　historical analyses of, 115–116
　as pluralist model of religion, 70
　as rooted in Protestant hegemony, 116

Zeller, Benjamin, 160
Ziakas, Gregorios, 210–211
Zuckerman, Phil, 202

www.ingramcontent.com/pod-product-compliance
Lightning Source LLC
Chambersburg PA
CBHW070312230426
43663CB00011B/2102